THE
COMMANDING
SELF

By the same author

Oriental Magic
The Sufis
Special Problems in the Study of Sufi Ideas
The Exploits of the Incomparable Mulla Nasrudin
Tales of the Dervishes
Caravan of Dreams
The Pleasantries of the Incredible Mulla Nasrudin
Reflections
The Dermis Probe
Thinkers of the East
A Perfumed Scorpion
Seeker after Truth
The Hundred Tales of Wisdom
Kara Kush
Neglected Aspects of Sufi Study
Special Illumination: The Sufi Use of Humour
A Veiled Gazelle: Seeing How to See
The Elephant in the Dark
Wisdom of the Idiots
The Magic Monastery
The Book of the Book
The Way of the Sufi
The Subtleties of the Inimitable Mulla Nasrudin
World Tales
Darkest England
The Natives are Restless

THE
COMMANDING
SELF

IDRIES SHAH

THE OCTAGON PRESS
LONDON

ISBN 0 863040 70 5

First published 1994
Reprinted 1994
First impression in this edition 1997

Printed and bound by
Redwood Books, Trowbridge, Wiltshire

CONTENTS

Quality, Quantity and Time
Flavour
Right and Wrong Study
Trust
Inconsequential
Value for Money
Bombardment
Stolen Property
The Five Animals
Your Share and Mine
Arguing with Gifts
Ants
Finding a Teacher
How to Tell
Imitators
Today He Understands
The Cook
Major and Minor Actions
The Indian Teacher
Whose Animals
Illiberal Behaviour of Sufis
Being Rude to People
Opening Another Door
Fierce and Mild
What is a Dervish
The Dervish and the Disciple
Dervish, Sufi, Disciple
The Trick
What a Teacher is
The Chess-Players
Way of Teaching
The Rope
Wisdom of the West

Sufi Thought, Experience and Teaching

Thousands of books and monographs have been written on Sufism and the Sufis, almost all of them from the point of view of other ways of thinking. The result has been chaos in the literature, and confusion in the reader. Over the centuries, some of the world's most eminent scholars have fallen into the trap of trying to examine, assess or consider the Sufi phenomenon through a set of culture-bound preconceptions.

All this may not be as foolish as it looks to us, today: after all, it is only relatively recently that students, including academics and people of the spirit, have begun to realise that their attitudes have traditionally been heavily influenced by subjectivity and unexamined assumptions. Although the pendulum is slowly swinging back, there is still no lack of people – specialists and others – who continue to look at anything, including Sufis, in anything but an objective way.

The main problem is that most commentators are accustomed to thinking of spiritual schools as 'systems', which are more or less alike, and which depend upon dogma and ritual: and especially upon repetition and the application of continual and standardised pressures upon their followers.

The Sufi way, except in degenerate forms which are not to be classified as Sufic, is entirely different from this.

Following closely after the primary misconception is the general impression that all spiritual entities must strongly depend upon emotion. Indeed, there is a marked confusion, even in the most lucid writers, between spirituality and emotionalism. Such confusion does not exist in authentic Sufi teaching or study.

The misconceptions of which the above two are typical produce in the student a frame of mind through which he or she will try to approach the understanding or study of Sufism, with predictably useless results. For this reason Sufi literature shows a

1

marked rejection of ultra-formalism, of mental fetishes, the over-simplifications which hamper understanding.

The Sufis refer to the action of the mixture of primitive emotionality and irrelevant associations which bedevil outside would-be observers as that of the *Commanding Self*.

It is only since the nineteen-fifties, with the discovery of the far-reaching effects of conditioning, brain-washing and attitude-engineering, that the subjective nature of virtually all approaches to knowledge has been perceived to the degree to which the Sufis, for centuries, have tried to establish.

The Sufis have always taught: 'Examine your assumptions; avoid mechanicality; distinguish faith from fixation'.

The Sufi teacher, in the first place, has to be someone who has experienced all the stages of the Way along which he will conduct his disciples. Outward observers are not capable of commenting upon Sufism, only upon its externals. They lack both the experience and the capacity to discriminate between real and degenerate forms. 'Who tastes, knows' is a Sufi saying. Equally, whoever does not taste, does not know.

The validity of this concept is, naturally enough, strenuously opposed by outward observers. But if, in any field, an unqualified person, lacking essential experience, decides to 'become an expert', it is inevitable that the specialist, the person with the experience, will – indeed must – assert the primacy of proper knowledge.

It has to be remembered here that the externalists (whether people of the spirit or of the pen and tongue) are themselves not particularly to blame. Reared on the concept that anyone can, at will, examine anything, they are victims of their own culture's assumptions. After all, this approach is adequate for a large number of disciplines. They have merely applied a principle which holds good in one area to a subject where it does not.

The Sufi, unlike the externalist, cannot, and does not, work mechanically. The projection of the message and the help which is given to the learner, must always vary in conformity with the needs of the time, the culture involved and the nature and potential of the student.

But as soon as we say this, we can see that Sufi organisation, teaching and learning differ fundamentally from all other 'systems'.

The Sufi, in short, is aiming for a development, not to produce conditioned reflexes. He is teaching, not training. He intervenes, to provide the right stimulus at the right time for the right person. Such an activity is seen as chaotic by those who cannot perceive its purposefulness; just as the way of life in some open societies feels unbearably disorderly to those who have escaped from regimented ones: something which frequently happens today.

The tendency to seek reassurance and regularity is common to all human beings. This is reflected in their cleaving to over-simplified systems. It explains why many people are drawn to organisations which offer authority and certainty. There is nothing wrong with order and discipline: indeed, these are essentials to all human groupings. But the misuse of this proclivity in areas where it does not apply attenuates or delays progress. It results in the uncomfortable feeling, even amongst the most regimented, that 'there is something else . . .'

And yet exposure to strong discipline does not of itself produce as a reaction a necessarily wholesome affinity for truth. It is noticeable that coercive, regimented or rigorously intellectualist societies throw up weird cults and aberrations, providing both the supply of and the demand for certain emotions.

There is a vast accumulation of Sufi teachings, much of it in writings, which would-be students plough through, looking for Sufism, and wondering why it seems, so often, self-contradictory. The simple answer is that this material is largely time- and culture-based. Most of it was prescribed for specific audiences at certain times and under particular conditions. Choosing the relevant materials for any time is a specialised task. To try to make sense of all of it would be like taking a bundle of medical prescriptions, issued over the years to a variety of people, and working out one's own therapy from such largely irrelevant papers: and without certain specialised medical knowledge. Sufi teaching is *prescribed*.

Such parts of the Sufi Classics, tales of the Masters, letters and lectures and so on which apply to the individual and the group today have to be selected and applied consciously and appropriately, by someone who is attuned to certain realities.

This concept is especially irksome to the academic worker, who always has a bias towards utilising every scrap of information he can find, not towards assessing contemporary applicability. He is, in fact, in a different field from the Sufi. His attitude influences even general readers.

If the scholar is unwilling to accept this concept, the conventional spiritual thinker is equally hampered. He, or she, does not wish to face the fact that Sufi activity is often carried out in a way which does not, for the conventionalist, resemble spiritual matters at all. The fact that the Sufi has to script and project his teaching in a manner which will work – not in a manner which will remind others of spirituality – arouses, if ever perceived, feelings of great discomfort in the conditioned 'devout' man or woman.

Yet the Sufi insists that the adherence to traditional forms is not a spiritual activity at all. It is only in recent years that he has been able to call upon the insights and experiments of the sociologists and psychologist to establish in current terminology, and hence in acceptable form, the fact that very many 'people of the spirit' are only religious in the sense that they have been conditioned to feel certain emotional responses. And that such people are, anthropologically speaking, little else than members of a tribe. These facts, written down and asserted centuries ago by Sufis, are now thought by modern thinkers to be a great new discovery...

The supposedly devout are, in Sufic terms (as well as in the new understanding of contemporary workers in the social sciences) cultists but hardly people of the spirit in the Sufic sense.

The use of authority figures, canonical literature, liturgy, exercises, special clothes, and similarly standardised elements, are now plainly seen as ingredients in training systems which differ, one from the other, only in the ideas and symbols used.

4

Yet these factors linger and confuse, producing blinkered minds.

The deluded 'Sufis', down the centuries, are those who have taken temporary teaching situations, parables and the like and stretched them to apply as perennial 'truths', 'exercises' and the like. This kind of development, or hypertrophy, has taken place in other projections than that known as Sufic. Indeed, it is this which is responsible for the existence of a large number of cults and religious bodies which are generally believed to be authentic and authoritative. In reality, the fossilization which is represented by such groups is the antithesis of a spiritual school. Instead of developing people, it imprisons them, as genuine Sufis have never tired of pointing out.

So far has this process gone that, in most cultures, the imitation has all but driven out the original. The result is that, examining certain existing religious cults (some of them involving multiple millions of people and possessing great influence) nobody could be blamed for believing this degeneration to be religion itself.

Recently, explaining this attitude to a famous spiritual leader, I received the answer; 'But it MUST be true: otherwise so many people would not believe it.'

He had, clearly, not heard of Gresham's Law: 'Bad money drives out good.'

I said, 'There are twice as many adherents of such-and-such a religion as there are of your own. By your logic, THAT one must be true. Its success proves it. Why don't you join that one instead of your own?'

It was at that point that he started to shout at me ...

Among the Sufis, the development of 'Orders' (*turuq*) gives us a conspicuous example of the process which I have been describing. Of all the major 'Paths' among the supposed Sufis of today, not a single one is traceable in its foundation to the man who is named as its founder. Each came into being only after his death, formulated from some of his specific teachings employed for local purposes, and soon turned into a cult. 'Orders' are temporary and time-limited. None was started by its putative founder. When the teacher died, his disciples, heroically but misguidedly, tried to preserve his teachings. The results we know.

Follow them and you will produce, perhaps, an excellent replica of a thirteenth-century man, and that is all.

All the distortions – and more – which have persisted in Sufic – and other – teaching are due to the presence and activity of the Commanding Self.

There is no intention of destroying or undermining the Commanding Self. But the Sufi activity insists upon asking: does it command you, or do you command it?

Cultural and Psychological Problems of the Commanding Self

The Western cultural milieu, more than those of the East, provides a background mentality which encourages the Commanding Self. Procedures designed for Eastern people are likely to have negative effects if adopted by Westerners.

Briefly, the Eastern tradition that one learns until one is permitted by a teacher to teach (an ancient tradition perpetuated in apprenticeship and the granting of degrees in the West), is not adhered to in many non-academic areas of the West.

The reason for this is not far to seek. In the West, the prevailing culture's emphasis is on haste, on getting something and passing it on (e.g. products or ideas, after value-enhancing) and so on. This has taken the form, in spiritual, psychological and other areas, of people trying to teach, to expound, to treat or cure, to communicate before they are properly fitted to do so.

The fact that, in the West, anyone can set up as an expert, a teacher, a therapist or an adviser, compounds this error.

The Commanding Self, always agile in its sophistication,

conceals from the individual that he/she is trying to run before being able to walk. When people start to approve of what the individual is doing, this is misread as a validation of his or her role. In fact, it is usually only the fact that some people are dependent characters by nature or formation.

This, indeed, is the aetiology of many cults and most examples of people who have become prominent beyond their true current capacity.

Someone has to pay for this. Sometimes many people pay for it. The reason is that the situation as just outlined is inherently unstable. Stresses within the individual cause distress, even breakdown. The stresses are the result of the battle between vanity, however well concealed, and the inner knowledge that the personality is false, is trying to run before being able to walk.

This condition is hard to treat. The Commanding Self will struggle hard to maintain itself, convincing the sufferer that the symptoms are essential parts of the personality. The sufferer will constantly imagine an inability to return to the baseline, become more modest, humble, less self-assertive, because he/she feels that this would mean a depletion of the personality.

The Commanding Self, though, can be seen as a sort of parasite, which first complements the personality, then takes over certain parts of it, and masquerades as the personality itself.

Breakdowns of communication are a frequent result. Sufi teachers, when describing this syndrome, are often accused of trying to keep the individual down, of saying 'You are not ready yet' in order to maintain authority. This criticism is invalid, unless there is plenty of evidence to support it; and, if there is, the supposed teacher is not a Sufi at all.

The answer? Time and service rather than wanting to take a place on the totem-pole. It is for this reason that Sufi teachers divert vanity from the spiritual area, by encouraging their disciples to channel the Commanding Self's activities to any worthy worldly ambition: while continuing to study the Sufi Way in a modest and non-self-promoting manner.

INTRODUCTION

The Pit . . .

A young woman who had been sheltered from many experiences of life found herself one day in the glittering foyer of a London theatre.

She had not been to a theatre before and she was almost totally unprepared for what she saw. Her indoctrination at home had been of an emotional religiosity which dwelt upon the delights of heaven and the horrors of the 'pit' of hell.

The lavish decoration of the entrance hall, where she had to wait for her escort to collect the tickets, was a completely new environment for her. The people were not only all strangers to her, but were dressed in a bewildering variety of colours and were characterised by a liveliness and sophistication which she could relate to nothing in her own life.

Suddenly, in the midst of the bemusement engendered by these impacts, she saw and read a sign which pointed towards the orchestra stalls. It indicated, *The Pit*.

What else could she do but give a scream of horror, run from the theatre, and – as soon as she could – seek solace and forgiveness in earnest prayer? And that is what she did.

Is this a fable? It is printed in the London *Observer*, as news and a record of a theatrical incident, contributed by a correspondent★.

Accounts of this nature, assuming them to be true, indicate both conditioned behaviour and the persistence of what we can easily recognise as a primitive pattern of reactions in the present day. The grafting of emotion-based ideas on top of the primitive, without maturing the latter, produces the 'Commanding Self', which affects much of everyone's daily thinking. There is no difference between the responses elicited by the experience of this girl and that of a savage who has been exposed to his own local training – or indeed any civilised man or woman. If the story is not true, the fact that it can be offered as possibly true

★ *The Observer* (London), 25th August, 1968, page 30.

shows that such primitive patterns can repeat themselves in contemporary society. The fact that people are expected to laugh at the story is extremely interesting. The unspoken intention behind the offering of the tale as humorous (which of course it is) is to draw a distinction, perhaps of relief, between 'us' and '*her*'.

And, singling out this kind of easily illustrated primitive behaviour, and imagining that because we can see its absurd side we ourselves do not act in a similar manner, is itself absurd.

The woman had been conditioned to respond with horror and an emotional storm to certain stimuli. Today, in the most barbaric and the most advanced societies, there are millions of people, many of them certainly in positions of authority and importance, who will react in a similar manner, providing that their 'horror trigger' is tripped.

The fit study of the anthropologist, surely, is his own society, although he may have learned his lessons by observing and studying other societies where, to him, patterns are more obvious.

It will certainly be seen in future as one of the anomalies of this society if this is not done. Certainly it is not done to any extent yet. We still say, 'Fancy that: the Chinese discovered gunpowder and the magnetic compass and did not develop the use of these instruments.'

Our successors, whoever they are, will perhaps be able to say of us: 'Fancy, they had these tools of investigation and illustration, but they used them only on people who were other than themselves.'

Purpose of Study and Research

The purpose of a Sufi book, or any Sufi activity, is to further Sufi development. You may think that this is obvious, but it certainly is not so to the hundreds of people who enquire, every year, for information and elucidation which shows that they are trying to operate in a direction which has no relationship with Sufi aims.

Let us take a simple example. We may publish a tale, probably in conjunction with one or more other stories, and perhaps in a context which makes this a 'teaching package'. No sooner is this material released than numerous individuals try to decode it, or to follow up all sorts of associations. Naturally, such attempted activity nullifies the effect of the package.

In some cases, perhaps in all of them, this tendency is motivated by a learnt pattern. The pattern may be scholasticism, or it may be puzzle-solving, or a tendency to seek emotional satisfactions or associations.

The problem is, of course, complicated by the fact that people seem unaware that the material, as presented and used, is purposeful and all of a piece. They badly need to note the story of the small boy who dismembered a fly. He ended up with a pile of wings, legs and so on, and then wondered where the fly itself had gone.

A further complication is the normal human desire to investigate, to assess, to make sense of data, and so on. This is fine: providing that you have the necessary expertise. In our field, to paraphrase a saying, 'Those who can't, try: those who can, don't have to.' Fortunately, it is quite easy to illustrate the dilemma for those who really want to understand it. If you are offered, for instance, strawberry jam, you have various options. You can taste it, you can try to investigate it, or you can follow up the etymology of its names and contents. The Sufis are, as they traditionally put it, engaged in 'tasting', not in research or testing. In any case, Sufism is not learnt by research or re-inventing the wheel.

Proof positive that many people who claim to be interested in Sufism are not interested in what it can offer is contained in the simple fact that, no matter how often you explain the foregoing facts, and regardless of how often they have been stated by the Sufis of the past, the requests for irrelevant information continue to pour in. And, of course, the piles of flies' legs grow larger.

The explanation is, luckily, quite simple. First recall that people will tend to persist in doing something after being told that it is absurd or unnecessary because continuing with this course pleases them more than adopting a correct one. Now apply this to the situation where someone is told that his (or her) insistence upon a certain course is absurd.

There are, of course, 'innocent' or naive reasons. In the case of academic workers, as we see from their often useless books, the training is such that the person is unable to operate in any other way. But this only means that little if any real communication is possible with people who have been narrowly conditioned in this or any similar way. Conventional scholars have denounced the Sufis for centuries for deriding academic work. This is only a manifestation of the 'give a dog a bad name and hang it' mentality, though: Sufis are, and have been, considerable scholars. But they know the difference between Sufi experience and scholasticism, and that the two are quite distinct.

It is, of course, not only Sufis who are at the receiving end of this kind of approach. Even if you are an engineer, you may well be approached by people who want to use engineering metaphors in dance choreography, or advertising, or something. And there is no harm in that. It is when – as it were – people imagine that engineering really is ballet that problems arise.

The tendency of seeking a panacea is also an aspect of this question. Not only Sufis, but all kinds of specialists, are regularly approached by people who want instant cures, improvements in their social, psychological or economic life, or – perhaps most frequently – some emotional stimulus. Of course, in the last-named kind of case, an internal, mental, censor usually ensures that the request is put in what the applicant imagines to be an acceptable form. And, although such behaviour is often regarded as hypocritical or self-deceived, it is much more likely to be socially conditioned.

Sometimes it is almost bizarre – where the conditioning has slipped. A few days ago I got a letter from a well-known but indigent person who asked for advice on how to make a lot of money in a very short time. Why? 'Not for myself,' he says, 'but because I could do so much good with it . . .'

What it all boils down to is that, regrettably, people have to know more about themselves before they undertake what are so often misconceived projects. Naturally, the more they are in need of such advice the less likely they are to take it; that has always been the case – but there are still Sufis who can carry out their work in spite of what might seem a considerable problem.

Not long ago I was saying something like this to a man who immediately insisted, 'But I have to know myself, which is the goal of all right-thinking people!' When I asked him what he meant by KNOW THYSELF, it turned out that he thought that it meant that he could make a breakthrough into a higher state of consciousness from where he was at the moment. He honestly had no idea that you have to get the lower state of consciousness into good order first. Trying to run, in this sense, before he could walk did not seem absurd to him.

On the contrary, he next assailed me with, 'If it were true that one has to attend to smaller things before attempting greater ones, why is this not taught more extensively? There is a long history of wise men saying, simply, KNOW THYSELF! They have not hedged it around with the qualifications which you are trying to impose!'

I give him due credit for speaking his mind. But, as I said to him, he had made no examination of his sources or assumptions, even within the field in which he was competent. Because, first, by tradition, simple statements are only 'headlines'. Second, many 'headlines' have been endlessly repeated by people who may have become reputed as authorities, but many of whom were only repeating slogans, however sincerely.

'It is the goldsmith who can assay the gold,' as Rumi said. But we constantly meet people who have read Rumi and taken no notice of this important and much-repeated statement of his. What do they take from Rumi instead? The dervish dance is one thing. And what is wrong with that? Only the fact that Rumi himself is on record as saying that he applied it specifically for the thirteenth-century people of Asia Minor, because of certain

15

characteristics of theirs: which are not to be found quite to the same extent among the thousands of people who have adopted dervish dancing recently in the West.

It is not only in the East that we have people busily turning themselves into imitations of medieval Orientals. But if they were to stop and look at what they were doing, it would spoil the fun.

Are you surprised that Sufis have so often said, down the centuries, that a large number of those who profess to want to follow the Sufi way do not really want it at all?

The fact is that people have their individual and common priorities. They will seek fulfilment of these, and through the channel and in the manner which appears to be appropriate: but those which appertain to the Sufi way, or any other specialisation, will often be quite different from these.

Sufis are not here to satisfy a demand. They exist to share what they have got. These two things are not always the same.

SECTION I

SECTION 1

Outworn Techniques

Q: *Is there any value in studying the teachings and activities of Sufi and other systems of the past? Some of them have died out, and some seem to belong to a past era, not applicable today . . .*

A: There is value in studying those which do have contemporary application. That means, of course, that the only people who can indicate which body of material – or what part of a body of material – to study are those who understand what they meant, for whom they were intended, and what their effect was designed to be. This, in turn, means that mere imitation is useless. Sufi study is prescription, not imitation or even tradition. There is, incidentally, no such thing as something 'dying out' in the Sufi sense. A medical prescription, for instance, does not 'die out': it is superseded. Broadly speaking, anything which is recorded (for instance on paper) belongs to a past era. Unlike the case of a doctor's prescription, it is not likely that the 'condition' for which Sufi exercises, say, were prescribed in the past, will recur today. We are not dealing with the human body's ills.

So we are back at the question of the teacher and his expertise. This is so important that you can actually discern a false or deluded teacher by noting that anyone who merely causes others to repeat Sufi exercises prescribed for dozens, hundreds, even thousands of years ago is not a Sufi teacher at all. He may be a traditionalist, a religionist, a ceremonialist: but he cannot help to develop the Sufi perception in others, or in himself. Tradition, colour, movement and so on have an undeniable appeal. They even have a therapeutic effect at times. But they are not Sufic activity. They are the degeneration of its externals: just as surely as the refilling of a medicine bottle with water and admiring its label is devoid of value except for the placebo, the psychological, effect. And that can be obtained in almost any way. Besides, there is no such thing as a spiritual placebo.

Recruitment and Education

Q: *Have you ever written on the subject of the importance of Sufi knowledge for the present day?*

A: Until recently, very little. The reason is that if you become identified with a stance, people will criticize it and write you off: and what you are trying to do will suffer, unless you condition people to support you – ending up with the kind of social group that improves tribalism but stultifies knowledge.

Hence I have instead worked very hard to get *facts* known and understood, first of all. This has really paid great dividends. The general stock of information has thereby increased; and information which was not accessible has been redistributed, bypassing personal prejudice.

I want people to have information *before* they decide to invoke their desires to support or to oppose an individual, a tradition or a system. This is, of course, making the distinction between a recruitment activity and an educational one.

Understanding Oneself

People are anxious to understand themselves. Part of Sufi preparatory activity is to make this possible, for the illustrable obtuseness of most of us is almost universal.

Certain approaches are worth noting from this point of view, for in this field it is quite possible, though not inevitable, that people may learn from the behaviour of others.

The first concern of all is to realise that we must study the wants and needs of people approaching the Sufis. Wants are not necessarily needs; even though wants may be the fuel and stabilisers of the present condition of the approacher.

I have here a bundle of correspondence from someone who wanted to work with us in making a film on the life of Al-Ghazzali. He has experience of film-making, and suggests that helping us in this way will be a contribution towards our work and also help him to learn by working with special materials.

We answer, informing him that, however theoretically desirable the project, we are already working on a plan of this kind. Moreover, and more importantly, we cannot work with 'externalist' perceptions of things like this. In other words, Sufi films have to be instrumental, planned for a certain effect. Only Sufis can do this, and in doing so would not necessarily choose this film-maker. His interest in the subject is not in itself a qualification.

Here is a selection of correspondence with a scholar, who is very friendly, and wants our help (and to 'help us') in finding out more, for publication, about a certain Dervish order. We answer to the effect that Sufis work with calculated methods. This is not the time or the place, and these are not the people, to undertake this specific activity.

A third collection of transactions concerns a lady who had written a book about our work, and seeks permission to quote from materials which we have published, which she is using to make certain points, so that 'we may become better known and understood'. We reply that there are two kinds of materials on Sufism: those written from an outside viewpoint, and those written to further the Sufi activity. The latter may not appear to be Sufi books at all, but they can be produced only by people with a certain kind of insight. The descriptive or propagandist book is not a Sufi one – therefore we are not able to support them. Indeed, we are ignorant of what they might be like. We add that, to include materials of ours might not only be of no use to our work; it might cause readers to imagine that the book represents something which we authorise.

Here, finally, is correspondence from a man of religion who assumes that all spirituality is the same, and seeks to have us ameliorate our 'harsh attitudes' towards various beliefs and activities in the religious sphere.

Now all these approaches have certain things in common, which (though perhaps visible to a completely outside observer) are unperceived by the writers.

The first evident characteristic is that the person has assumed that he or she is doing something useful, without knowing whether this is true or not. Secondly, it is also inherent in this assumption that we are working as randomly and on an equally shallow basis: that, in fact, we have no long-range insight. Thirdly, the assumption is here that the particular aspect, item, and so on, is useful; fourthly, that we are not already working on a plan; fifthly, that there is no other plan in which this person might take part; sixthly, that one can start in the middle. That is to say, that this individual can adopt an idea and that it is sure to be good, without any of the absolutely essential learning which alone can qualify someone for meshing into such programmes.

In short, the question which should have been asked is: 'Can I learn? What, if anything, can I do?'

All Sufis teach this first. It is hard to do so, because this bald statement ('you need to do something else first') is very often taken, by the *Commanding Self* as a rejection or as a challenge, instead of it being taken for what it really is, a constructive and well-meant description of the other person's current position and needs.

This is what lies behind the concepts of *Taubat* (repentance, turning back from ignorant assumption in these cases) and *Khidmat*, (service, which means to serve oneself best by not trying irrelevant things, just as much as being in the service of Truth).

Criticism and Learning

Q: *Sufi teachers in their books and in the stories about their teaching interactions often complain about the problems there are in dealing with*

people, and criticise their followers and all kinds of other people con-
stantly. If circumstances are as bad as that, is there any hope of teaching
getting under way?

A: In the first place, what some people regard as criticism is also
to be seen as being descriptive of a situation. Secondly, the
description of people and their behaviour is itself an integral part
of the teaching process. When you see, hear or read of such
interchanges, you are in fact seeing the teaching under way, so
there is no question of 'when will it start'. Part of the effect of the
teaching is to observe this, so that if you have not noted it, it
is you who are not learning, not that the teaching is not
operating.

Q: *Then, presumably, if one has not observed these things, one cannot
be taught?*

A: Not at all. Not to have observed something in one way or on
one occasion – or in one of many ways or on many occasions – is
no indication that the person cannot be taught. Persistence in
teaching is paralleled by persistence in learning. People are, in
fact, induced by various approaches to expose different facets of
themselves to the teaching, so that they can eventually learn.
Indeed, reverting to the first question, it is often the very forcing
of an inhibition upon certain approaches that induces the learner
to stop playing what are in fact games and may induce him to
focus seriously on what is being taught. But if, because of his
arguing and wrangling, this process cannot be carried out, he
cannot learn. That is why dialecticians cannot teach anything in
the Sufi Way, and why intellectualist or emotional approaches
from the students cannot yield results beyond mutually stimulative reactions, which are absent in the Sufi teaching situation
and are avoided or suppressed by the kind of 'criticism' to which
you refer.

Why Should I Change Now?

There was once a merchant who bought a pair of shoes. He wore them until they were almost worn out and then, because they were comfortable, he had them patched and wore them until even the patches were in ribbons. Patches were then put on patches and, although misers and people who did not think much about things applauded his economy, the shoes were unwieldy and unpleasant to look at, and they scuffed up a lot of dust in the street. When people complained about the dust, he always answered: 'If the dust were not there, the shoes would not raise it – go to the municipality and complain about the streets!'

The shoes made a lot of noise as the merchant clumped down the street, but most people had become used to this, and the others were in a minority and eventually had to get used to it.

So, with enough people applauding his carefulness with his money and plenty of people prepared to get used to his nuisance-value, what the rest thought was of no account. It became understood that the merchant's shoes should be as they were, by the merchant and by everyone else. So accepted was it that something quite unusual would have to happen for people to start to think about the matter afresh.

And, sure enough, one day it started to happen.

The merchant had bought some rare glasses for a low price and expected to resell them and make a huge profit. In celebration, he decided to go to the Turkish baths and have a luxurious steaming and soaking. While he was in the bath, he started to wonder whether he should not buy a new pair of shoes out of his expected profits on the sale of the glasses; but then he put the idea out of his mind, saying to himself: 'They will do for a time yet.'

But somehow the idea stayed in his mind, and somehow it seemed to have affected his thinking, the shoes and even the glasses, and much else, as we shall see. The first thing that

24

happened was that, as he left the bath-house, he automatically put his feet into a pair of very expensive slippers and walked away with them. He had left by the wrong door, and the slippers which were there, in a corresponding position to his own terrible footgear, belonged to the Chief Judge of the town.

When the judge came out of the baths he missed his slippers and could only see the awful shoes of the merchant, which he was forced to wear back to his house. Of course, like everyone else in the city, he recognized the monstrosities.

In less time, almost, than it takes to tell, the judge had the merchant brought to his court and fined heavily for theft.

Bursting with indignation, the merchant went to the window of his house, overlooking the water, and threw his shoes into the river. Now, he thought, he would be rid of these instruments of loss, and he would be able to escape their influence. But the power of the shoes was not yet exhausted...

A fisherman pulled the shoes up in his net soon afterwards. They tore his nets, so heavy were the nails with which they had been studded in the course of their many repairs.

Furious at the merchant – for, like everyone else, he could see whose shoes they were – the fisherman took them back to the merchant's house and hurled them through a window. They landed on the precious glass which the man had bought, and smashed it to tiny pieces.

When the merchant saw what had happened, he almost exploded with rage. Going into the garden, he dug a hole to bury them.

But the neighbours, seeing him so unaccustomedly at work, reported to the Governor that the merchant seemed to be seeking treasure, which, after all, belonged by law to the State. Now the Governor, convinced that there would be rich pickings here, spent on credit and got into debt for some very fine porcelain which he had always coveted. Then he called the merchant and told him to hand over the buried gold.

The merchant explained that he was only trying to get rid of his accursed shoes; and, after the Governor had had the garden completely dug over, he fined the merchant a sum which covered his trouble, his porcelain and the cost of digging, plus something for causing the officials to waste their time.

The merchant now took his shoes far away from the city and threw them into a canal. Presently, carried by the water into the irrigation channels, they blocked a pipe and deprived the King's garden of water. All the flowers died. The merchant was summoned as soon as the gardeners had found and identified the shoes, and he was again fined a large sum.

The merchant in desperation, hacked the slippers in half and buried one piece in each of the four main rubbish-dumps which surrounded the city. Thus it was that four dogs, scavenging in the dumps, each found half a shoe, and each one carried it back to the merchant's house, barking and growling for rewards, until the people were unable to sleep or to walk in the streets for their aggressiveness and fawning. When the dogs had been placated, the merchant went to the court.

'Honoured Judge!' he said, 'I wish formally to relinquish these shoes, but they will not give me up. Please, therefore, execute a paper, a legal document, which attests that anything done by, with or through these shoes shall henceforth have no connection with me!'

The Judge thought the matter over. Eventually he pronounced: 'Since I am unable to find in my books any precedent for the assumption that shoes are persons in any sense of the word, capable of being allowed to do anything or prohibited from doing anything, I cannot accede to your request.'

Strangely enough, as soon as the merchant bought a new pair of shoes – he had been going barefoot – nothing untoward happened to him again.

This of course, is the answer to the question: 'Why should I change my ideas, my ways or my thoughts now?'

Such questions can only be answered by allegories, claiming that things are happening as a consequence of doing nothing. And these things, unfortunately, are not as obvious in their connection with our ways as the shoes were in the case of the merchant. After all, if things were so obvious, nobody would need to ask the question, would they?

Science and Philosophy

Q: *What do the Sufis think of the controversies between science and philosophy, and between similar groups of people with varying formulae for the reorganisation of the world? There are so many systems, though, no doubt, we can adjudicate between them since we are – so to speak – their employers.*

A: Perhaps you have not heard of the story of the two masseurs at the bath-house, their employer and their customer? The ancient author Hamadani, in his *Maqama of Halwan*, explains this point very subtly, showing just how deep – and how superficial and irrelevant – such systems can be, in the absence of knowledge:

THE BATH-HOUSE

There was once a man who, returning from a pilgrimage, entered a town and had careful enquiries made as to the very best bath-house where he could refresh himself and obtain good attendance with warm water and pleasant perfumes.

He eventually found himself at the most highly recommended of such establishments. As soon as he entered its door, an attendant massaged his forehead with clay, as is the custom, and then went out. Soon afterwards, another masseur entered, and kneaded and pummelled the client.

Now the first man returned, and immediately attacked his fellow. 'Leave that head alone – it is mine!' he shouted.

The second man denied the claim. They fought, rolling on the ground. The first was crying, 'This is *my* head, for it was I who massaged it with clay!'

'Not so,' said the other claimant, 'it was, rather, I who rubbed the body upon which the head sits!'

When the two were exhausted, the owner of the place was called to adjudicate. He, in his turn, asked the customer to give an opinion as to which of the men owned the head.

The traveller cried out, 'For goodness sake! It belongs to neither of them – it is mine!'

But the owner of the bath-house was infuriated by this. Turning to his employees, he said, 'May God curse this damnable individual, for his head is obviously useless: I do not see why you are bothering with him! Let him go to hell...'

Human Development

Q: *How long does the process of human individual development actually take?*

A: As long as it takes the teacher, the individuals and the group to be in the right harmony. In your terms, this might be ten minutes or ten years – or more or less.

Q: *It is said that only one in a hundred thousand can make the grade.*

A: Is it?

Q: *Is this correct?*

A: It is not correct for us and those in our situation. I am not responsible for what others have said at other times, in other places and situations. If you want to lump together what various people have said to you or to other people and use the result, you are an anthologist or synthesist, not a Seeker in the sense in which we use the term.

Q: *But I never heard of such an idea. Surely the teachings of the great ones who have come before us are still valid?*

A: They are still as valid as they ever were, given the same conditions and students. How they are to be understood and made use of depends entirely upon the right experience and ability of those who are trying to make use of them. The melancholy fact is that the conditions and seekers have changed. Their curriculum is correspondingly inappropriate.

The Quality of One's Search

Q: *Is it not better to have spent some time, even years, in trying to find some sort of truth, than not to have tried at all?*

Surely we cannot say that one has not gained something through having spent time with books or people connected with an esoteric or higher search?

A: If it has been a wrong search, there is probably no advantage, and certainly a great deal of disadvantage. This is a question which is asked again and again by people who want reassurance.

If they are prepared to face it, here is the rest of the answer: They have spent years with books or people – therefore something must have been attained. The reasoning, from the point of experience from which we speak, is false.

'A donkey eats a melon, it remains a donkey'; 'You will never reach Mecca, because you are on the road to Samarkand' are two sayings which are intended to illustrate the position of some of these people. What, exactly, have they gained, apart from a sense that they must have gained something?

The answers to this question, from the people themselves, generally consist of assertions that they feel better, that they feel happier, or that they have been able to 'help others'. There are a lot of other answers too.

The situation really is that, unless they know what they have gained, how much of it, and where they are going, the 'gain' if any, is at best latent. It cannot be regarded as useful at the time. It has no worth at all until activated by harmonisation with a significant activity in the real tradition.

I meet many people who have worked hard in this field, have tried so hard that they did not know when they had reached the end of their constructive development. They needed certain other developments, and consequently have deteriorated through repetitious activity until they are, in fact, no use at all, though they may feel that they are, and may contrive to transmit this sensation to others.

The worst are those with vague, sporadic, incomplete connections with an 'invisible world'. In fact, such feelings are mere distortions or the stirring of a potentiality, which their own subjectivity endows with fantastic, distorted entities and meanings, and often attempts to systematise. And the worst of these seek similar equally distorted individuals or examples of literature, and 'prove' their experience by reference to these.

They suffer from concealed arrogance.

The World

People follow one creed or system after another, each one believed to provide the answer, the thing that will solve all problems. In the West, for instance, people followed religion and then threw it up for 'reason'; then they put all their money on industry and finally on technology. Until they have run out of panaceas they are unlikely to cure this habit.

There was once a man who took a flock of sheep and some bags of grain to market. He sold the grain and hid the money about him, and was looking for a buyer for the flock when a trickster approached him.

'I know someone who wants a flock of sheep just like that one,' he said, and led the farmer to a gate. 'Just wait outside this house,' he said, 'and I will drive the sheep into the yard and let the owner look at them. He knows me, and is suspicious of rustics.'

He drove the animals through the gate and through an alleyway at the back of another road. Shortly afterwards he sold the sheep very quickly and cheaply.

Disguising himself as a pilgrim, he hurried back to where the dupe had just realised that he had been cheated. 'Good Sir,' he cried, 'I have just seen a man such as you describe driving a flock of sheep like yours into a certain barn. Come with me and I will show you.'

When they arrived at a large barn the trickster said, 'Go in there, quickly. I will hold your horse.'

As the farmer walked to the barn, intent on getting his sheep back, the thief galloped away with the horse and sold it in the market for one-tenth of its value.

The farmer was deeply distressed and ran hither and thither, crying out, 'I have been robbed.' The thief now disguised himself as a scholar and found the distraught man once again. 'Have you nothing left, my poor friend?' he asked.

'Well, I have the money I got for my grain, so I had better walk home to such-and-such a place where I live, and count myself lucky that something remains to me.'

'As it happens,' said the trickster, 'I am going that way myself, with this bag of money, which is to be used to build a new college.'

He indicated a bag which he had filled with stones.

'Let us travel together, for safety on the road.'

The farmer agreed, and they set off.

After some time the pair were crossing a bridge over a stream when the thief let his bag fall into the water.

'Oh!' he cried, 'I am ruined... I am too old and frail to descend into the river, and the money is lost. I shall be disgraced...'

'I'll get the bag,' said the farmer, 'if you give me ten per cent of what is in it.'

'Willingly,' agreed the villain – and the farmer stripped off his clothes and left them, together with his own profit from the grain, on the bridge.

The thief made off with the money and the clothes.

31

When the naked and dripping farmer reached the bank and opened the bag, he found only stones.

The shock finally turned his head. He is now convinced, they tell me, that all he has left – himself – will be stolen from him, and he ranges the streets of the town alternately calling for his lost goods and cursing the thief whom he so often thought to be his friend.

The Short Cut

Q: *Is there anything wrong with following a path which has been trod by thousands, or even millions, in the past?*

A: None whatever, providing that you don't mind ending up like the man at London Airport who followed the route taken by millions before him.

Q: *What did happen to him?*

A: He followed a sign which said: 'To the Aircraft'. He found that it led to the gangway of an aeroplane. When he had boarded and the plane had taken off, he asked the stewardess: 'Where do I get the connecting flight for Rome?'

She answered: 'Under the circumstances, you will have to change at the end of the flight – in Tokyo!'

Ass and Camel

Q: *People make the most intensive study of contemporary problems and of history, and they set up all kinds of organisations and institutions to provide justice, health, education and peace, amongst a hundred other things. How is it, then, that terrible problems persist, and new ones constantly arise?*

A: You have evidently not heard the tale of the donkey and the camel.

A donkey and a camel were walking along together. The camel moved with long strides and the donkey moved impatiently, stumbling every now and then. At last the donkey said to his companion, 'How is it that I am always in trouble, falling and grazing my legs, in spite of the fact that I look carefully downwards as I walk; when you, who never seem to be aware of what surrounds you, with your eyes fixed upon the horizon, keep going so fast and yet seemingly at such leisure?'

The camel answered: 'Your problem is that your steps are too short and by the time you have seen something it is too late to correct your movements. You look all around and do not assess what you see. You think that haste is speed; you imagine that by looking you can see; you think that seeing near is the same as seeing far.

'You guess that I look at the horizon. In fact, I am merely gazing ahead so as to work out what to do when the far becomes near. I also remember what has gone before, and do not need to look back at it and stumble once again. In this way what seems to you baffling or difficult becomes clear and easy.'

Similarly, donkey-minded people are those who believe that they can learn enough to improve themselves or their lot by short-sighted means. This includes not looking towards the future or even into it. It includes demanding a certain pace without realising whether it is counter-productive or not. The ass is the ordinary person, the camel is the Sufi.

33

Telling the Time

Q: *Why do you use quotations from modern writers and from newspapers, if Sufi ideas have already been sufficiently well formulated centuries ago?*

A: I think that the best way to illustrate this is by means of a modern joke. There was once a wrist-watch salesman who found that he could sell watches well enough to townsfolk who knew what time was. With rustics, however, it was more difficult.

One day he found himself in the country where a man was chopping wood. He promised himself that he would get the rustic to understand the value of a timepiece.

So he shouted out:

'What time is it?'

The old fellow looked at the pile of wood.

'About twenty logs to dinner-time,' he said.

The Teacher

There are certain characteristics which run through teachership. This is a very large question, though in its real essence a simple one. By this I mean that it can be *touched on* in a hundred thousand words – or understood without words; depending upon the approach.

But observe this. The Sufi guide teaches from a position which is at times 'in the world' because he has to maintain contact with his environment. He follows the 'arc of ascent' to learn; and when he has completed the 'arc of descent' he is among the people. He is now transmuted. This means that although his outward form and even a part of his essence may be visible, his whole depth only unfolds to those who are developed enough to understand and perceive it.

There is more than an analogy here with teaching or leading in other fields; because leadership in the more ordinary things is a 'shadow' or distortion of the essence of 'teachership'.

If you are teaching a child, or a student, something which you know and he does not, you have to draw yourself to what you call 'his level', and pull him up, slowly. Again, you have to withdraw from involvement, in order to see the thing objectively. As in the ordinary, so in the extraordinary: hence the teacher is in a way (or in what seems to be many ways) apart, or has been set apart, from the mass. He does not belong to the mass, and yet he does. His relationship to the mass is like that of the refined gold compared with the ore.

He is not 'in his own land', because his own land is already cultivated. The concept and the detachment are clear if you look at both spiritual and other teachers, seeking the general law which permeates them. Disregard for the moment the element of personal difference or authenticity; even of quality, nationality or teaching. Look at the people.

Buddha operated in a milieu outside that of his royal palace. Before he taught, he detached himself from his 'land' as prophets and others did. Napoleon came from Corsica to France; Jesus from Nazareth – and ultimately, from beyond the 'world' or land as we know it normally. All the nuances of this 'strangerhood' as the Sufis call it, have to be felt if the paradox of the 'saviour from afar' is to be apprehended and made to work within the organism in which he appears.

Knife and Fork . . .

Q: *I notice that, in your lectures, you style our Western adaptations of Eastern thinking, such as Christianity, as being superficial and robbing*

35

the thing of its depth. But, surely, you would not object to anything
being adapted to suit its local usage?

A: My dear friend, interestingly enough you have been – albeit
unwittingly – answered by Lord (formerly Sir Geoffrey) Howe,
speaking in another regard.

He said: 'It is hardly progress for a cannibal to use a knife and
fork.'

The whole point is not in the adaptation, but whether the
adaptation is in accordance with the possibilities, or whether it
may even be deleterious.

Mystical Formulas

Q: *What is the point of mystical repetitions? They seem to exist in all*
religious and magical traditions, whether primitive or otherwise.

A: The 'point' as you call it, depends entirely on their application, which must accord with their true nature. There is a Sufi
story which makes this 'point'.

A man once climbed onto the roof of a place where a Sufi was
privately instructing a disciple, in order to learn their secrets. He
heard the Sufi say: 'You shall now repeat, seventy-seven times a
day, the phrase "Is it worth it?"'

The eavesdropper went away and decided to put his new
knowledge to work. He repeated the phrase as prescribed for the
other man, but it was not a suitable one for him, because he soon
became unable to say anything else. Whenever he went into a
shop to buy anything, he would say, 'Is it worth it,' until he was
thrown out of the town and had to live on whatever he could
find growing wild in the countryside.

One day he found a piece of paper on the ground, and, still
thoroughly imbued with the phrase, wrote on it:

'Is it worth it' is the secret phrase of the Sufis, which has to be repeated.

It happened that the Commander of the King's guard, who also wanted to know about Sufi knowledge, rode past and saw this paper on the ground. He picked it up and read it, and went on his way, dutifully repeating the mystical formula. Presently he arrived at the court of the King, who was planning a war, still mechanically repeating the words.

'What was that you said?' asked the King.

'I was saying, "Is it worth it?"' said the officer.

The King had him beheaded for defeatism. And, as for the eavesdropper, he is the ancestor of those people who believe that they can teach Sufi knowledge by rote. The piece of paper has been found again and again, and people have published what it says in books. The eavesdropper, of course, did not write (because he did not know it) on the paper that the phrase was prescribed for one individual. That is why so many people use it and try to make it work...

Repeatable Experiments

A good deal of the time and energy devoted to research into higher perceptions is expended in the attempt to devise experiments which can be repeated. This is, however, often like trying to feed a horse by telephone: the objective may be praiseworthy and its reason known, but the method selected is rather uninformed, unlikely to succeed.

As to the objective, however, it and its praise-worthiness too, depend upon what the experimenter's orientation is. It is considered a good thing, by some people, to 'increase knowledge' by finding repeatable phenomena and using them to lead one to a general rule, law or principle.

In the case of Sufi experience with extra-sensory phenomena, the principle claimed by the Sufis is different. Their investigation shows that the following of phenomena yields diminishing returns. This, they aver, is because the increase in knowledge of localised phenomena cannot be carried out beyond a certain point. The detail, or secondary manifestation, of 'psi', in their view, actually emphasises that there is no further progress along that road. The progress comes, rather, by way of the holistic approach.

It might be said that the scientific approach has most often been: 'I shall make this phenomenon yield its secrets', while the Sufic attitude is: 'Let the real truth, whatever it may be, be revealed to me'.

The former is the 'heroic' mode: attempting something with insufficient knowledge; the latter the 'self-evolution' mode: fitting oneself to perceive that which is to be perceived. It eliminates heroism.

In the latter mode, experience is needed before knowledge can be perceived. In the former, experience provides knowledge. One pitfall in the way of the 'heroic' may be glimpsed in the story of the professor and the carpet – in which this gentleman generalises only from such data as he has got:

There was once a professor who lost a book and could not find it anywhere. One day he had just taken off his hat and was rolling back a carpet for some reason, when he saw the missing volume on the floor.

This lesson was not lost on him. Not long afterwards, someone told him that a valuable ring had been lost.

'There is no real problem there,' said the professor, 'for all you have to do is what I did, which yielded results. Take off your hat and roll back the carpet – then you will find the ring almost at once.'

This pitfall is avoided by those who insist on repeatable experiments. But supposing another pitfall is that those who try for repeatable experiments are relying upon a mechanicality which itself frustrates the manifestation of what they are trying to produce?

It is by no means unknown among members of authentic mystical schools that trying to force something is the best way to stop it happening. Probably many more attempts will have to be made to storm the gates of heaven, though, before it is realised that this storming is a way of shutting them.

So the parable of the professor is not quite so inappropriate to the scientist if it portrays someone who relies on something which the experience of others shows cannot work. At the same time, the results of the experiments themselves (including negative results) may be 'trying to tell you something'.

In one widespread tale of the land of fools, a number of yokels decide to move their house a few yards to the left. They take off their cloaks and leave them on one side of the building, to mark the place they want to reach. Then they go to the other side of the house and push with all their might. Returning to the first place to see how far they have moved the building, they see that the cloaks are gone: in fact a thief has run off with them. 'We have lost our cloaks!' they exclaim. 'That means that we pushed too far and rolled the whole building over them.'

How Things Seem To Be

Q: *The first time I met you and heard you talking about ordinary things in an extraordinary way, I was puzzled. I often thought that this was no more than an intellectual exercise. It was a temptation to put the whole thing out of my mind.*

Then I said to myself, 'There may be something in this. Am I not judging too soon?' Then, as we met, different planes seemed to unfold. Things you said on earlier occasions seemed to make sense and join into the pattern. Some things I began to appreciate on different levels.

It is difficult to know how to put it, but I might say that a word or a story seemed to be used again and again in the mind, as if its power was not just a single-shot one. The barrage is over, but the bullets are still taking effect. This is a strange experience.

Now I am wondering, since I have read a great deal of psychology, especially in the past ten years, whether this is merely a phenomenon of my mind. I have the idea that something is forming in my mind.

A: Everyone has the compulsive habit of relating everything that comes into his mind with as many other things as the pattern of his thoughts allows. You can interpret what is happening to you in any way you like, or in any way you need.

Among us, the variety and parabolic nature of the impact is so arranged as to address itself to parts of the consciousness which are least conditioned to automatism. You can, however, interpret the phenomenon in accordance with whatever pattern of thought you are dependent upon.

For instance, various schools of psychology will provide you with tailor-made frames of reference through which you can account for the process.

If you need the protection and reassurance of such a system, you will find it in that system. What we are really doing, however, is beyond the formal limits of a psychology as generally understood at the moment.

Misunderstood

Q: *It is often said that people do not understand even the most explicit Sufi writings, and that people simply take the meaning which they think is intended. How can one identify this tendency, and how can it be overcome?*

A: You hardly need to identify the tendency: if you assume that it is there, you will generally not be far off the truth.

But take this example, almost at random. In his *Bostan* (The Orchard), Saadi tells a story about kindness to the unjust.

There was once a man who wanted to destroy a hive near his house, and his wife prevented him. Then, one day when she was stung by a bee, he reproached her for not having let him take action when he wanted to. Saadi goes on to say that 'If the watchman shows kindness, people remain awake through fear'. Patience with the evil only increases their evil, he emphasises.

Certainly it is human experience that ignoring that which may harm one can increase the danger. This is the apparently explicit message from Saadi, and one for which he has been greatly applauded, except by those who say that evil can be conquered by inaction or by humility.

But, in Sufi circles, the Sufic message is as clear: that the only remedy for injustice in the world appears to be to oppose it; but the Sufi's capacity is to understand what justice and injustice really are, when and where they really are operating, and what means other than superficial, instant reaction, may be taken to deal with this phenomenon.

For the Sufi is asking you to wonder what is really happening in the world – do you see it as it really is: are your remedies and those of your authority-figures based on any such perception?

Simplifying Sufi Teaching

Q: *Many people find it difficult to understand Sufi ideas. Would it not be better if they were put more simply and with a more gradual introduction, so that people could become accustomed to this unusual way of thinking?*

A: I think that we must be fair to the very large number of people who do *not* find it difficult to follow Sufi ideas, and say that we do not find a great problem of communication with people who are ready to give the right kind of attention to the materials. I do not think that it is a question of simplifying, but of having the right approach. When one approaches anything with, say, impatience, anxiety or by interposing a mass of assumptions, these are the things which we find, in common with the traditional Sufis, act as barriers which filter out the ease of understanding which others are able to experience.

This kind of question rather reminds me of the fact that some people who have heard of one, after a conversation, say, 'What a horrible man! I thought he would be marvellous...' And of some others, in similar circumstances, who say, 'How marvellous, and I thought he would be horrible!' Which assessment is the correct one?

Most cultures specialise in the inculcation of prejudice. The Sufi one tries to help remove it, so that the reality of anyone or anything may be perceived. But it is not possible to ignore the fact of the existence of this prejudice (for or against, or towards what one wants something to be) and instead of facing it as the major problem, to look for ways to tinker with the Teaching, whether you call this 'simplifying' or whatever else you may call it.

Perils of Imitation

Q: *What happens when genuine teachings, as distinct from diluted ones, are offered to a society which has not had them before?*

A: This has to be done with the greatest caution. I do not vouch for its truth, but I was told the following story by a Yogi in India:

A genuine Yogi, visiting Britain, heard that a highly popular Yoga teacher, much hailed as 'a master', was very ill.

He went to see him, and found him in bed, surrounded by his Western disciples, all of them with eyes closed and crouching in approved positions such as you see in the attractive photographs which are nowadays published everywhere.

The real Yogi said: 'I shall now demonstrate to you the secret healing postures which may cure this man.'

The self-styled Yogi, imitated by his followers (who of course were all agog at this dramatic and exciting intervention) carried out the exercises which the true Yogi demonstrated.

And, miraculously as it seemed, by the power of the authentic Yoga, the false master was cured.

It was only his disciples who became ill, unable to stand the strain of the advanced techniques...

The Mouse and The Elephant

You may care to hear another (this time ancient) but still current tale: that of the love affair between the elephant and the mouse.

Despite the opposition of their respective families, an elephant and a mouse who were in love decided to get married.

On their wedding night, the elephant keeled over and died.

The mouse said: 'O Fate! I have unknowingly bartered one moment of pleasure and tons of imagination for a lifetime of digging a grave!'

So, when you try to ask questions, see whether you can descry the logical and other shortcomings in them.

Intolerable Mishmash?

Q: *What can be done about the intolerable mishmash found in the books on the Sufis which pour from the presses? These are often written by reputable people, but they take no heed of the different epochs, cultures and so on in which their materials were projected. The result is chaos, and I think that there is a real danger of people adopting these materials as authentic renderings of what the Sufis have been, and are, doing.*

A: You have to note two things. The first is that, for these self-appointed experts, the whole matter is really at a very early stage. They are the equivalent of the pre-scientific writers who accumulated, and confused, information on, say, herbs or precious stones. It is not that they do not know what they are doing; it is that they think that what they are doing constitutes an adequate study. Time will put this right, as it did with stone-lore or herb-wisdom. Secondly, you should remember that authentic materials are also available. It does not take too much common sense to see, when comparing these with the ones to which you take exception, which is more likely to be correct. In this respect, at least, Gresham's Law can be reversed, so to speak: 'Good money drives out bad'.

The only exceptions are the credulous and the inadequate, who will prefer the jumbled materials because they have a taste for such things. It is not our function to 'do anything about' the situation. This happens inevitably, with the wider currency of correct materials. Naturally, we cannot protect the credulous or fortify the inadequate: but there are people and institutions whose function this is.

Rather than deplore the shortcomings of inferior work too much, I think that we may allow ourselves to feel some satisfaction that legitimate materials, and the proper response to them, do exist and become stronger almost by the day.

Appearance and Content in Sufi Tales

Q: *I note that Sufi stories are nowadays very widely used in all kinds of publications and lectures. What are the advantages and disadvantages of this explosion of interest and experimentation?*

A: The main disadvantage is that the story will be used in such a superficial way that its internal dynamic is not available for its real purpose. More and more people write to us, asking to use stories or saying that they have found them useful. The interesting thing is that in many cases the stories are not even being adequately used for the lower-level purpose attempted by those who adopt them in this fashion. What has actually happened is that someone wants grist for his mill and lacks the desire for truth which alone makes it possible for him and for the story (let alone his students) to reach their potentiality.

You may recall a story about this: there was once a man who, when a ship was sinking, called the passengers together and instructed them how to break up the lifeboats to make a raft!

There is no substitute for knowledge. Trying to put things into practice prematurely is not confined to people who teach or are interested in Sufi tales.

Tales, like fruit, contain such things as colour, flavour and nutrition. The apparent effect (say the refreshing quality) is not the end of their operation. The difference between fruit and tales is that, while the fruit's nutritional effect will take place automatically, the tale needs awareness on the part of the person giving out the tale. At the very lowest level, such a person should keep the door open by emphasising that there is this other content: or that those who produced the tale assert that there is.

It is often said that others have used the tales for superficial purposes. But this hardly justifies everyone's taking it on themselves to dilute materials intended for a higher purpose. Transpose this into any analogy you like (say one of high technology employed for lesser purposes) and you will see what a waste it is, and how it encourages ignorance.

Supreme Importance

Q: *You have published more anecdotes concerning the ancient Sufis than anyone else, I think, in the history of Sufism. Since these refer to people well known in Eastern culture but generally unknown in the West, does this not fail to convey the great importance of these teachers?*

A: In what sense?

Q: In the sense that if, say, Junaid or Nuri said something, we know that it must be of supreme importance, and really true. How can a Western person feel this if he does not know the rank of Junaid or Nuri?

A: If Junaid or Nuri said it, it is indeed of objective importance, and nobody needs to know for learning purposes who said it or to feel that it is true. It must have an effect.

Q: Then why mention Junaid or Nuri at all?

A: Not to authenticate a statement or to influence people; merely to keep the framework so that the materials may be of use to both Eastern and Western students.

What it is Really Like

Q: *What can one do if one's closest friends or spouse object to one's attending study-meetings?*

A: I suggest that you tell such people the following story:

MISINTERPRETATION

There was once a man who used to go out at night to study spiritual and psychological subjects with a number of others. His wife objected, and she was always complaining that he was selfish and peculiar.

One day he managed to get her to go along, just to see what it was like. She sat there among all those strangers, listening to incomprehensible things. Finally, when they left, she said: 'What a lot of ridiculous nonsense! I could hardly stand it . . .'

The husband said: 'Well, now you know what it is like, you surely don't still think that I enjoy myself there, do you?'

This tale brings out two points. First, that things that you are not used to, or from which you are excluded, seem unpleasant or awful. The second point, which may well be true in many cases, is that a great number of these groups have an atmosphere which really do tell newcomers that they are not normal. So the test always is whether your friends in this kind of interest are acceptable to relatives or other, normal, friends. If they are, well and good. If they are not, you have to discover whether you are in a weird group, and whether your other associates might not be right, after all.

Escape

Q: *I want to get away from 'things of this world', and as a result I have immersed myself in the study of all kinds of books on occultism and experiential religion.*

I feel that I am on the way to 'finding myself', and wonder whether you would agree with me that this is the right thing to do?

A: Have you ever heard of the man who jumped into a river to get away from the rain?

Books on occultism and religion will merely make you think of such things in a 'worldly' way, if you are a worldly person. What you have to learn is how to find the unworldly in everything. Can you do that? Obviously not, or you would not have asked the question.

It is not the immersion alone, as you call it: it is very much a question of who or what is being immersed. Some things are cleaned by immersion: others merely become waterlogged.

Inner Space

Q: *How can one remove vices and shortcomings, so as to become a truly spiritual person, in the Sufic sense? There are so many accounts of struggles carried on by holy people against temptations and sins . . .*

A: Nothing which you have said accords with Sufi diagnosis, theory, practice or experience. It is, in fact, something snatched from a half-understanding of spiritual exercises, at one remove. *Note this:*

Sufic spirituality can help a person to deal with what you call 'vices and shortcomings'. But this does not mean immediately plunging into activities intended to fight temptations, and so on. Such efforts do not work, which is the best argument against them. What, then, does work? The first thing to observe is that Sufis are not against, say, human emotion: they are against the over-activity of emotion, which leads to vice or to the other extreme, imagined holiness and spurious spiritual experiences.

This means that the Sufi learning system needs first to induce the learner to settle for the minimum emotional stimulus which he or she needs to operate the various functions which require emotional inputs. When this has been achieved, there is a 'space' into which the developing function can be 'poured'.

Many familiar religious systems have over-simplified matters. They have assumed that, say, emotionality is bad, so they have tried to get people to destroy their emotional life. This has only produced delusory effects. Or they have channelled emotions into what they have decided are 'good' or 'spiritual' emotionality. At best, this is, of course, only another form of self-indulgence. What has to be done, as with any other input needed by the human being, is to regulate it (whether it be the desire for gain, the need to achieve, or whatever underlies the 'sin' or 'vice') so that the necessary 'space' may be found. And that first step is the combined work of the teacher and the learner.

SECTION II

SECTION II

Three Significant Modes of Human Organisation and Learning

All human efforts are organised in one of three 'departments':

> The General and informational,
> the More Specific or specialist,
> and the Personally Experiential.

Hence, for example:

Information about food; organisation of food; consumption of food, in that area. In the area of religion, we have information and general exegesis (doctrine), followed by application of religious organisation (rules and worship), and finally, personal experience of spirituality.

All religious systems are based on personal experience (stage one) which has been codified (stage two) and applied to a community (stage three). When the three ranges become confused or if one or other is forgotten, people imagine that the organisation is all, or that the rules are paramount, or that neither of these matters since they are seeking only personal illumination.

When people agitate for personal experience, they may attack institution or dogma, imagining that these are what stand in the way. What they have in fact encountered as problems is the growth of those areas until they claim to represent, extinguish or replace personal experience. What has happened is that the balance between the three elements is lost, not that one or another of them is paramount or interchangeable with others.

Thus: we may know about food or have the apparatus to obtain, taste and digest it. This does not mean that we are organised to do so; or that we can taste it without obtaining it. Similarly, if we have tasted it, this does not imply that we have the information or organisation to recognise or obtain it a second time.

This simple formula is so little known that one almost

hesitates to enunciate it. It is, however, essential for restoring the balance in access strategy – the retrieval of Truth and awareness of fact.

'The Donkey which Brought You Here . . .'

A man came to see me recently, and I could see that he was very agitated. He had read a lot of books, and had been in many groups of 'seekers', and he had made himself desperate to get into a learning situation.

I told him that excitement of this kind, emotionality at this pitch, was a barrier to learning.

Now he had obviously been informed by others in the past that 'agitation is next to spirituality', and he was not going to give this up without a struggle. He said that it was anxiety and emotionalism which had brought him to me, so how could it be bad?

The very fact that he saw things like that, and could not see the flaw in his own reasoning was a sufficient symptom of his state. So I had to explain it to him. I said: 'If you had come to this house on a donkey, which brought you here, you would not have been allowed to ride it into my study. It fulfils its function, and then other functions take over.'

Again, such was his state of excitement that, instead of this appearing, as it was, to be a wholly reasonable statement of the situation, he regarded my information as a kind of masterly inspiration, or esoteric analogy.

Of course, when one of the symptoms of a person's state is that he cannot understand that he has them, talk tends to be of little use; and that is why people have to be dealt with, not talked to. He will have a chance to recover if he can be induced to behave in the sort of ordinary way in which someone without such pretensions behaves.

Because, sadly, aspirations to greater things can sometimes become transformed into a form of pretentiousness; and that is why all valid traditions demand humility. This posture, so often called a virtue, is rather to be looked at as a necessity, a technical requirement.

Another example from very recent experience is also a useful illustration of postures. Someone who has been writing to me about one or two people who have tried to attack me keeps trying to get me to hit back, and feels that he himself should take some part in this. I have been writing to him in a calming and reasonable way, but this does not satisfy him. He insists that he should do something because people like that shouldn't be allowed to do what they are doing. The fallacy here, of course, is that my correspondent has no overview and little context. He has failed to ask himself whether *he* is the man to do the job. People come to me all the time trying to put the world right, or even to put tiny parts of it right. But before you can do that you have to have the knowledge of how to be truly effective. Heroism is no substitute for effectiveness. And *that* is the lesson that is needed here. Unluckily, because of the warp in current cultures, one cannot exactly spell this out because people want approval, not information. If they will accept information, they can gain skill and then can become effective. We say this to them. If they won't accept it, this really means that they are rejecting us and in effect dictating policy and even tactics.

How does this accord with *our* role? In any teaching situation, one must teach and the other learn. This is why we say, 'Will you allow me to teach?'

People who are saying 'Will you teach me?' seldom really want to learn. Or, at best, they have a priority: that they shall be allowed to carry out their own subjective role first. They are, as it were, interposing a sort of circus between themselves and the teaching situation.

The only answer to this is for them to satisfy themselves first of all that they want to learn, and as to whether they accept the teacher and the teaching. If they do not, they are wasting a lot of time, both ours and theirs.

Timing

Q: *Can one predict an individual's actions? Can a Sufi teacher help someone to avoid wasting his life in studies and searches, or in unnecessary experiences?*

A: With enough information, it is almost impossible *not* to predict people's action. As to a Sufi helping someone to avoid wasting time: that is what the Sufi is for, as far as students are concerned. But do they accept it?

An ancient tale, which is partially found in the Persian *Thousand and One Days*, was written by the Dervish Mukhlis of Isfahan:

FATE AND ACTIONS

There was once a wise man who left a great deal of money to his son. On his deathbed he told him:

'If you should ever reach a state of real despair, but not before, open that door yonder, and not until you have literally no food left for even one day's sustenance.'

As soon as the father died, however, the youth, full of impatience and curiosity, opened the door. Beyond it was a room, and within that room was a rope and a wooden block. A notice on the wall instructed him to get onto the block, put the suspended noose around his neck, and jump.

He said to himself, 'This is a fine way for a father to behave towards his son!'

As he turned and left the room, he saw a piece of writing on the wall:

> If you have not heeded and applied what has been offered to you, much confusion and unnecessary suffering will follow you. Your own actions will cause these events, until you learn: you will have to travel
> from premature action and curiosity to wild assumption;
> from profligacy to ill-luck;
> from despair to insufficient remedy;
> from carelessness to derision;
> from misery to desperation;
> from obedience to fulfilment;
> from testing to enlightenment.

He left the room, unwilling to give any credence to his father's words, and plunged into a life of gambling and speculating with what he had inherited, acquiring many companions who helped him to spend his money and to sell his estates.

He was deeply in debt, and at last came to the point where he had no money for food. He collected the last few small objects in the house and took them to the market where he sold them for a trifling amount, buying some bread and yoghurt. As he was going home, a dog jumped up, spilt the yoghurt and carried off the bread.

The youth was now quite desperate, and went to the houses of all his supposed friends to ask for food and a comforting word. But they merely laughed at him, and one after another turned him out. 'You can't be as poor as that!' they said.

As he sat, hungry and miserable, he thought to himself, 'From carelessness with the bread and yoghurt to derision from my friends; this is the time of misery, as predicted by my father: and misery of this kind certainly leads to desperation.'

With that he again entered the room with the rope. He read the notice again: 'Stand on the block and hang yourself.'

Standing on the wooden block, he put the rope around his neck and jumped.

Immediately he did this, the rope broke loose, and the ceiling fell, releasing a huge hoard of gold coins which had been hidden in it.

'Obedience to fulfilment!' cried the youth. He paid his debts and bought back his property. Then he invited all his former friends to a rich banquet.

'When I spoke of my poverty,' he said, 'you did not believe me. Now I will tell you a story. There are a lot of rats in this town, who are so voracious that they will eat stones. Some of them specialise in gems, and will live only on rubies and emeralds. Hands up everyone who believes this...'

Everyone present raised a sycophantic hand.

'You did not believe in my poverty when I was hungry and wanted something although it was just a morsel and a kind word which I needed,' he said, 'and now you believe everything I say, because *you* want something – my wealth. From testing to enlightenment is my father's teaching, that of a wise man. Get out of my house, all of you, and allow me to return to the path of learning that my own stupidity made so hard for me.'

Look to The End

Although loosely used to denote a Sufi, a dervish, in reality is simply one who is on the path: a learner who may too often think or behave in a stereotyped way.

There was once a king who was fond of the company of dervishes. Meeting one who had all the outward marks of great devotion, the King asked him for a single phrase which would help him in his spiritual development.

'Certainly,' said the Dervish; 'Repeat, several times a day, the words, "Always think of the end before you make a beginning." I do that myself.'

Expressing his gratitude, the King made a practice of repeating the formula whenever he thought of it: which was generally when he was in a relaxed frame of mind.

It so happened that the King was sitting quietly in his palace one night, repeating the form of words and pondering their wisdom, when two thieves who had climbed in through the window heard him. Thinking that the King had mystical or clairvoyant insights and had seen them although he had his back to them, the thieves were seized with terror, and confessed all. The King was delighted.

Not long afterwards, the King was sitting in his chair, very relaxed, while his barber prepared to shave him. Now the barber had been bribed with the promise of the post of Grand Vizier by an enemy, if he would cut the King's throat. This the barber was just about to do, when he heard the King mutter, 'Always think of the end when you make a beginning', two or three times.

Terrified, the barber let his newly-sharpened razor fall to the floor, as he prostrated himself before his monarch, imploring him to forgive him and confessing all.

The King was overjoyed at the continuing power and effect of his mantram, and called the whole Court together to hear the wisdom of the Dervish, and how it had saved his life. But there was a Sufi present, well aware of the limitations of the philosophy of dervishes. He said to the King:

'Know, O King, that you should allow for unforeseen possibilities.'

But the King, who liked simple solutions, refused to listen.

Then the Sufi took a small stick from the folds of his robe and held it up. When he tapped it three times on the floor, a dog ran into the throne-room, in answer to the signal.

'Now,' said the Sufi to the dog, 'bring us some refreshment – shall we say a pitcher of cool sherbet. But when you come back, change into the shape of a beautiful maiden.'

The dog trotted off and in a few minutes a beautiful girl

entered, with a jewelled pitcher and two amber cups, to serve the sherbet.

The King was delighted. 'Sufi,' he said, 'give me that magic stick and I shall give you a bag of my choicest jewels.'

When the exchange was completed, the King tried out the stick, but nothing happened. He looked at the Sufi with anger, demanding an explanation.

The Sufi bowed and said, 'Majesty, you look for an end when you make a beginning. But your idea of both the beginning and the end was useless. You did not begin with the real beginning, which should have been to have your own mind matured.'

Adventurous Frogs

In the country of Iraq lived two frogs: one in Baghdad and one in the city of Basra.

At about the same time, a similar thought occurred to each frog. The Baghdad one thought he would like to visit Basra; the Basra frog yearned to go to Baghdad.

And, at about the same time, each started out on his travels.

Halfway between the two cities, or as close to that as makes no difference, they met.

'Where are you going?' asked one frog.

'To Basra. And you?'

'To Baghdad.'

'And where are you from? I'm from Basra myself.'

'I am from Baghdad.'

They sat there for a time, thinking. In the meanwhile, a fool came along and asked them their origins and destinations.

When he heard their stories he said, 'There's no point in your travels at all. Each of you should go home.'

The frogs were unconvinced.

Then a wise man came along. When he heard of the frogs' plans, he gave the same advice as the fool.

But the frogs were not interested in the words of the fool or of the wise man. They hopped on their respective ways.

When, however, the frogs had been at their destinations for some time, they realised that both the fool and the wise man had been right.

Because, for a frog, no matter how he might feel delight at the journey and its experiences, Baghdad and Basra were so similar it made little difference where they were.

Before you start hopping, you may have to cease being a frog...

Heat and Thirst

Q: *Do Seekers always recognise a real Teacher? If they do not, what happens to them?*

A: What happens to them is, in its own way, equivalent to what happened to the Five Dervishes.

A group of wandering dervishes came to Baba Farid's* house complaining that, although they had covered enormous distances in their search, they had not yet found one true Sufi.

'Be seated,' said Farid, 'and you will find one.'

But the dervishes refused to tarry, saying that they had to continue with their search.

As they were leaving, Baba Farid said:

'I beg of you not to take the desert road, for it is dangerous for you.'

They took no notice of this advice, however. As a result, four died from the heat and the fifth, although he eventually found water, expired from drinking too much.

* Baba Farid died in 1265.

This is a metaphor of what happens to those who, in ordinary life, are fixated upon seeking and hence not only miss the finding but suffer for it, and all to no purpose.

The Conversation of the Birds

Q: *I am resolved to enter upon the enterprise of seeking knowledge, and I am determined that I shall succeed. Whatever sacrifices and problems this may involve, I shall read all the books, carry out all the exercises, travel anywhere necessary, until I reach my goal. Is there anything wrong about this?* ·

A: There is a classical Sufi story about a king who was setting out to war. He was accompanied by everything necessary, from gold to arms, from fierce warriors to military bands. No detail of his enterprise had been forgotten. On the way he met a Dervish, a poor and weak wanderer who was yet a wise man, reputed to know the language of birds.

The Dervish told the King:

'I know the language of birds, and what they are saying about your Majesty.'

The King said:

'Are they pleased that I am set on this path, and that I am determined to succeed?'

'They are delighted, your Majesty,' said the Dervish, 'for they say: "This King will ruin so many cities that we shall have abundant nesting-places for the rest of time among the fallen buildings."'

This is the answer to your question: you may arrive at a goal by the methods which you mention. The question of the effect which this will have on others, and what your own fate will be, are not reckoned into the scheme. That is why we have the institution of teaching and learning: so that people will not only go forth on the path, but will do so in a manner which is advantageous to everything and everyone involved.

THE BASIC AND THE UNFAMILIAR
HUMAN COMMUNITY

All human societies are based upon, and their continuity and growth are reinforced by, the use of hope, fear and repetition.

Although this simple structure is not visible to the overwhelming majority of people, everyone who is concerned with human groupings uses and approves the application of hope, fear and repetition.

The structure is employed in every type of organisation: whether tribal, national, political, religious, recreational, educational or other.

Two things militate against the recognition of the structure by the people in it and those operating it:-

1. The seeming diversity of objectives of the societies in question;
2. The very simplicity of the structure. It is so obvious as not to be self-evident in the way in which people think things are self-evident.

There is also an unspoken, because unrecognised, consensus in human thought upon this matter: Because everyone is accustomed to being manipulated by hope and fear, and because everyone assumes that repetition is necessary, the possible progress in analysing this situation is virtually at a halt. It is as if one might say: 'We make sounds. Why should we turn these into words? They suffice us.' – in a pre-verbal condition of man.

Such a hypothesis (about words not being necessary) would be adequate only under circumstances in which there was no real need for coherent speech. In a society, in other words, where there were no dissatisfaction and no real curiosity leading to investigation which might result in the production of a useful instrument (that is to say 'speech') and the removal of a source of

63

tension and annoyance leading to frustration (for instance, superabundant grunting and chattering!).

When such statements as the foregoing are made clearly enough, experience shows that they tend to elicit two main automatic reactions. These reactions may be presented as attempts to avoid or resolve the challenge. In fact they are capable of doing neither.

Summarising the first reaction:

'Man can learn only by these methods. To abolish them would be to prevent learning and reduce the chances of human cohesion.'

Summarising the second reaction:

'This contention does not prove that there *is* any other way of learning or organisation, or that quality and measure in these techniques exists or needs to exist.'

Now, it is always difficult to deal with prejudices which provide people with advantages – such as not having to think. It is equally difficult to satisfy people who inwardly but not admittedly fear that they might be revealed as shallow; or who fear that the consequences of admitting something unfamiliar might 'change' them. It is difficult – it is not, however, impossible.

If it were impossible, the human race would have died out through lack of adaptive capacity. It is true, though, that those who cannot or will not adapt to constructive but unfamiliar information are members of the segment of humanity which does, in the cultural sense, die out. Those individuals, schools of thought and societies which have *not* adapted to 'now' (that is, unfamiliar) information and environmental changes *have* died out.

The two main reactions just quoted are less plausible than the contentions which they oppose. For that alone they could be dealt with merely by ignoring those who hold them, and regarding the actual fact of holding such opinions as evidence of the incapacity of the person to adapt to unfamiliar ideas: evidence of his relatively poor survival ability.

But there is a mechanical trap here, and it is worth observing in passing. People who oppose 'now' or unfamiliar concepts can be made to accept them if the 'new' conception is sufficiently energetically projected. That is to say, there would be no real difficulty in conditioning, by fear, hope and repetition, these objectors to 'believe' that fear, hope and repetition were undesirable in quantity or quality. The trap is that you would now have plenty of conditioned people who objected to conditioning because they had been conditioned to object! They would be useless to further understanding, almost by definition, certainly by the crudity of their operational capacity.

So agreement with your original statement, or 'belief' in it, are not what is aimed at. This in itself is a very unfamiliar concept, since virtually all human societies prize above everything agreement and belief. What do you seek, they will (and do) ask in bewilderment, if you do not seek converts, heroes, martyrs, believers, dedicated supporters, disciples, propagandists, enthusiasts, representatives, common denominators, and so on.

What you seek, because it is an essential prerequisite to understanding, is people who can accept the possibilities which follow:-

1. That virtually all human communities are established and maintained by the reward/punishment and repetition mechanisms;
2. That there might be an alternative;
3. That this alternative might not require the abandonment of membership of one or several of the 'basic' types of grouping; the basic type is a grouping produced by hope and fear and maintained by repetition.
4. That it might even be necessary for man to remain, for some of his purposes, formerly grounded in one or more 'basic' grouping;
5. That it might be possible to *add* the unfamiliar form of relationship to one's range of experience, without disturbing the 'basic' type already implanted;
6. That there may be a value in some form of understanding which could be *prevented* by conversion;

7. That it might be useful to observe and recognise the occurrence and operation of the 'basic' structure in all forms of human association which surround everyone;

8. That it might be advantageous to absorb this 'new' information rather than to react to it as if it were a key, panacea or magic wand;

9. That it is being suggested that it could be the *exclusion*, (not the cultivation) of emotional or intellectual bonds based on hope and fear and operated by repetition, which could open a door to knowledge of a kind different from that which is available through the single system just described.

Imagination

Q: *How can we explain the fact that many people, even very learned and respected ones, make up their minds on insufficient information and are often found having to withdraw or change their opinions? And why some of them refuse to withdraw, even when wrong?*

A: We do not have to explain it, only to observe it, so that we do not make the mistake of believing that people's ideas are reliable. You can prove that people haven't yet understood this, by the way, by asking around. People think that their own minds are reliable.

Nowadays, however, the reverse is shown by one psychological test after another: trusting of eye-witnesses, of memory, of learned materials, of opinions, and so on. Here is an example of a common delusion: Nobody imagines that the television serial *Colditz* was factual, or that the British actor Anthony Valentine was really a Nazi officer. But, interviewed by Tim Ewbank, he complained that a waitress refused to serve him tea (in real life) on the grounds that he was a Nazi officer and reading the mail of prisoners-of-war. He also mentioned that a car park attendant at Waterloo 'looked me up and down and said that he didn't like my sort'.*

The Birds

A large number of people approached a Sufi master, seeking to become his disciples. He gave each one of them a box and a key, with instructions not to open the box, and to bring it back to him the following day.

When they returned, he opened the boxes and found that most of them were empty. There had been a bird in each, which had flown away and could not be caught again, when the would-be disciple, unable to restrain himself, had tried to peep.

It is reported that, when they were faced with this fact, few of the applicants were pleased. Some said that it was not a fair test; others complained that it was unkind to shut up birds in boxes; yet others said that their particular boxes had, by an oversight, not contained any bird at all.

'These explanations and expostulations,' said the Master to the lot of them, 'are as important and as revealing as the restraint of the successful candidates, for they will teach something to us all.'

* *The Daily Mail*, London, 14th January 1974; p. 7, cols 1–4.

Knowledge or Experiment?

The Sufi contribution to the release of human potential is dependent upon the understanding of the need to clear away barriers to understanding.

The major barrier to understanding is wishful thinking and following that which pleases one. Hence, if a person is desirous of achieving spiritual states, he or she will pursue this end in a manner which corresponds not with the way in which it can be done, but which gives him (or her) satisfactions.

This is the mainspring of all human movements, whether political, national, religious, economic or other. First there is the objective, then the mechanism for attaining it. And the object must always be one which pleases the aspirant; after that, the method must be one which gives him satisfactions.

No other pattern, no other formula, is needed to explain why people believe things, of such a diversity of organisations and systems.

And the pattern is perfect, the system delivers results, subject to a single caveat. This may be stated in the phrase: 'An attractive objective and a satisfying procedure will always produce results, providing that the objective is possible and the methodology is effective.'

A very large number of aims are not realistic, and very many procedures are ineffective. An aim of the ancient Egyptians was to cure bilharzia; a very attractive one. The chosen method was circumcision. Its single flaw was that it did not work. Countless generations of people have wanted to make gold; this was their aim, and a very attractive one. Their methods (which included 'getting the impurities out of lead') did not work.

Today it is widely known that bilharzia is caused by a parasite and that gold is not purified lead. Therefore either the aim or the method loses its appeal; sometimes both lose it. The cause of this failure of the appeal of the aim or of the method is – factual knowledge.

The aims of contemporary people, pursuing power, pleasure,

fulfilment and so on can also easily be seen to be, in some cases at least, modifiable or capable of being vitiated by an increase in factual knowledge which would illuminate the false assumptions on which the enterprise and/or its methods are founded.

These false assumptions, reinforced by greed and other subjectivities, are the barriers to knowledge, even factual knowledge. Until people start to ask the equivalent of 'What exactly is bilharzia?', and 'What really are metals?' the 'circumcision' and the 'purification' will continue.

This is the single reason why all Sufi effort is directed towards knowledge. From this viewpoint, all effort without knowledge must be seen as speculative, therefore wasteful of energy and perhaps even impossible of achievement.

Sweet Water*

A story is related among the wise of a man who believed that pleasure in this life was the highest human purpose.

One day, on a journey, he became thirsty. He knocked on the door of a Dervish and asked for some cool, pure water.

The Dervish, perceiving both his outward and inward states, brought him a cup of warm and brackish liquid.

'This is undrinkable!' spluttered the visitor, 'I asked for clean, cool water...'

'Friend,' said the Dervish, 'we are prisoners of this world, and captives do not get the best nutrition; although, true enough, they crave it in their dreams more than anyone else does.'

* A very similar tale is found in the *Silk al-Suluk—The Thread of the Way of Life*, by Khaja Ziauddin Nakhshabi (d. 1350–51).

Direct and Indirect Learning

When there is an obstacle to spiritual progress, it is not always to be approached head-on. The application of knowledge can make possible the dissolving of problems through special techniques.

The tale of *The Chests* allegorises this process:

THE CHESTS

A Central Asian was on his way to Mecca and decided to leave a chest containing his valuables with a merchant of repute in Cairo before setting off, and to take with him on the pilgrimage only such few things as he would actually need.

He made enquiries and found himself in the shop of a man regarded by his fellows as of the highest probity. The box was entrusted to him, and the pilgrimage set off.

When he returned and claimed his property the merchant denied ever having been given it, and even said that he had never seen the pilgrim before.

Even the neighbours refused to believe that a man with such a reputation as the merchant could possibly be lying.

The pilgrim, with very little money left, without friends and in a foreign land, wandered down the road in a state of shock and dismay, unable to decide what he should do next.

It was at this point that a certain wise woman, dressed in dervish garb, noticed him and asked him his trouble.

When he had explained what had happened, she said:

'What would you propose to do about this?'

'I can only think that I might resort to force, or go to the police,' said the pilgrim.

'The police will not be able to help you, since you can prove no crime,' said the woman, 'and as for force – that would just get you into jail.'

'If, however,' she continued, 'you care to repose complete

trust in me, I can devise a plan which will secure the return of your property.'

The pilgrim agreed to do whatever she asked. She helped him to hire, for one day, ten beautiful and valuable-looking chests, which she filled with earth and stones. Then she asked another friend to accompany the chests on a cart, to the merchant's shop. He was a Dervish, dressed as a rich man.

When the man and the cargo arrived outside the shop he pretended to be a stranger in the town and asked the merchant if he would agree to look after the ten chests while he went abroad.

'The chests look as if they are full of valuables,' thought the merchant, and he agreed to take them in, for a small fee, and have them looked after.

As the boxes were about to be carried into the shop the pilgrim played his part. He went up to the merchant and the disguised Dervish and said:

'I have come for my chest of valuables, may I have it now?'

Fearing that he would not be trusted by the owner of the exciting chests of 'valuables' if there was any argument, the merchant handed over the pilgrim's property, full of smiles.

Then the disguised Dervish said, 'Thank you for your trouble, but I have changed my mind – I think that I shall take my own chests with me, after all.'

And that was how the pilgrim's difficulty was resolved...

He thanked the Dervishes for their help, saying, 'I cannot imagine how you thought of this ingenious solution.'

Starting to Learn

Q: *When can I start to learn?*

A: You have started already. You are learning all the time. A great deal of what you are learning is imperceptible to you. A great deal of what you know is not suitable knowledge for what we are engaged upon. When we talk about 'Learning how to learn' we also require a sense of discrimination as to which parts of what you learn are of developmental value. This, again, also means when, how and where you use learning for deliberate development.

Remember the tale of the ignorant fishes who swam to the wise old fish asking him to describe to them this thing called water that they had just heard about!

At your present stage you have to try to see that a person groping, or asking certain questions originating in an unprepared mind, is not capable of assimilating an answer except in his own terms of thinking, which may be inadequate for profiting by that answer. Your attitude should not be, just vaguely, 'How can I start to learn?' – but 'What am I to do about myself?'

Imagine that you have a deep undirected desire to progress. This, passing into your normal thinking pattern, is considered to be 'thirsty' because it lacks information on how to progress. The mind then 'processes' this assumption again, trying to see how it can formulate the desire. It goes through the mechanism which contains experience and the result of thought, opinions and other elements. These work upon it. It is bent by this mechanism into a query which may or may not (a) convey what is really originally intended: (b) show whether the mind in which the query originated is at this point capable of handling effectively any response given to it. In asking the question the mind is assuming several things, such as:-

1. That the person asking the question is sincere, and not just asking for reassurance or passing the time;
2. That the person asked knows what the answer is; or will 'track back' to convince, or attempt to convince, the questioner that he does know what the answer is;
3. That the question is correctly formulated and does express the real needs of the questioner;
4. That the taking-in and handling mechanism of the

72

questioner is capable of understanding the answer and profiting by it;

5. That this is the time and place to ask and/or to answer this question, on the assumption that 'Questions can be answered anywhere'.

And so on. Comprehensive work and the work-situation provide the real context and the hope of understanding.

Advice and Seeking

Once upon a time there was a poet who went to see a famous Sufi master, and in whose assembly he sat for many months, without anyone taking any notice of him.

When he became completely disenchanted with the Sufi, the poet asked permission to leave, as he wanted to go on his way and seek his fate.

The Sufi said:

'Would you rather I gave you a present of some money for your journey, or would you accept instead three pieces of advice?'

The poet said that he would rather have the money, since one could buy advice with it, but you cannot eat advice.

So he went on his way, and robbers got his money and he concluded that the Sufi life was not for him. He leaves our story here.

Now a second man, this time a merchant, went to sit at the feet of the Sufi. He spent years working for him, and was not even allowed to enter into companionship with any of the other disciples. After several years, he decided that he had had enough. He, too, asked permission to go.

The Sufi offered him money or advice. The merchant thought 'I can make money, being a trader, but advice cannot be had everywhere.' So he chose the advice.

The Sufi said, 'The first piece of advice is "Never take the new path, even though it is attractive".'

The merchant thought to himself, 'There went one-third of the money! What kind of advice is that?' But he kept outwardly calm, and the Sufi said:

'The second piece of advice is, "Choose the smaller even if it seems the lesser".'

The merchant thought, 'Two-thirds of my money are gone! That does not sound very coherent advice to me...'

To the Sufi he said: 'O great master! Be kind enough to give me one-third of the money instead of the last piece of advice, so that I may be able to pay my way for at least a part of my journey!'

The Sufi laughed and said, 'So be it!' and gave the merchant a hundred pieces of gold.

Now the merchant started on his way and presently found that the road was very rough and the incline steep. Eventually he came to a place where a new tunnel had been made through a mountain. As he was about to enter it, for it seemed an easier way, the words of the Sufi suddenly came into his head: 'Never take the new path, even though it is attractive.'

So he turned away from the tunnel and clambered over the mountain. When he got to the other end, he heard from other travellers that the tunnel had collapsed at the time when he would have been in the middle of it.

He continued on his way, until he came to a town. Here he found a man selling large hens for a small amount and another man offering small hens for much more. He thought he would invest in fowls, and was about to buy the larger ones. Suddenly the Master's words came into his head: 'Choose the smaller even if it seems the lesser.' He bought the smaller hens and started a farm. Soon afterwards he found that the small hens were great layers, but that the large ones which the first man had offered him, did not lay at all.

Ultimately, however, a war started, and he was impressed into the army. He lost his farm, which was usurped, and he found himself, a penniless soldier, captured and enslaved by the enemy, wielding an oar in a slave-galley. One day when the galley was taking travellers across the sea, he recognized a fellow-disciple from his days with the master Sufi as one of the passengers. 'I wish I had taken the third piece of advice and not the money,' he said to the other man.

'That might have been the best thing to do,' said the other man, 'although I do not know. The Master told us, after you were gone, "A hundred pieces of gold, which I have given this man, will not compensate him for the third piece of advice, which is 'If you start a farm, sell it as soon as possible and journey to another country!'"'

In the meantime, a third man had enrolled as a disciple of the Sufi teacher, this time a scholar who had vowed to give up narrow pedantry. After years of associating with the disciples and carrying on meaningless tasks, he, too, asked permission to leave. The Master said: 'Leave if you must, but it is best to wait until dismissed, for in company there is safety.'

The scholar decided to stay until dismissed.

Finally, one day some years after this conversation, the Master said:

'You may now start on your travels. Do you want some money or three pieces of advice?'

The scholar chose the advice.

The Master said to him:

'The first piece of advice is: "Never eat what you can comfortably go without".'

The scholar memorised this sentence.

The Master continued:

'The second piece of advice is: "Always refuse to take short-cuts".'

The scholar nodded.

The Master then said:

'The third piece of advice is: "If something is offered you, you need seek no further".'

The scholar assured the Master that he had understood.

'We shall see,' replied the Sufi.

Presently the scholar had prepared himself for the road, and he went to say farewell to the Master. The Sufi offered him a meal at his table. 'I can comfortably go without, and I remember your first piece of advice,' said the scholar.

'Very well,' said the Teacher, smiling, 'but if you are in such a hurry to get away, you can join a caravan which is leaving the cross-roads soon; but you will have to run.'

'Master,' said the scholar, 'I cannot forget your instructions, "Always refuse to take short-cuts".'

'In that case,' said the Master, 'I am able to offer you enlightenment, for you are ready for it.'

'Thank you.' said the scholar, 'As your third piece of advice has it, "If something is offered you, you need seek no further".'

The High Cost of Learning

Q: *What does it cost to learn?*

A: Learning cannot be expressed accurately, of course, in money terms. But here is an example where money is used as an allegory:

There was once a sage who set up business in the market-place as a seller of knowledge.

One of his customers was a young man, newly married, who wanted to test out this strange form of commerce.

'How much is your knowledge, if I buy it piece by piece?' he asked the wise man.

'It can cost as much or as little as you can offer, but the advice will be proportionate to the price in its usefulness,' was the answer.

'Very well,' said the young man, 'I'll try a piece for one copper coin.'

'The advice is,' replied the sage, 'Don't eat more than you have to, and get exercise – or you'll get fat!'

'Nothing cheap without reason,' thought the customer to himself. Aloud he said:

'What can I have for five pieces of copper?'

'For five I can tell you that if you neglect your duty you may lose eighteen years of your life!'

'I shall certainly try not to have that happen to me; but what will you tell me for one silver piece?'

'For that I can tell you that if you attempt to act without a proper basis and lack understanding, you will ruin your life.'

Partly out of politeness to the older man, whom he now thought of as perhaps a little mad, or perhaps just a minor swindler, the youth thanked him and said to himself, 'Perhaps what I have learnt today is to follow my own good sense and not to try to buy advice when I should gain wisdom by experience.'

He put the whole matter out of his mind.

Not long afterwards, the young man was walking along a street when he saw a beggar, who said to him: 'It is your duty to give alms, and I call upon you in the name of that duty, so that good shall befall you and so that evil shall be averted!'

Instead of giving the man anything, he started to walk faster, muttering, 'May God give you something!'

It so happened that his increasing his speed brought him face to face with a military patrol whose task it was to capture strong young men for the army, for the king of his country was waging a war. He was seized and spent the next eighteen years in fighting and captivity.

This gave him a great deal of time to think, and the words about the eighteen years which would be taken from his life if he failed in his duty now bore strongly upon his mind.

Finally he was ransomed, and he found himself back in his native town, looking for the house where he had left his wife, such a very long time before. No sooner had he approached the building than he saw a woman, whom he recognized as his wife, going in through the front door with a young man, holding him by the hand.

The blood rushed to his head, and he put his hand to his sword, thinking, 'I might as well die for murder, but I cannot stand the sight of this infidelity!'

Then he remembered the words of the sage: 'If you attempt to act without a proper basis and lack understanding, you will ruin your life.' At that moment he could not see that there was any lack of understanding, or that there was no proper basis for killing the miscreants. But somehow he restrained himself, just in case there was some better course of action.

All that day he walked about, tortured by the thought that his wife had played him false, or, at the least, had given him up for dead and had taken a new husband or a lover. When evening fell, he went back to the house and lurked by the lighted window, almost resolved to commit the double murder.

Inside the room he could see the couple sitting together on a sofa. Then he heard the words of his wife: 'I have been told that another ship has arrived in port, from foreign parts. Tomorrow morning you should go, my son, and enquire from the sailors, as we have done for almost twenty years, if there is any news of your father.'

Thus it was that five pieces of copper were shown to be the price of eighteen years of suffering: while one silver piece was the value of three lives, although, without an understanding of how life works, nobody would have suspected it.

Whom Do You Imitate?

It is one of the commonest things in life to imitate. People copy kings or sages, according to whether they are snobs or spiritually-minded (as they call it). People applaud or deride the act, instead of noticing the common factor, mimicry.

Mimicry is trying to look like someone or something else.

But what about looking, feeling or being like *yourself?*

A wise man once said:

'In the next life, you will not be asked, "Why did you not behave like such-and-such a person?"

'You will be asked:

"Why did you not behave like your real self?"

'If you know who and what you are, you can start to be that person, instead of a copy of the ideas, the behaviour or the image of someone else, or some collection of people. Then you can really *be*.'

Deeper Things Affect Surface Ones

One of the reasons for having a school and a teacher is that the teacher and the curriculum are responsible for dealing with learning in a manner appropriate to the student, irrespective of his own priorities.

People who want to learn will naturally choose what they want to do, unless they realise that there may be a better way known to specialists.

A good example is in human predicaments. People seek from spiritual sources solutions to problems which are themselves generally only symptoms. The real spiritual school deals with the cause.

When the spiritual experiences have been achieved, they remove the problems which trouble people. It is not the other way around.

This is a good analogy:-

A shopkeeper had a cask of oil, which he sealed with his ring-impression after filling it full. His assistants, however, found that they could steal oil by drilling a hole near the bottom of the barrel and plugging it until they wanted to draw off the oil from there.

When the shopkeeper opened his cask and found that, although the top was secure, the level had gone down, he was baffled. He asked a wiser man, who was a customer at his shop, what this might mean.

The wise man said, 'Some has been drawn off from the bottom: why don't you look there for the source of your problem?'

'Fool!' shouted the shopkeeper: 'I am talking about the oil that is missing from the *top*!'

People 'On Different Levels'

Q: *When I attend these meetings I am grateful for the easy natural way in which you answer questions and think of the interests of the people asking them. I have also noticed for some time that there must be some of the questioners who are far ahead of me, because they are dealing with matters which had never occurred to me, and your exchanges with them often puzzle me. I am quite sure that they are engaged in an advanced form of work. They have meetings which are not the same as the meetings which I attend. I have been trying to keep silent, and I have also realised that I have been coming here far less often than the others.*

Is there anything that I can do to prepare myself for the progress which seems evident in others? I am emboldened to ask this because you have said that you will answer absolutely any question, which should be asked without double-think as to whether it will please you or display ignorance.

A: A tree, in order to grow properly, needs roots and correct nourishment and climatic conditions. What we are doing here is analogous to that, in as much as we need a certain climate for growth. Some people have perceived that climate, others not yet, others to a small degree. It is my function to enable you to make progress without ruining its movement through your own impatience. The impatient man is his own enemy; he slams the door on his own progress. You are absorbing climate. You are also within your own exercises, making yourself ready for an understanding which is impossible to you at one leap.

There are 'wheels within wheels'. In initiatory societies, there are degrees of initiation. These, in most of such societies which are with us today, are merely the relics of separate assemblies held for specialising groups of people who share a common range of experience and potentiality. Originally such organisations were compartmented to prevent people of various 'degrees' from having a delaying influence on each other. What we are doing is so arranged as to reduce this possibility. Where it arises on the superficial ('psychological') level, such explanations as I am making are sufficient to deal with it.

Uncertainty, Dissatisfaction, Confusion

Q: *I am uncertain as to whether I should study Sufism. I have often been confused by psychological and spiritual studies. I find that confusion makes it difficult for me to approach these subjects, and, once in them, the confusion and dissatisfaction continues or gets worse. What should I do?*

A: I have no doubt at all that what you should do is to learn that 'information comes before illumination'. You certainly do need information. Our information and experience is that people are uncertain, feel dissatisfaction and suffer from confusion when, and only when, they really do not want to learn. The part of them which is resisting the learning provides the confusion, etc. The secondary self which is what people interpose between themselves and knowledge, the bundle of subjective and conditioned responses, resists truth. This is similar to the reaction of, say, addicts or obsessionals when they feel that they want to do something but cannot.

So, in answer to 'what should I do?', you should get used to this idea. It is not the materials, the school, the individuals, or anything else, which are confusing, making dissatisfied or causing uncertainty, but the clash between the materials (etc.) and the personality which feels itself threatened.

If you can learn this, the difficulties disappear. This is because the secondary personality learns that it is not in danger of being punished or extinguished. The 'need to oppose' which so many people have but which they always call something else (like 'a desire to understand' or 'difficulty in understanding') has to be put in its place. Nobody can do this for you: there are some things, after all, which you must do for yourself. But your question is rightly put when you couch it in terms of 'what should I do?'

Remember: 'If you yourself do not cause difficulties, difficulties will not be caused for you.'

Of course, if you decide that you cannot avoid these reactions you talk about, then there is nothing you can do until you have tackled this problem. That is the price of admission, as it were.

Time and Occasion

Q: *When we are not carrying out real 'work' what are we doing? Can we be said to be preparing ourselves for 'work'?*

A: That depends upon whom we are talking about. I will answer you in terms of a group carrying on real work. This means a group which fulfils these requirements:-
  (1) A need for the work, calling forth someone charged with it in a given place and in a certain human community;
  (2) Capacity or preparation of the individual to carry out work;
  (3) A group of such people.
When these conditions obtain, the activities – both individual

and communal – carried out by these people are work activities, when 'designed' as such.

These activities may be partial, may be preparing for something, but they are not preparing for work – they actually ARE work.

Only a group of people who are NOT charged with the work mission could be said to be preparing themselves for work. And even then, they would be hoping that they were preparing themselves for work, because they have no guarantee that their 'work' will be *accepted*. When I say *accepted* I mean here that the positive gain, the substantial or 'baraka' aspect of what they are doing, in more than one depth, can be made available to them – they can get 'paid' for it, only if they are fortunate enough to get into a work situation. Only, that is, if they become involved, at some time, even after they have accumulated potential capacity, in a school of work.

Approaching Eastern Teachings

Q: *Why is it that we in the West have so much difficulty in getting to grips with the mystical thinking of the East, in spite of the fact that so many people have spent their lives studying Eastern mysticism, and indeed, have become great teachers?*

A: Take a deep breath, because in the interests of truth I am going to have to shatter idols, even in the small part of the question which I am going to answer. First: in the West, there is very little perception as to the vast range of teaching and quality of that teaching which exists in the East.

The problem of the investigator collecting information about it is that he does not know how to learn. He is a mere assembler of facts or experiences. As a collector, he organises and passes on information gained from what may seem to be the same, but are frequently different varieties of a central fact or activity. He passes on these distortions, sometimes further complicated, to you. In the process, if he is an academic worker, perhaps a sanskritist, he transmits 'cold' material. If he is an emotional type, he will himself become involved in the conviction of truth which his teachers have. He will not realise that they themselves are the possessors only of an attenuated, incomplete or warped tradition.

Not all Eastern mystics are in touch with a total reality or anything of the sort. They may appeal by their detached saintliness or orgiastic techniques, to something in the Western student. But they do not necessarily represent truth as a process or an activity which has a function to develop man. This last sentence is the key to the whole thing: 'What kind of business are we in, anyway?'

The written and other material available in the West (and often in the East, in unregenerate circles) is studied and puzzled over, or accepted and made a basis of a search for truth in an experimental spirit which applies well enough to certain matters, but does not apply in this field. There is often no significant relationship between the material, the teacher and the taught. Thus we have a whole litter of quasi-mystical effort. 'C'est magnifique, mais ce n'est pas la guerre!' First of all this must be understood.

To wallow in mud is something done by a hippopotamus. A man who has a correct perspective of the use of mud may make bricks out of it. Both are excellent uses of the material. But when the hippo thinks that he is a man...

However, this sort of talk is very unfashionable, because, for social reasons which are currently at the very root of our behaviour here, we must allow the other fellow to believe that he has the equipment to understand. To suggest that he has to learn how to learn is not socially acceptable. At the very least you are accused, overtly or otherwise, of trying to score a point over someone.

Meditation and Other Topics

Q: *Why do real Sufis not teach meditation and other spiritual practices as a matter of course? Surely everyone can benefit from them?*

A: For the same reason that good gardeners do not plant productive crops among, or on top of, weeds.

Q: *How can prayer be 'a barrier to progress', as eminent classical Sufis have said?*

A: In the same way as a plug, even one made of gold, placed in a tap, may be a barrier to the flow of water. Both gold and water are essential or valuable. When are they to be used?

Q: *How can a sensible person allow anyone else – even a Sufi whom he respects – to tell him what is true and what is not?*

A: A really sensible person would not have to be told, so the question would not arise. The Sufi's role is otherwise, in any case. He has to help remove the barriers erected in the other person, which have reduced his sensitivity.

Q: *When can one get spiritual satisfaction from Sufi work?*

A: When one stops expecting emotional stimuli, and therefore 'stops desiring spiritual satisfaction'.

Q: *Why is it that I find difficulty in believing some of the things which Sufis say, and also find their writings, too often, turgid?*

A: The answer to the first question is that you are looking for someone or something to induce you to believe, and that is not what the Sufis are about. Hence you must feel such problems as you mention. Without knowing it, you are seeking a persuasion system which isn't there. Similarly, with the supposed turgidness of written materials: your assessment is based on the disparity between your expectations and the facts. We would all like wetter water...

Q: *I looked at a book put down by a dervish, and found that many passages were crossed out. He had also written in it a list of six copies of the same book, with dates against them. What was this man doing?*

A: The opposite of what people usually do with books. They mark passages which strike them, to return to. The dervish will cross out a passage which has impressed him, so as to concentrate upon the equally important content of the rest of the book. People ordinarily, again, have only one copy of a book. But a dervish may have six copies. He works through one at a time, marking passages and dating the book. Then, subsequently going over the whole exercise he can see his progress and therefore make it permanent.

Q: *I am not supposed to become credulous or to be sentimental in higher studies. I should not be too intellectual or too emotional. There are so many things to do and not to do. How do I find the proper level of attention and quantity of emotion, etc.?*

A: The reason why you are given a course, or written materials to work through, is so as to maintain the right quantity and quality of attention. Someone with a headache who is given an aspirin does not say, 'How do I get rid of my headache?'

Q: *Why are the Sufis trying to teach?*

A: Look first at each one of the possible 'reasons'. Every one of these represents a barrier: one of your possible opinions. When you have got them all out of the way, you will realise why, and this kind of realisation alone is worth while. The real reason, of course, is therefore not contained in words, but beyond them.

Q: *Is there any idea as bad as that 'Knowledge can be bought'?*

A: Yes. This is the idea that 'Knowledge must be free'. You see, thinking in such terms is so restrictive that it prevents learning, and fills the mind with low-level activity, raising the barriers to perception.

Q: *I have had dreams, visions and even, I believe, messages.*

A: Good. Now you can get rid of that phase and we can start to approach Reality.

SECTION III

Quality, Quantity and Time

Consider the method of seasoning a certain dish. The pot is put on the fire, together with some of the ingredients. Little by little, other items are added. As they cook, they release their substance and flavour, contributing to the total effect. In addition to this, certain spices are used. These condiments are not merely dumped into the stew, they are measured out and put into the pot at certain stages of the cooking. This sort of technique is familiar to all cooks.

There is an additional technique, however, which is less familiar. This is it: an individual condiment is not all added at once. It is measured into several portions. Each portion is added at a different time. The result is that each portion of the same condiment is giving off a flavour slightly different in accordance with its stage of cooking. Such a condiment, may therefore, contain more than one 'flavour'. It is working with subtleties of this rarefaction that distinguishes the prowess of the accomplished cook.

Flavour

Q: *Many of the things which Sufis say should be approached with caution or avoided altogether except under special conditions, move me deeply. And many of these are things which people of all religions have used for centuries: music, invocations, rituals . . .*

A: This is precisely why some people, in all religions, have warned against: mistaking excitement for spirituality.

If you have to flavour a hundred kilograms of ice-cream, you will need one-third of its weight in real fruit juice. If you put less in, you will be adding goodness, but it will not be perceptible.

If, however, you add instead synthetic flavouring, you will need only one three-thousandth of the volume to produce the fruit flavour.

Now decide: do you want the easy way to get flavour with no nutritional value, or the flavour and the fruit content as well? The smallest pinch of the false fruit flavour will give the impression of fruit: and it is easily obtained.

How many people, however, will say: 'Why should I not have the synthetic, since it is so easily added?'

Right and Wrong Study

Any subject, including that of the Sufis, may be studied or carried out by absolutely any method.

The results obtained, however, will always depend upon how correct the method was.

Equally, the understanding of these results depends upon sufficient knowledge to evaluate them.

It is for these reasons that learning, both among the Sufis and in education and teaching in general, require expert guidance from outside, if that guidance does not exist inside the learner.

Such guidance may be unfamiliar in form or associations: but it is never random. It mediates the manner, the time, the place, the company, involved in the learning process and its applications to specific instances.

There are three erroneous 'paths' which have become

associated with Sufism, due to ignorance of the matters just referred to. These are:

1. Scholastic study which takes the literal for the figurative (or vice versa); which works selectively, using only some sources; which tries to organise through an unsuitable pattern, and so on;
2. 'Guruism' (called in Persian *piri-muridi*) producing a circus, running on the energy of crude emotion, imagined to be spirituality, and may be either self-deceived or spurious;
3. The morbidly religionist, characterised by a sad and depressing approach but excitatory movements, sometimes of a revivalist nature.

Real Sufi study is based on design and measure. The design is perceived only by those who have the experience to know it, the measure is the consequence of this perception.

Ignorance of the existence of the design and measure reality has caused all legitimate spiritual teachings to fall into the hands (in part at least) of the personality-types which distort the teaching's outer shape into one of these three categories. Effectively, they are, all three of them, cults.

Trust

Q: *How can a person learn to trust?*

A: By overcoming stupidity through exercising the mind.

Here is a tale to ponder:

ALTERNATIVE

There was once a man who fell over a cliff. His clothes caught on the branch of a tree which was growing on the cliff-face. He hung there, halfway down, in imminent danger of falling into a river foaming far below.

The man looked up to the heavens, and called out in his fear:
'Is there anyone up there?'
A voice immediately answered:
'What do you want?'
He replied:
'Tell me what to do!'
The voice said:
'Let go and fall!'
The man thought for a moment, looked down again, and then cried heavenwards:
'Is there *anyone else* up there?'
At that point the tree's roots separated themselves from the earth...

EYEBROWS

A man looked at his wife's face and said:
'When did one of your eyebrows become thinner than the other?'
She answered:
'It was first noticed when you started to look at my exterior, and became less appreciative of the inner Me.'
So runs the Sufi tale. It continues:

So, too, when the potential Seeker asks how he can trust a

Master, he is approaching matters superficially. If he could discern inner worth, he would not of course need to ask the question. But, as he cannot understand, the only answer to him is, 'There is no answer for you!'

Inconsequential

Q: *I went to see a Sufi, and he only spoke a few inconsequential words to me. How can I respect such a person, as we are supposed to respect teachers? I have even heard of a Sufi who made an appointment to see someone, and then said nothing to him at all. I have, moreover, read of Sufis who spent their time chaffing their companions, and gave out no teachings at all.*

A: It is all a matter of perspective. Have you considered whether you were wrong and he was right? I suppose not, from your question. So let me just give you a small analogy from my own experience. I was once on a journey, and I saw before me, at a great distance, a hill which was all that stood between me and my final destination. I estimated that it would not take me very long to climb the hill, and so I did not take much in the way of provisions. But when I had gone forward for some miles, I realised that this 'inconsequential hill' was in fact a very high mountain. Not only was it a barrier, but I could not climb it at all! That which appears inconsequential to you, even a few words, from where you are, may be of the greatest possible importance, like a mountain. If you take this into consideration, by giving attention to your teacher, you will have thereby the provisions. And, unlike me, you will also find that you can traverse the mountain. When you get to the top, furthermore, you will be able to see your destination. And, looking back from the peak, you will see the reality of what you have traversed.

93

You will then understand both what is behind and what is before. This is the reality of the Sufi way.

Value for Money

A man went to a Sufi master and complained that although he felt that he was getting some spiritual guidance from his current Teacher, he would like something more attractive than the form of instruction which he was receiving.

The Master allowed him to join his community for a time, and put him through such severe exercises that he could not stand them, and returned to his original mentor.

One of the Master's disciples said:

'I am sure that if this newcomer had been treated more gently at first, he would have accustomed himself to hardship, and would not have been lost to the Community.'

The Master called the disciples together and told them:

'Once upon a time there was a judge who used to insist on being given a bribe before he would hear a case or even sign a document. The people resented him, but since he had been appointed by higher Authority, there was nothing that they could do.

'When the judge died, his son was given his position. He, in turn, forced people to pay him money whether there was a case or not, or whether there was a paper to sign or not. Before long the people were praying for the return of their dead and formerly reviled judge. "At least," they said, "he used to leave us alone and give us some justice ..."

'The disciple who has returned to his former mentor had to

have experiences which would allow him to value the teaching which he was in fact receiving, which was all that was indicated for him for the time being. I was the means of applying that lesson...'

Bombardment

When someone's self-esteem is linked to his 'spiritual search', he can achieve very little until he has seen that this is a wrong connection. Generally, of course, people are unaware that they *pride* themselves on being serious 'travellers on the Way' or whatever they call it. They more often imagine that they are humble: but this humility is quite often easily exposed as an unwitting cloak for a sense of personal importance.

A young man came to see me. He had read many books on spiritual matters, but felt that 'his faith in the Path was faltering'. He wanted me to restore it, and to be his teacher. This sort of approach, more often than not today – as with the Sufi records of the past – is found to be a demand for attention, not knowledge.

I asked him if an allegory of his history, present state and desires would suit him. He brightened up and said something like: 'I had not dared to hope that you would give me anything as comprehensive as that!'

Now I wanted to demonstrate whether he meant, by 'comprehensive', only flattery. So I told him the following anecdote:

> A young soldier was sheltering from a bombardment in a trench. He suddenly noticed his old recruiting officer beside him. The young man said: 'Do you remember how you told me when I was a potential recruit about the pleasures of army life, and how if I joined, I would avoid the horrors of civilian automatism?'
>
> 'Yes,' said the recruiter.

'Well,' continued the youth, 'would you please tell me again, as I find that my enthusiasm is weakening!'

My visitor, who had originally written pleading for an interview, and pledging total and eternal acceptance of anything that I might say, now became quite annoyed...

Stolen Property

Q: *Some people give knowledge free – why should others charge for it?*

A: That which is given free is never knowledge. It may be information, or it may be something with which one can work, but knowledge does not come in that manner.

What does come in that way, however, is something which can never be your own.

There is a saying which implies this:

'If a man has stolen a herd of horses, why should he not sell them for a penny each?'

You have to know that something valued at even a penny or less may not be your property, and may never become such.

The Five Animals

After quite a number of adventures, five animals came together one day on a highway. Each discovered that all the others had a single belief and a single aim. In short, the cock, the dog, the donkey, the cat and the monkey were all convinced that he or she had a beautiful voice: and one, moreover, which was not appreciated. Every one of them had thus separately set out to find this appreciation.

Not unnaturally, they decided to continue their journey together.

First of all they came to a village. The monkey set off, mounted on the dog, to see what the villagers were like. 'It is no use our looking for appreciation here,' he reported on his return, 'for as soon as they saw us the ignorant peasants fled in all directions, saying that the Devil had arrived, mounted on one of the fiends of Hell . . .'

They therefore avoided this village, and approached the next one.

This time the white cock, with all his beautiful plumage, wandered into the village on the donkey's back, crowing a little to test the effect of his voice on the people. To this sound the ass could not help adding some of his own melodious notes.

At this unusual sight the people crowded around, at first unable to fathom the meaning of the demonstration. Then, suddenly, some bumpkin cried: 'These are supernatural creatures: the white cock is a saint, and the donkey is his faithful disciple, honour them and they will bring us peace and plenty . . .'

So intense was the emotion of the crowd as they sought help and healing, riches and satisfactions of all kinds, that the bird and the quadruped turned tail and fled.

'It is no use,' they reported, 'nobody wants to hear our voices, they only want us to hear theirs.'

Well, the group of creatures, having decided that this village was not the one for them, continued along the road until darkness began to fall. They decided to shelter in some woods, and to start off again the next morning.

The dog and the donkey lay down at the foot of a tree, and the cock floated up to roost on its lower branches. The cat and the monkey, being more inquisitive, climbed right to the top. Suddenly the cat, wakeful as nocturnal creatures are, saw a bright light not far off. He roused the others:

'There may be food near that light, for people cook by flames. Let us go and investigate: besides, there may be someone there who realises the value of our beautiful voices.'

Thus it was that the group found themselves, not many minutes later, in a clearing in the woods, where lights were showing through the windows of a cottage.

They crept forward. The monkey sat on the donkey's back, and the cock perched on his head, so that they could see through the window.

Now it so happened that the owners of the house were away, and a party of robbers had broken in and were regaling themselves with the food and drink which they found there. At the sight of the revelry, and hearing the discordant singing of the thieves, the cock let out a cry of surprise. Hearing this, the robbers looked at the window. To their horror, they thought that they saw a gigantic cock with a monkey's face on his breast. Screaming and howling with alarm, the miscreants fled into the night. And the animals took over the house.

When they had eaten, the animals settled down in the ground floor room, happy to be fed and warm. But the thieves, after their first headlong flight, began to wonder whether they had imagined what had happened. They crept back to the cottage and went in through the door.

They saw nothing at first, so the first thief struck a light to find a candle. Immediately the light was reflected in the eyes of the cat, sitting high up on the warm mantelpiece. The thief sprang back in alarm, and he was kicked by the donkey, who was sprawled on the floor. This disturbed the monkey, who spat at the other thieves, while the cock pecked them and the dog growled. Once more the thieves took to their heels. Piecing together their experiences later, they decided that the house was inhabited by an immense demon with fur and feathers, glowing eyes and a hideous growl, which could bite, scratch and kick.

They still believe that this is how things are in the cottage. In fact, it is said, they have a way of thinking about things which is very similar to the way in which people imagine this world to be.

Your Share and Mine

The Sufi teacher Anwar Abbasi was asked:

'What was it that put you on the road to knowledge?'

He answered:

'I had spent many years looking for a teaching and a teacher. I found something to which to object in each one, until I despaired of ever reaching my goal.

'Ultimately I reached the house of a certain Sufi whose actions seemed to accord with his words, and whose followers impressed me very much.

'For some time I felt that this was where I should be. Then, unfortunately, a demand was made upon me for money, and I thought to myself, "Men of wisdom do not charge for knowledge." And I left the place that very day; without, however, mentioning my reasons to anyone there.

'That evening I shared my evening meal with an old Dervish whom I met by the wayside. I had not conveyed any of my thoughts to him, but he sufficiently perceived them, for he said:

"When you give money, do you seek to donate your valuation of what is to be received, or do you give what you think you can spare? Perhaps, on the other hand, you find reasons for not giving at all, imagining that you are virtuous at the same time?"

'I was so shocked by this, by seeing so suddenly that my attitude was only a mask for stinginess, that I returned to my last teacher. As soon as he saw me, he smiled and said, "Those who say that one should not charge money for knowledge cannot receive it even as a gift. This is because one can learn only after the matter of charging or not charging, the mentality of the world, has been expelled from the mind so that wisdom may take its place. There is no room for both 'I do not want to pay' and also 'I want to learn' in one and the same person. To deflect a greedy person, or to show him his shallowness, we always ask for money."'

Arguing with Gifts...

The ways of learning, the knowledge of the nature and needs of learners, and all other things which are possessed and made available by Sufis, are known by them as 'gifts'. These therefore are 'things given', which can be of use to the recipient.

When people ask for guidance or teaching, they are in this sense asking for gifts. But, as with more material gifts, they cannot stipulate the nature, extent and timing of their bestowal.

'Gifts' are not only given, but they can be given only within the framework which governs gifts of this kind.

This conception of bestowals of capacity and of their reception and employment is very helpful in understanding that one cannot bargain with someone who has gifts to give; that one may not appreciate their worth unless one is shown what they are or how to use them; that one does not really, for the most part, apply for gifts to be given.

Ants

Q: *Lots of people are giving lectures, running groups and enrolling disciples, all over the world, in the name of Sufism. How can we tell whether they are Sufis or not? I am sure that most of them are not, from what I have seen of some of them...*

A: Here is a report from the Press:

The American 'Crazy Ant' has arrived in Britain. Correctly named the Long-Legged Ant, this creature was first identified in the United Kingdom in a Preston psychiatric hospital.

Was this deliberate? Did the Crazy Ants head straight for the psychiatric hospital when they climbed off their jumbo-jet? I would say that they found themselves there, or near to the hospital, and settled in because there was something – perhaps the central heating – which they found congenial.

Similarly, people who think that there is something in the Sufi Way which corresponds with their ideas will 'adopt' it. They will settle down by enrolling as disciples and so on.

How can one tell, you ask; and then you answer it. You are sure that most of them are not Sufis. How do *you* tell? By using common sense. There is always something odd and unacceptable about these 'adopters', even if it takes some time to be noticed. The formula is to use common sense before the 'ants' take it away from you.

TRUE AND FALSE TEACHERS...

Since there are so many people all over the world claiming that they are spiritual teachers, many of those who want to follow them – and those who want to refute them – spend much time trying to work out which are real ones and which are not.

What is rather remarkable is that a great many of these self-styled teachers are discernibly not teachers, if studied with the normal rational apparatus which is of some value even to seekers after truth.

There is a story about a man who went up to another one who was selling what he described as 'the most delicious and irreplaceable honey in the world' in a market-place. 'If it is so marvellous,' he asked, 'why are you selling it?'

'I wouldn't try, you may be sure,' answered the honey-seller, 'if a mouse hadn't fallen into it!'

Now, in spiritual matters it may be claimed that the seeker, however sincere, cannot tell whether there is a mouse in the honey of the teaching which he is offered. But if he would only steel himself to look at the honey with dead mice floating on top, he would start to learn how to recognise the real thing. If you can test a verifiable counterfeit, you will eventually find a coin which is gold. Those who start at the other end: who can test gold without being confused by counterfeits, are a different lot of people, sad to say.

Finding a Teacher

Q: *Is a teacher absolutely necessary in the Sufi Way?*

A: Yes. For practical purposes, absolutely necessary.

Q: *How should people seek teachers?*

A: By fitting themselves for the search, by familiarising themselves with the materials which a teacher provides for primary studies. Then by approaching a teacher and asking whether one can become a pupil.

Q: *But is that not what people always do?*

A: Very far from it. They do not bother to think whether they have taken the trouble to absorb what a teacher may have provided, preferring to look for a teacher and to put all the onus upon him to teach them. This attitude debars them from learning, because the assumption is based on the vanity which the preliminary familiarisation is designed to help to reduce.

Q: *Where exactly is the vanity in just looking for a teacher?*

A: It lies in believing that one can and should be taught direct by the teacher without taking the necessary preliminary step of getting to know his work on the primary level.

How to Tell

Q: *How do you tell a genuine Sufi from someone who is only pretending to be one?*

A: There is a Roman Catholic anecdote about a certain gentleman in the Philippines who, introduced to the Pope, said, 'Are you a Catholic? I am, too!'

According to my informant, someone who could think and talk like that could not really be a Catholic.

Among Sufis, certainly, you may be sure that those who call themselves 'Sufi' are not such at all. Sufis are recognised by other Sufis.

But there is a capacity to perceive truth and deception. This is enough for those who want to learn. This capacity is not developed: it is inbuilt. It can be overlaid by cant and bias: therefore the first step is to deal with these things, to liberate oneself.

There is a story current in England about six men waiting in an anteroom at Buckingham Palace, to be received by the Queen. Three were white, one was yellow, another black and the last was brown.

An equerry came in and said, 'The distinguished guests will now follow me.'

The three Englishmen stood up and started for the door. The courtier stopped them, saying, 'No, I mean these gentlemen – His Highness, His Eminence and His Excellency...'

The yellow, black and brown men trooped out of the room.

The three Englishmen looked at one another, and one said, 'Whose country is it, anyway?'

Imitators

I have had endless difficulties with people, both men and women, who purport to 'give out my teachings', but get everything wrong.

In desperation, I asked a man and a woman who were terrible offenders, to come to see me and told them that they were just indulging themselves and were misleading people. I objected to their exploiting people, to their random collection of students, to their 'teaching' when they understood nothing, to using the wrong materials with the wrong people, and so on.

They listened carefully to everything that I said – and then carried on exactly as before: with one difference.

The difference is that they now claim to be 'personally instructed by Idries Shah'!

Today He Understands . . .

In my early days, I was puzzled by the behaviour of a Sufi who, like many others, was a business man. A would-be disciple of his (whom I knew) was told to donate a very large sum of money for the purposes of the Sufi's business: and he was startled at the request. Accustomed to believing that men of the spirit sacrifice themselves unstintingly for their work, he was puzzled by the words, 'This is to compensate the business for time given to you in teaching'. He would get nothing, he was told, until he paid the money, not a single lesson.

The rich but puzzled student spoke to me, in a pained voice, as we sat together on the steps of the Sufi's centre. 'I don't know whether I trust him,' he said, 'so why should I be faced with such a decision: why should I have to wonder whether I can give him money?'

I agreed. If the object was simply to make the disciple pay, why not nominate a charity, I thought, some organisation unconnected with the Sufi? We agreed that a bad construction was more likely to be put by anyone on such an approach, even from such a man as we thought the Master to be . . .

'What is more,' said my friend, 'I wonder whether the teacher realises that I now have his reputation in my hand. Saintly, a man of God, learned and all the rest – that he may appear. But how would it look to the world if I – unenlightened perhaps, but certainly a man of great probity – told all the world that this spiritual man would not teach without first being given money?'

Quite true, I thought. One should never put one's reputation in another's hand. I got up and went away, shunning the Sufi and never returning to his abode.

Five years passed, and I was in another country, working very hard on a difficult assignment. Sometimes I did not leave my small room above the Souk in Damascus for days on end. Sometimes – and this was one of those days – I felt I simply had to get out, to see other people, to have a change of scene.

Thus it was that I got up from my little desk, and went downstairs, into the crowded market, to walk among the people milling past the shops.

No sooner had I reached the street than I saw, standing in a doorway, my friend the rich man, dressed as a wandering Dervish, with a conical cap, a patched cloak, and a string of rosary beads. I took his hand, and led him to a café table where we could talk.

I immediately asked him what he had decided, in the end, about giving the money to the Sufi. He sighed, and then said certain things which are among the most important I have heard in my life.

'In the end,' he began, 'I gave him the money, because I decided that it might be a test of some kind. After a week he called me and handed back the package of notes, and drove me from his presence. As he was sending me away, he said, "You try to test me, and all the while you flatter yourself that I am testing you."

'I returned again and again to his assemblies. I ate at his table, and listened to his lectures: but I did not really understand anything of value, I am sure of that.' He stopped talking and shuddered.

'And then?' I asked.

'And then, not long afterwards, the Master died. I thought, "He has put himself beyond my reach".' He fell silent again, and I had to remind him that I was still there.

'Tell me, brother,' I asked, 'what the consequence of all this was.'

'The day after the Master died,' he went on, 'I was sitting in contemplation when he appeared before me as in a vision. His hand was extended towards me, but I could not reach it. He frowned, and I felt fear and love, both at once. Then he spoke to me.

'"My dear friend," he said, "money was your god, and not God himself. Greed produced doubt, and I could not teach you while you still had greed and doubt."

'"But you played on my doubt and made it worse," I cried.

'"I brought to your attention your disabling characteristics. I did not make them worse – I only made them manifest themselves to you. This gave you a chance to assess yourself as well as judging me." He paused, and then showed me how he had been reading my mind all along. "You reflected that you had my reputation in the hollow of your hand. But why did you exult at having something that everyone else also has? Do you not know that every ignoramus on earth can safely defame every single Sufi in the world. He will be believed by every other fearful, suspicious, greedy person. Do you not know that the dog sees an

106

enemy in every shadow – even in the shadow of his own master who brings him his food?"

'I fell on my knees and implored him to help me. "You will not help yourself, and yet you ask to be helped!" he said; "And I can return only when it is possible for me to help you again".'

With tears in his eyes, my wandering Dervish friend jumped up from his chair and, although I followed him, was immediately lost in the Friday evening throng.

That was thirty years ago, and I have not seen him since. Today, however, I had a message from him. It said, 'First I was ignorant, then I learnt a lesson in my mind and feelings, and thought that this was a spiritual lesson. Today, at last, I understand. Spirituality is understanding, not imagining. Praise be to the Lord of All the Worlds.'

The Cook

We can take life as a journey and, looking at the way in which people imagine things are going to be, find that there are interventions, now and then, which change that course. Once changed, of course, that destiny is again assumed to be linear, and it goes ahead, until another intervention once more confounds the pattern. Then, by hindsight, people start the process all over again, assuming that the linear form will continue...

The best illustration of what happens and what people imagine is going to happen turns out to be a story: and we can present one here which will allow us to examine what is really going on.

Once upon a time there was a caravan of rich and self-important merchants, which set off from Syria to make the long and dangerous journey to Mecca to the south. Not long after their departure, an ancient and self-assured looking man, riding a donkey and accompanied by two laden mules, asked to join the party.

While the caravan-master was discussing the possibility with him, some at least of the merchants objected to the newcomer. He did not look prosperous; he had mules and an ass rather than camels. Besides, he did not look able-bodied enough to bear arms, which might have been a reason for his coming along, since the desert was infested by bandits...

The man, moreover, confessed that he was by profession nothing more than a cook – a master chef, perhaps, but nevertheless a cook. He insisted that, since he was 'protected', his accompanying the caravan would only be for the good. Finally, since time was being lost, the merchants ceased their objecting, and the cook was allowed to tag along.

When the caravan reached a particularly barren part of the desert, it was surrounded by robbers. Well organised, they hobbled the camels and shut the merchants into a zareba, a corral of thorns, while the bandit chief sat down surrounded by his men, to plan the sharing of the spoils.

They had been thus engaged for some minutes when they became aware that someone had been overlooked. The cook was outside the corral, and had busied himself with laying a long strip of white cloth from his saddle-bags, on the ground. As the thieves watched, he took numerous delicious-looking pies from his baggage and laid them out on the cloth.

'What are you doing?' roared the bandit chief. 'Don't you realise that you are a prisoner?'

'Prisoner or not, people have to eat, and I am a cook,' replied the man, and he went on laying the meal.

Now the bandits, attracted by the food, gathered around and cuffed the man out of their way. They sat down and wolfed all the pies.

In half an hour, drugged by something in the food, they were lying fast asleep...

The cook opened the thorn-barrier and released the prisoners. The bandits were taken as prisoners to be handed over to the authorities, and thus it was that the least likely saviour turned out to be the means of the saving of the caravan.

I told this story this evening because someone had shown me the draft of an article about us, which expressed surprise that such a band of people could really be involved in anything important.

As it happened, though, among the people present were some who had sent me various questions. Among the questions were:

'Is there anything beyond what we can see in our lives?'

'Can the unseen content of something affect events?'

'Does failure to see reality hold us back?'

'At certain points it seems as if our destination is impossible to reach. Is it?'

The story, it seemed to me, covered every one of these questions, and many more besides . . .

Major and Minor Actions

Q: *If the great Sufis, such as the past and present Masters, have such tremendous importance, such cosmic tasks to perform, how is it that they are so often seen to be doing such simple things as instructing minor disciples and giving out elementary teachings?*

A: Failure to understand this is due to an incomplete knowledge of the function of real Sufis. Having capacity and functions means that these may be used as and when indicated, though not randomly. Hence, if you have at your disposal, shall we say, electric light, you may switch it on either to look at a trivial book or else to see your way to write a Nobel prize winning thesis. But if you just switch it on because you have it, or only to light your prize thesis, you would appear – and be – absurd. Knowledge and function means that the Sufi knows what he can do, can do what he knows he can, and does what he can. Imitators are those who disdain supposedly lower actions, or who specialise in doing simple things from humility. They may be useful, but not so useful as one who knows the consequences of what he does.

The Indian Teacher

I was very surprised to hear you say one day here that the attitude towards the teacher in Hinduism, the teaching personality with which we are so familiar in the West as of seemingly immemorial origin, is not, in fact, original to India or Hinduism as we know it. You said, according to notes which I made immediately afterwards: 'The Hindu teacher who is followed today in India, and who is the guiding figure which has attracted the mind of the Westerner for some time, is often attractive to him not so much because in him resides a true successive transmission of knowledge, but because he is a secondary manifestation of Sufism. In short, the theatrical version which panders to cruder thirsts for guidance attracts in a special way because of this Sufic, dervish content. The Hindu and his imitator in the West pays court to the living representative of an unbroken chain of transmission. This is not the same as the ancient Hindu teaching, in which there is no such concept of a continuous mission of transmission, but simply a theory of quasi-divinity in the individual.'

Trying to do some research on this question, which is what you told me to do, I found that there is indeed a confusion, and that the Sufi concept had indeed been taken into Hinduism in the Middle Ages, giving us today what is not a consistent Hindu teaching on preceptorship, but an amalgam. This factor is known only dimly to many Indians and Indologists, but some individuals have, in fact, pointed it out.

110

The result of my research can best be summarised by a passage which I found in *Influence of Islam on Indian Culture*, by Dr. Tara Chand, the Hindu authority on Indian culture. If I may present this here as the essence of my undertaking, I quote him:

> But it may be urged that the reverence to a teacher is an ancient Indian idea ... The student is asked to regard his *Guru* as more than his father, to pay him perfect Obedience during the period of studentship and to hold him in reverence throughout life. The teacher is even compared to God. But this ancient homage that the disciple paid to the preceptor is not the same thing as devotion to a spiritual director who is human yet divine, who is a link in the hierarchical chain of preceptors... This Sufi conception of the deified teacher was incorporated in medieval Hinduism ... the idea spread all over India.★

Whose Animals?

Q: *Why do Sufis concentrate so much on other people's defects and on their own virtues?*

A: In fact they do not: it is only others who imagine this, because of a bias towards these subjects.

This kind of mind is illustrated by the Nasrudin tale about the animals:

MENAGERIE

Mulla Nasrudin went to a psychiatrist, who tested him by showing him symbols on a sheet of paper.

★ From *Influence of Islam on Indian Culture* by Dr Tara Chand (1954) page 114f.

First there were three dots. 'What do those stand for?' asked the doctor.

'Three wolves,' said the Mulla.

'And these two dashes?'

'They stand for two elephants.'

'What do you make of these dots and dashes together?'

'They illustrate a herd of ponies and donkeys.'

The doctor told him:

'I am afraid that you are obsessed by animals, and we'll have to do something about it . . .'

'Do something about yourself first,' said the Mulla, 'for all these creatures belong to *your* menagerie!'

Illiberal Behaviour of Sufis

Q: *Why are Sufis sometimes so hard on society, on people and on ideas?*

A: For the same sort of reason, more often than not, that the owner of the bath-house clubbed one of his patrons . . .

THE TRAVELLER AND THE BATHS

A man once arrived in a town after a long journey and decided to go to the baths to refresh himself. He also needed rest after many days in the saddle.

No sooner had he located the baths, however, than he saw the proprietor rush up to a third man who was doing no harm, and beat him with a club. This man, in his turn, struck a blow at his assailant, and then cried out for help and began to heap vituperation on the aggressor.

Now the traveller turned away from the baths in disgust;

and ever afterwards related to people whom he met of the extraordinary aggressiveness of the owner of the baths in such-and-such a town.

One day, many years later, when he had once more spoken of this incident as illustrative of unprovoked aggression, one of his audience stood up and said:

'I am a native of that city where you spent one day so many years ago. Now, match your recollection of an instant with mine as a resident. There was a bath-house keeper of the most exemplary life and conduct. An irresponsible evil-doer formed the habit of going to the baths and annoying everyone there. The proprietor abstained from intervening because he refused to allow his anger to get the better of him. Ultimately, however, all the people who had been deprived of baths due to the behaviour of the evil man insisted that their interests should also be considered. Indeed, each of them actually held the owner of the baths responsible: and even the police agreed that it was a private matter. In the end, to the satisfaction of all, including the evil man who mended his ways, the proprietor belaboured him – in front of you.

'The fleeting vignette was enough for you to make assumptions and be judge and raconteur, but now you may care to interest yourself in the truth: if truth is anything of concern to you, rather than emotion.'

Being Rude to People

Q: *You sometimes seem to be very rude to people, and I have seen you take something someone has said and answer it in a way which did not seem to be intended by the questioner. Then, at other times, you seem to misunderstand what is being said. Another thing, why do you show vehemence and even intolerance? Surely calm and a reasonable attitude are essential if we are to examine things with an open mind?*

A: There are lots of questions there, and questions within questions. To many people the assumptions upon which they are built will be immediately obvious. Let us run through some of them. The first, of course, is that the questioner can assess what is happening. The answer to that, in the words of the-run-of-the-mill schoolmaster, is 'If you could assess, Madam, you would be sitting here, and not me'. This remark immediately seems rude.

'Rude' is a difficult word. It implies that one has said something which is rough; or outside the accepted form for the group in which we find ourselves. It would be rude of a Sheikh not to offer you, as the guest of honour, a sheep's eye at a feast. But if you handed a sheep's eye to your guest at a genteel tea, it would be rude. You see the difference?

'Cruel to be kind', is another factor not to be forgotten. You slap the face of an hysteric, without thinking yourself 'rude'; or apply rough artificial respiration to a drowning man. The genteel convention that these methods are not used in polite society does not apply on a different sort of occasion. One reason why polite society is unproductive of our sort of activity is that it is based on gentility made into an art.

Deliberately misunderstanding a person can be a 'polite' rebuke. If a person asks me 'How many beans make five' and I reply about bean-soup, I am doing two things. First, I am politely ignoring the question. Secondly, I am supplying the information which is in some way associated with the question. If I happen to be teaching cookery, I will naturally talk about bean-soup.

The point about the answer not being in the sense intended by the questioner is important. It gets to the root of a problem. You see, a great many questions are 'loaded'. That is, they are automatically intended to elicit a certain answer. This is an answer desired by the questioner. What kind of business are we

114

in? Certainly not that of providing reassurance for people who could get it by mutual admiration, over a cup of tea.

The words 'calm' and 'reasonable attitude' are 'loaded'. For example, you can only know what a reasonable attitude is and what calm is in relation to the situation.

Mulla Nasrudin points this out in his story about a number of stones in his earthenware jar. He counted hundreds but told a questioner that there were forty. 'That is impossible!' said the man. 'If you only knew the truth,' said Nasrudin, 'you would know that not only did I not lie, but I even reduced the number.'

'Temper the wind to the shorn lamb' depends on how fierce that wind is, and how shorn the lamb is. Direct talk is a favour as well as an inconvenience.

Opening Another Door

Q: *Why is it that Sufis, in the literature and apparently in the flesh as well, tolerate others who are often obtuse and who seem to make mistakes in understanding something of the most elementary kind?*

A: This is hard to answer fully unless we know which instances are being referred to. There are, however, two circumstances under which this frequently happens:

1. When the interchange is tolerated in order to provide illustrations for others – 'speaking to the wall so that the door may hear' – and also so that the obtuse person may 'wake up', though not necessarily at the time;

2. When people are obtuse because they are unconsciously suppressing their perception of the facts or of
   truth. There are many people who act against their
   reliable and accurate promptings for some delinquent
   reason. This reason is generally because something in
   them fears the intrusion of truth, either because this
   unsettles them or because they are partly hypocrites.

This tendency, by the way, has been illustrated in cases where
people, trying to guess a card or dice, will make so many
mistakes that it is statistically impossible for them to be wrong so
many times. This has shown that there are people who are in fact
guessing right, but that some inner censor prevents them from
admitting it, and actually reverses the facts.

The 'censor' is that part of the Commanding Self – the
artificial personality, which seeks to protect the existing ways of
thought of the person, who therefore is suffering from an inward
conflict: half of which knows the truth and wants it, admitting it
into his brain, the other half inhibits the acceptance of this fact,
since it is dedicated to maintaining what it takes to be an
equilibrium. If it were to admit the truth, so its reasoning goes, it
would face the unknown; the personality, it fears, would
change, or else the person would then be motivated by
something else (truth) not by the small bundle of ideas and
reactions with which it is familiar.

While you keep certain doors open, such as the door of
imagining that you can dominate your own learning with
insufficient tools, you cannot open – and go through – the door
of a greater understanding. This is why Saadi, for instance, says
(in his *Bostan*, The Orchard): 'The door of illumination is open
to those for whom other doors are closed.'

Fierce and Mild

Someone has asked why I am 'so benevolent to some people and so hard with others'.

Put it into the framework of this parable:

A man went into a merchant's shop and argued fiercely over prices – and the proprietor was very attentive to him.

Then another came in, and the owner dealt very firmly with him, bargaining closely and not sparing his comments.

When both had gone, the assistant asked his master:

'Why did you behave differently towards each of those two men?'

The merchant said:

'The first one wasn't going to pay, he was not even going to buy, as I knew from experience. So I took no real interest in him professionally. This left me free to allow good behaviour to have its full expression. He was superficial, but I pleased him, which was all that could be done.

'The second customer was serious and genuine: and so I treated him as a colleague and dealt with him professionally. Naturally, the discussion took a different form.

'The first transaction was planned to avoid unpleasantness with the unreliable (who always demand politeness as they mistake this for something real); the second was to provide mutual advantage by concentrating on what was really relevant to both of us. Naturally we could not guarantee amusement as well.'

What is a Dervish?

People in the West tend to think that dervishes are madmen ('the dervishes of the Sudan') or 'Mohamedan monks' (sundry encyclopaedias) or else 'profoundly wise' (various occultists and esotericists).

In fact, as this true story from the East shows, they are more generally ignorant people, aspirants to being Sufis – or real mystics.

A group of dervishes was visiting Afghanistan from neighbouring Iran, whose dervishes like to call themselves Sufis, possessors of higher consciousness.

They constantly asked unnecessary questions, were preoccupied with trivia and religiosity, and generally behaved in an irascible manner.

One of their party, however, spoke intelligently, conducted himself very well indeed, commented wisely and with much background information on the history and symbolism of the shrine of Gazargah.

It was at this place that the local Governor, pleased that at least one of the twenty self-styled contemplatives should show real promise, asked him if he was the Chief Dervish of the group.

'I am afraid not,' answered the man. 'In fact, I am the hired groom who looks after the animals of these devout people, while they do their spiritual exercises and wear their special robes...'

The Dervish and The Disciple

There was once a Dervish who lived in a hut with his disciples camped in other simple dwellings all around. Like all real dervishes, he wore the clothes of the country in which he lived, and neither he nor anyone else regarded his resting-place as an abode: for the enlightened do not abide on this earth.

He had a disciple, however, who always wore strange cloaks and a wild head of hair and a beard, and insisted that he dwelt in an abode, contrary to the attitude of the elect. This disciple, of course, was one of those who went by contraries and could only learn by reverse behaviour. He even gave out that he was himself a teacher, to anyone who would listen to him.

At the same time, greedy for secrets, this disciple always asked the Dervish for instructions when he could.

One day, when the teacher was about to set off on a pilgrimage, he called all the community together and, in their presence, addressed the disciple in these terms:

'When I am away, you are to be my deputy. You must have everyone obey you. Under no circumstances should you study these books. Further, you must grow your hair and beard, wear a strange cloak other than those of this country. And you must not live anywhere near a large city.'

The disciple was very pleased to be put in charge of the community, and all the others were, of course, quite distressed, for they knew how difficult he was to deal with.

When the master returned, however, he found that the disciple had decamped, and gone to live near a large city. Sitting in his evening assembly, the sage addressed the pupils:

'I am glad to hear that you have been in harmony while I have been away, since I left nobody in charge of you.' One of the disciples murmured, 'But, Master, you told the disobedient disciple to look after us.'

'Of course I did! But to tell such a person to do something is equivalent to telling anyone else the reverse. Did he take charge?'

'No,' they chorused.

'Did he stay here at all?'

'No, he went away almost immediately.'

'Did he trim his hair and beard and put on normal clothes?'

'Yes, he is now dressed in a manner which obeys your traditional instructions,' said the disciples.

'But only,' observed the sage, 'when he was instructed to do the reverse...'

Dervish, Sufi, Disciple

Q: *What is the difference between the Dervish, the Sufi and the Disciple?*

A: One cannot answer such a question in simple structures. But if you get to know the various tales and illustrations featuring these people, you will acquire the feel of the matter, and understand it.

Here is one story which says a lot about these relationships:

There was once a Dervish who wandered from one town to the next, giving his standard lecture, talking to the people in almost the same words each time.

He took a disciple with him. This man, after some months, said to his master: 'I have heard you so often that I often feel that I could give your lecture myself.'

'Why not?' said the Dervish. 'At the next town, you give the lecture, and I'll pretend to be your disciple.'

The disciple gave the talk at the next town, and sat down amid thunderous applause. People crowded forward to kiss the hem of his robe, and everyone agreed that here, indeed, was a great man of the spirit.

Then one of the audience stood up and asked a question.

The disciple could not understand a word of it.

So he said: 'The level of comprehension of this audience is so low, that I am illustrating it – and giving you the answer – by having my disciple of a few months answer the question.'

The people were chastened when they heard this, and even more amazed when the 'disciple' gave them the answer to the question with great lucidity and knowledge.

And this part of the story is told to illustrate such concepts as that, although one may be able to repeat words, flexibility of understanding and teaching is something else.

'Learning,' someone has said of this story, 'brings humility. So the Dervish was not ashamed to pretend to be a disciple.'

When the story stops at this point, too, people use it to

indicate that quick-wittedness – such as that of the disciple – may be useful: but it depends for its success on the presence of the teacher.

But, as with many other traditions, it is only the first part of the tale which is generally remembered. There is more, and this is it:

Dervishes preach, and their words can be repeated, with great effect.

Sufis act, and their actions have their own effect. The action can be blocked.

One day, a Sufi was visiting the same town, attended by a number of disciples. When the people heard that he had come, they flocked around him. They clamoured for him to speak; but, as often happens, the Sufi said: 'I only speak when something useful can come of it.'

Then the people said: 'Perhaps this Sufi is a fraud. Let us question his disciples.'

So they asked all kinds of questions from the Sufi's followers, who did not answer either.

'There you are!' shouted the townsfolk, 'If the Sufi had been genuine, his disciples would have been able to answer every question, just like the follower of the Dervish!'

And the Sufi, with his disciples, was hounded out of the town. Many years had to pass before the action and being of the Sufis, as distinct from the beliefs and impact of the Dervish, could be introduced to those people.

The Trick

Many dervishes, to encourage the faith of those who heed them, resort to tricks to impress.

There was one such who had a disciple, a young man, who helped him in his deceptions.

Every time the pair entered a town, the Dervish would perform the 'raising of the dead' hoax.

He first dug a deep pit and the youth climbed in, up to his neck. Then the Dervish, using a special platter with a hole in the middle and hinges, fixed this around his confederate's neck, at ground level. The Dervish then called out, 'O people! Come and see this severed head, which can talk and prophesy! See the blood in the plate! Watch the eyes roll!'

People would crowd around, and the 'severed head' would talk, giving answers to their questions, for a fee. When all was quiet, at dusk, the youth would get out of the hole, and the two would be on their way.

Now the deception worried the young man, who really did want to find truth, and realised that this was the complete opposite. He went to see a Sufi, who gave him certain instructions.

The next time the two came to a town, and the Dervish had collected his audience, he commanded the 'talking head' to speak. Instead, to everyone's amazement, there was a flash of fire and the youth, head and all, completely disappeared, having been made invisible.

The Dervish was beside himself with fury.

'Fool!' he cried, 'That wasn't the trick I told you to perform!'

What a Teacher Is

The world is full of teachers, people who collect disciples or who in various ways instruct others.

Now the wonderful thing about all this is that very few people ask what the teacher knows about teaching. The act of behaving like a teacher, or rather like people think a teacher would behave, establishes them.

If a teacher is not what he appears to be, how is he to be defined?

Try this: an ancient statement which is found in teaching materials such as the Tale of the City of Brass, in the *Thousand and One Nights*:

I AM

A real teacher was asked how it was that he could teach, and he answered:

I am what you will be:
What you are, I once was.

The Chess-players*

There was once a king who used to play chess with his court jester.

The jester was a good player, and he won the game. This so annoyed the king he punished him.

Then the monarch insisted on playing another time.

The jester was reluctant, but he had to continue.

When he was again on the point of winning, and the time had come to call 'Checkmate!', the jester jumped up and ran into a corner. There he covered himself with rugs, to avoid being beaten by the king.

The king asked him what he was doing.

'Checkmate!' called out the jester; 'I am hiding here because nobody can dare to checkmate you unless he is hidden, covered up...'

* Rumi, *The Masnavi*.

Like the jester, the Sufi teacher is at the mercy of the people of the world, who have the power to make him appear ridiculous and also to punish him in a myriad ways. He is not allowed, by the unconscious censorship of the general will, to say directly things which will annoy ordinary people; so he 'covers himself in a rug'.

Way of Teaching . . .

Students must sit and listen to the teacher until understanding comes to them.

This requires a form of alertness and concentration – while relaxed, which alone allows the meanings to penetrate.

People have to unlearn the compulsive habit of trying to puzzle things out as their ONLY response to a teaching situation.

This effectively means that they have to ADD a capacity, not to lose anything.

This can only be done by practice and by allowing the teacher to guide the student's thinking, at least at the beginning.

This 'dynamic attention' enables the psychological breakthrough to take place, where the words and writings of the teaching become plain, and the student no longer needs the guidance of the teacher.

People who have been too deeply conditioned to a single mode of learning (which effectively cuts out wider forms of understanding) sometimes object 'I want to understand first, before I learn, or as I learn'.

The problem here is that you can't revive an unconscious

man who's drowning – first you have to get him out of the water. What the ignorant would-be learner is asking is to be taught HIS way, even though that way does not work!!!

The Rope

Q: *Why do Sufis so often refuse to discuss other Ways to Truth? Surely they can lose nothing by comparison with the efforts of others in the same field? Surely their techniques are not the only possible ones? Discussion costs little, in my opinion. If you know better, as I imagine you may, please enlighten me.*

A: As to knowing better, listen to a parable and decide for yourself. Supposing that you are in a boat and you find someone who is in danger of drowning. In that boat you have a rope, and you call to the drowning man or woman to catch hold of it. Now, if that individual starts to want to discuss matters such as the rope and the boat and any possible alternatives, what is the situation? There may be a drowning.

Now, someone else may come along, on the bank of the river, well-meaning but trying to give instructions and encouragement and all kinds of messages to the drowning person. What is your responsibility? Do you try to get the rope to the threatened one, or do you oppose the interrupter, or spend time in explaining what you are doing?

'Discussion costs little', you say. In the circumstances just outlined, does it? The comparison of efforts of others, if seen from the perspective of the rescue operation, is irrelevant. It is simply because you have the means and the perspective that you offer the rope and not talk. It is merely because of lack of it that the threatened person does not see the situation. It is for the same reason of lack of relevance at that moment that the well-wisher on the bank is concentrating upon opinion and reassurance. This is as far as we can go in words, while the water threatens and the means to escape it are to hand. We must use only the minimum of words and the maximum of actions. But the success of the effort still depends upon the rope being thrown, and the other individual grasping it.

Wisdom of the West

'*Tenterden Steeple was the cause of the Goodwin Sands.*'

Sir Thomas More, it is related, was sent on a commission to discover the cause of the Goodwin Sands and the shelf which blocked the Sandwich Haven.

An old man told him that he was sure that he knew how this silting up had come about. He remembered, many many years before, when the steeple at Tenterden had been built. Before that time, there was no sand-shelf at the Goodwins. Sandwich Haven, therefore, was silted up because of the building of that very steeple.

This is like a story straight out of the Eastern corpus of the Land of Fools: like a classical example of drawing false conclusions from coincidental data . . .

Now you can make this into a joke, and take the laugh at this point. To do so might be to stop the process, obtaining a satisfaction and perhaps a feeling of relief or superiority that you are not like that.

But suppose that there is a further dimension? Suppose, even, that the old man was right?

If you add a little more information, you see quite a different picture.

It is said, you see, that for a long time large amounts of money were collected for the purpose of building a dike to prevent the sea from silting up the area. The money had been entrusted to the Bishop of Rochester. Instead of using it for the purpose for which it was intended, the Bishop endowed the church and built the steeple of – Tenterden.

All propaganda, religious or secular, is generally built on a narrow factual base. This is one reason why all propagandists resist the broadening of contexts as much as they do any direct opposition to their activities.

It may only be a coincidence that it was the wife of another Bishop who, informed of Darwin's theory, said, 'Let us pray that it is untrue. Or, if true, that it is not believed.'

SECTION IV

Hypocrite

Q: *I find it hard to understand how, if man is a spiritual creature, at least partly, things of the world can help him to recover his knowledge of the Divine. Words, actions, teachings, of the Sufis, surely, must all be considered things of the world?*

A: Think about this story, for it is the only way in which your question can be answered:-

> Once upon a time there was a man who was very greedy and objectionable to his poor and harmless family, though he was such a hypocrite that nobody else knew of his true nature. This man had heard that there was a certain cave, in which a priceless treasure had been hidden, and spent years seeking it. One day he was going through a thicket when he came across the cave. Entering it, he saw that it was full of treasure, gold and silver. He loaded as much as possible onto his donkey, and went back into the cave to get his staff – he was so greedy that he would not leave it behind. But this was a magic cave; before the man could leave, the time came for the entrance to close by itself, and the door swung shut, not to open for another ten years. The donkey, becoming hungry and tired of waiting, made its way back to the family home. As the greedy hypocrite was never seen again, his innocent family shared the treasure which the donkey had brought back, and lived happily ever after.

So, you see, in order to obtain the treasure, the *innocent* may have to depend, to some extent, upon things which seem to have no connection with their needs, and do not seem to be related – until the pattern works out.

On The Way . . .

Q: *Do you find that it is hard to carry on your work, because of the irrelevance of many of the ideas of those who apply to you?*

A: Resisting the temptation to call that an irrelevant, hindering question, I'll tell you a brief tale showing what it feels like – and then say something more.

There was once a traveller who was making his way between two cities which were very far apart. From time to time, because of the heat or through hunger or fatigue, he lay down by the road and slept.

No sooner had he got to sleep than people would wake him, asking for directions.

Finally, he had an idea. He wrote a notice: 'I DON'T KNOW THE WAY TO ANYWHERE!' – propped it up beside him, and went to sleep.

An hour later, the traveller was shaken awake by a kindly man. 'Friend,' he said, 'I have seen your notice, and I shall be pleased to direct you anywhere!'

The misunderstanding was due, as you can see, to a mixture of two or three things: such as an equivocal notice and impatience plus lack of any special sensitivity on the part of the new arrival.

So, each party has a responsibility. For my own part, I do find that people like you, who are considerate enough to think of the problem as it might affect me, are not in need of any information on harassment. And, I am glad to note, the absence of too great self-absorption usually makes them good students – good 'travellers'.

The Shroud Has No Pockets

Q: *Why will Sufis, although they may write books on literature and Sufi thought, so rarely co-operate in social or scholarly research? Why will they almost never discuss other people and their work?*

A: For much the same reason that fish do not dig mines, or a bird which can fly does not walk. Real Sufis are not operating information bureaux or debating societies. Their time and attention are consumed by teaching, and not by doing things that other people can do.

They are not collecting things – ideas, material, social activity. They have not forgotten the saying:

> One day we will all wear a garment which has no pockets...

Both Sides of The Road

Q: *I have heard you say that in twenty years hardly anyone ever said to you 'How can I learn?'; they instead asked you to accord with some preconception. There can scarcely be a more startling illustration of human absurdity than this proof of people's erecting barriers against learning. But how can one avoid such alarming stupidity as you mention?*

A: The first thing to learn is not to assume that one wants to learn, when it is possible that one only wants preconceptions reinforced. The next thing to do is to register that higher study is less the provision of activities than it is the effective increasing of the ability to learn: which may have to be done by any means necessary. Action because one wants movement or emotional stimulus may be study *of* Sufism, it is never study *in* Sufism.

Modern people are in the same relationship to spirituality that backward people are to technology. That is to say, they know so little about it that they are unable to perceive their own ignorance.

Such people may know that they want to learn. They do not know how; they should understand that if someone else knows the 'how', this is what has to be followed. Only too often, the desire to know, which is perfectly laudable, is overtaken through haste by the assumption that one should learn in a manner which the *learner* wants or approves.

This recalls the story of the Englishman who said to someone in an under-developed country of the East:

'We drive on the left-hand side of the road at home, and most other countries drive on the right. Tell me what you do over here, so that I can teach you.'

The oriental answered:

'We are not slaves over here. Everyone has a right to drive on whichever side he prefers. If we had cars, we would be allowed even to drive down the middle of the road!'

Doctor and Patient

A man went to see a doctor:

'I have nightmares, and I've got sores all over my hands!'

The doctor looked him over. 'You may have the symptoms you describe, but think of your perfectly shaped ears.'

'But what about my symptoms?'

'Just remember that you have reached the age of 54 without dying...'

'And these green stripes on my feet?'

'Mr. Smith, they do not affect your nose, which is in very good shape.'

'My knuckles are stiff...'

'...But you have all your hair and teeth...'

The patient gave a cry, snatched up his clothes, and ran, sobbing, out into the safety of the street.

The patient went to see another doctor.

'I am taking this tonic, prescribed by a friend, but I still feel ill. Anyway, I am not much better.'

The doctor said: 'No wonder, it is only making your symptoms worse.'

'But how can that be?' the man asked: 'I do not actually feel WORSE.'

'You would have been much better if you had not taken the "tonic" at all.'

'Surely that can't be true – the man's such a nice chap. When I talk to him I always feel happy. He is a good man.' He continued, 'Well, my knees ache, too.'

'That,' said the physician, 'is because you walk pigeon-toed. This places a strain on certain muscles, and you feel the pain in the knee.'

'I ask you about knees,' said the other man, 'and you talk about toes! What kind of doctor are you?'

The doctor continued, 'I notice that you are peering at me from two feet away. You need glasses.'

'The more you say, the more you seem like a fraud to me,' the patient said; 'I remember how it happened. It was three years ago, just after I'd eaten turnips. Now, if only you had diagnosed *that*, and if you knew what the antidote to turnip allergy was, then all would be well.'

The doctor threw down his stethoscope and ran.

Maximum Effort

Q: *Why can't people reach enlightenment within a reasonable time, even when they are exerting maximum effort?*

A: That does not apply to all people. But the ones you are talking about are those whose quality of effort is affected by vanity and other factors, which undermine their effectiveness. Hence, though they think that they are using maximum effort and that time is a-wasting, the reality is that their efforts are crippled and time drags because events are waiting for an improvement in this individual's quality. Here's the story of the man who couldn't see what there was for him in situations:

THE MAN, THE TREE AND THE WOLF

A man who was dissatisfied with almost everything in his life set off to find prosperity. His aim was to see a wise man who would give him the clue where to begin.

On the way he saw a fish, floating on the surface of a stream.

'Where are you going?' the Fish asked.

The Man told him.

'Then please ask the Wise Man, for me, why I cannot dive and swim under water as I used to be able to do.'

The Man promised that he would, and went on his way.

Presently he lay down to rest under a tree. As its branches creaked in the wind, the Man was able to hear it ask where he was going. When he told it, the Tree said:

'Ask the Wise Man why I cannot grow taller; my heart tells me I should, but for some reason I cannot.'

The Man promised, and went on his way.

As he neared the home of the Wise Man, he came upon a wolf. 'Ask a question for me,' said the Wolf. 'Namely, why am I so thin? I freeze in winter.'

The Man promised and, soon afterwards, he arrived at the door of the Wise Man.

'O Wise Man!' he said. 'I have travelled far to find out, if you will tell me, how I may become prosperous. And, further, I have three questions from others whom I met on my journey.' He told the Wise Man what the others had asked, and the sage gave him advice for each of them. Then he said:

'Return to your own land, and you will have all the opportunities you need, to achieve prosperity.'

The traveller set off homeward. First he saw the Fish, floating on the surface of the river, and called to him:

'The Wise Man says that there is a stone stuck in your gill. When it is removed you will be able to dive and swim under water.'

The Fish came to the bank, and the traveller took out the stone. 'That's a huge diamond!' gasped the fish. 'Take it as a reward for your kindness.'

'Diamonds are only a nuisance; some of them are under a curse!' said the traveller. He threw the gem into the water, and went on his way.

Next he sat down under the Tree, and told it:

'The Wise Man says that there is a large earthen jar blocking your roots. If it is dug up, the roots will be able to spread, and you will grow.'

The Tree begged him to dig up the jar, and the man did so. It was full of gold coins.

'I want prosperity, not coins!' he shouted and, abandoning the wealth, went on his way.

Finally, as he was nearing his home, the traveller came upon the Wolf.

'What did the Wise Man tell you?' asked the animal.

'He said that you are thin because you do not seize every opportunity to eat,' said the man.

'Then I'll not make such a mistake again,' said the Wolf. Pulling the man down, he ate him up.

Duality

A famous man of learning went to El Shah.

He had decided to be modest, and had formulated his request. He said: 'Guide of the Age! I seek that you should teach me in the Sufi Way, and that you should give ear to some of my problems.'

Bahauddin answered:

'The first thing that you should learn is that if the one is accomplished, so will the other be. You imagine that to learn Sufism and to have your problems attended to are two distinct things. It is this flaw of duality in the mind which makes people unable to approach Truth on their own. If your problems are solved, you will be on the Path. If you are on the Path, your problems will be solved.'

The scholar exclaimed: 'By coming to you for teaching, I have admitted that I need to learn. Therefore what I think and say is sure to be defective. Give me, then, the medicine for my illness rather than speaking of it, I beg of you!'

The Teacher said:

'If you regard me as a Teacher but at the same time try to tell me what I should do with you, you must first solve this second duality: the one in which you do not know how to think or act, but still you tell me what to do to cure you.'

The scholar said: 'I realise that my occupation makes me sensitive to criticism.'

Bahauddin said:

'What you call criticism may also be seen as description. But whatever it is, the important matter is how it is received and what the result of it is. If you relate it to your personal feeling of well-being, you will not be able to benefit from its alchemy (transformation power).'

Two Swords

Because there is so much information, so many pieces of knowledge and diversion going about in the world, few people can still their minds long enough to take in real learning beyond a very primitive stage.

They believe that you can add, as with a collection, one piece of knowledge on top of another.

This is true, if they know where to put the various kinds of knowledge.

Unfortunately they do not.

There was once a man, in an ancient story, who wanted to be taught spiritual sciences by a sage, while he was already full of all kinds of beliefs and theories, of fads and fancies, and so on.

The wise man said:

'I shall certainly teach you, if I can. You must stay here and serve me in every way.'

The disciple took up residence in the wise man's house and did everything he was bid.

One day he said to a fellow-inmate:

'I have doubts about our teacher. He says that he will teach me if he can. What sort of instructor is this, who may or may not be able to instruct?'

The wise man had overheard him. Calling him, he produced two swords and said:

'Put these into that scabbard.'

'Noble One!' stammered the disciple, 'as a man of peace you may not know what I do, as a former soldier. You cannot get two swords into one scabbard...'

'But that,' said the old man, 'is exactly what I was attempting to illustrate. You may have been a soldier, but that experience did not teach you about the possibilities of time, place and people.'

Confrontation and Support

Q: *What do you think of the people who try to 'confront' you?*

A: Confrontation as a form of behaviour can best be understood by looking at it in conjunction with its opposite: support. People who want to confront someone, and also those who have a strong desire to support anyone, very often do so because they have a desire for self-assertion which is not finding any other outlet.

It is for this reason that people who imagine that they are gentle, relaxed or benign feel a need to confront or to support. It is most usually a matter of the underlying aggressiveness finding an 'acceptable' outlet. This is well known to ancient as well as modern psychologists; though less well understood by other people, if they look at the apparent reason for the support or opposition, not at the mainspring of it.

The problem of making this clear is not eased by the fact that, since the desire to oppose, for instance, is so strong (it is an appetite seeking satisfaction) one can generally not reason with the sufferer.

Vanity and self-importance, if denied other outlets or if suppressed and not correctly refined to vanishing-point, will further fuel this desire to attack or support.

The phenomenon is strongly marked in religious circles where the teaching has not acted correctly upon the individual or the group. People who, for reasons of misapplied modesty training have been denied self-expression in a way which will provide socially acceptable outlets, are especially prone to this ailment. It also occurs throughout history (with a wide geographical distribution) among those who feel that they have been rejected by a source of authority.

Sufi teachers who have been unable to accept particular pupils have often been targets for this behaviour: it is a version of the 'sour grapes' behaviour of the fable in such instances. It is usually more harmful to whoever suffers from it than for the target, because the misapplied emotion activates all kinds of desires for power, envy and eventually results in unbalance. Such unbalanced people, oddly enough, often influence others quite strongly until they start to crack up. This gives us the emotional cults which most people now know about.

This problem is one reason why Sufi teaching tries to allow self-expression while the elements of vanity are being refined.

Rukhsa

After I had invited questions on things I had written, someone sent me this one:

'Among the Sufis, there are certain things which should be done, and certain others which should not be done. And I have heard that Sufi teachers can give their students *rukhsa* – permission to do something or to omit something in the rules of the school. Is *rukhsa* ever detrimental?'

Now the answer to this depends on our having much more information than the questioner gives. Perhaps he does not have it. Perhaps he does not realise that circumstances alter cases. What kind of a 'Sufi teacher' is he talking about?

But I think that you could work out my answer if I replied in a less laboured way than the question, for the question seems to me to be tiresomely wordy. I attempt this as follows:

At the Court of Versailles there was a lady – the Queen in fact – who was much addicted to card-playing. But it so happened that, one day, the Court had been informed that an unimportant German prince had died and cards were not allowed when there was mourning.

The lady was distressed at the deprivation (of the cards, naturally) but the adroit Monsieur de Maudepas, who was present, solved her problem for her. He merely said, 'Madame, I have the honour of assuring your Majesty that playing the game of piquet is equivalent to deep mourning.'

Etiquette

I have just had a letter from a reader who is annoyed by my alleged opposition to etiquette. He says, 'There is only one way to do right things, and often only one person who can or should do them. This is an important principle of religious actions, and it is seen to good advantage in etiquette as practised everywhere and at all times.' He concludes, 'Learn spirituality from etiquette, which is never wrong, or acts to anyone's detriment, nor does it produce unhappiness.'

Now that's a thought! I would not ordinarily take much notice of a letter like that, except that it is the latest of quite a number.

If things are, and always are, the way my correspondent puts it, he is right. But my attitude towards hidebound custom masquerading as social or religious sanctity can also be justified by reference to etiquette. Never wrong? Never acts to anyone's detriment? Does not produce unhappiness? Let us see.

I shall choose an example which is sufficiently far from most people to avoid too much offence, and leave you to seek similarities in more contemporary and immediate areas.

Spanish etiquette is said to have been one of the most developed systems of the kind in the world. And, of course, Spanish court etiquette was the best example of it.

One day the Spanish Queen, wife to Charles II, was riding when she slipped from the saddle, hanging upside-down by her stirrups. Luckily, at the time, she was attended by forty-three courtiers and others – etiquette demanded it. So far so good. But who was to go to the aid of Her Majesty? Etiquette said that nobody was permitted to intervene in such an event except the Grand Equerry. The only problem was that the Equerry was not present: so the forty-three remained frozen where they were.

Surely someone would break the rules and save the Queen? Sure enough, a man who was passing the Royal band saw the difficulty and ran forward, releasing Her Majesty's feet. He only did this, it was noted, because he was not aware of the very strict protocol which prevented anyone except the correctly appointed person to aid the Queen.

Was he rewarded? Yes, indeed: he immediately received a number of gold coins. But one question remained: the stranger, even though ignorant of etiquette, had committed the crime of touching the Queen. This could not go unpunished, and he was duly banished from the Kingdom for his insolence.

It would have been etiquette to leave the lady in her predicament. It was wrong to go to help her. It was right to reward the passer-by. Etiquette demanded his banishment: but ... 'Never to anyone's detriment? ... Does not produce unhappiness?' Perhaps the man really wanted to be banished.

Fellow-Feeling

Q: *There is a community of feeling and harmony which surely indicates that those affected by it are on the right lines. Have you any comment upon the importance and value of this unity of people and experience, this communion with something higher, which surely must be the mark of true experience?*

A: This feeling, in almost identical words, is expressed by members of human groups whose members profess diametrically opposite and often mutually hostile ideologies. In history, it has been recorded both by the oppressors and the oppressed,

143

on many occasions. Indeed, it has even been held by an oppress-ing community that it is this very feeling which makes it important to oppress (or 'bring to the truth') the oppressed community.

The claim or belief that this feeling is limited to those who are attuned to the truth can only be sustained in the absence of such information as this. It flourishes among people who have done no comparative study, or who want to believe that only they – and not people who differ in beliefs or attitudes – can experience the sensation of which you speak.

In reality the social and subjective feeling which you mention is not the one to which people allude when they speak of a truly universal and cosmic experience. True gold, as Rumi says, exists: that is why there can be false gold. The feeling which you mention is a form of what the ancient scientific historiographer, Ibn Khaldun (also a Sufi) describes as *Asabiyya*, 'group spirit'. It is valuable when employed for constructive purposes, but can be dangerous when accompanied by an ideological posture. To settle for this when there is something higher is a form of greed.

Fate

There was once a Dervish who had divinatory powers, having arrived at the Fourth Stage of Understanding.

A certain woman who had four young sons and was anxious for their future, approached him and begged him to take them under his protection.

The Dervish pondered, and then said:

'Ask me not why; but make sure that the first boy becomes a shopkeeper, the second a priest and the third a soldier. If they do not take up these occupations it will not go well for them: but if they do, they will be protected.'

The four youths grew up and followed the careers indicated by the Dervish, with the fourth becoming his disciple.

Every year the men visited the Dervish, grateful for the success which attended them in life and convinced that it came from the benediction of the sage.

After many years the fourth lad, now himself a respected teacher, asked the Dervish why people placed so much reliance on the Fourth Stage of Understanding. He himself, after all, was widely revered, and he had not received this illumination.

'I can illustrate something of its use,' replied the ancient, 'by referring to the day when your mother brought you boys to see me. I perceived by my inner powers, from the Fourth Stage, that the first lad would become a thief, the second a liar and the third a killer. Their occupations licensed or protected them in these tendencies...'

'And I?'

'You were the only one who sought Truth without desire for gain or protection.'

Living Forever

Q: *Why do you say that one-half of a person's mind does not know what the other half is thinking?*

A: Here is an example:

An hour ago you came to me and said that you had had 'veridical experiences of the Future State'; that you had had 'ecstatic joy connected with the Beyond'; that you were 'going to go to Heaven when you died'; that you were 'a man of the Spirit', and much else. Is this true?

Q: *Yes.*

A: Very well. Then, when you had finished, I said:

'Would you like me to give you a recipe which would keep you young and healthy for a hundred years?' Your answer was "Yes". Is that so?'

Q: *It is.*

A: Now I shall show you the split mind. One part cannot wait for the experience of Heaven, which you have tasted, so you say. If it cannot wait, why is another part (it cannot surely be the same part) interested in staying on this earth for a further century?

The Raft

Q: *I do understand that there are several, all equally valid, ways of describing the human inner condition and the means of its solution. But can you give me one which, perhaps by its unfamiliarity, could help one to get closer to the Teaching?*

A: Here is one. The real, inner self of the human being is trapped. Two things hold it thus: the assumptions and operation of the secondary Self, and the shallow but strong bonds of conditioning and environment. The Sufi has to do what he can to approach that inward Self and, with its co-operation and eluding and otherwise negating the effects of the opposition, help in self-realisation.

Q: *Yes, I understand that as being the skeleton of what the Gnostics in the West and the Sufis in the East say about humanity. In fact, I dare say that such a diagnosis could be made of every religion. But how is this to be conceived so that one might hold it in the mind?*

A: I can give you a brand-new parable, which seems to be what you want. Visualise a man who had to try to rescue a prisoner from a castle on an island. He made a raft of weeds, just strong enough to bear his weight, and floated by night to the castle's shore. The soldiers guarding it saw the raft, and ran onto it, whereupon the raft sank, while the rescuer hid himself in the dark. Some soldiers said, 'That raft is not much good, for it sank the moment we all ran onto it. This is not a serious attempt.' They also concluded that, as it had sunk, the prisoner could not escape. Some of them thought that the raft *had* carried someone, others not. The prisoner himself, hearing these speculations, imagined all sorts of things.

Now the rescuer is the Sufi, seeking the captive through the raft, which is the means which he uses to approach the problem. The 'new transport', which shall be used later, is the methods which are devised by the rescuer on the basis of his expert knowledge. The castle is the environmental beliefs and the soldiers are the subjective ones, including assumptions.

Impossible

One of my constant critics has been good enough to write again, giving me material for what – I hope – may be an instructive passage.

He says that, twenty years ago, he was given 'certain spiritual exercises' to carry out by his mentor of the time. That man is now dead. If he (my critic) were to take notice of things that I have been saying and writing, he would have to consider 'abandoning what has given me so much, in favour of something else from someone whom I don't respect'.

I can see his quandary.

Perhaps he (and you) would like to share with me a true story of Philip III of Spain. He was sitting by a fire lit by the Court Fire-Maker, when he found that it was too hot. Turning to the Marquis de Pobar, who happened to be handy, he asked for it to be put out. The Marquis, though anxious to obey any Royal command, was unable to comply. This was on the wholly reasonable grounds that the Duke de Useda was the man appointed to quench flames. Accordingly, no action was taken, the Duke being away at the time hunting in Catalonia.

The King, for his part, was unable by reason of his dignity to withdraw from anything (including fire) and so he remained where he was. The fire became stronger and in the end it so damaged His Majesty's health that he died of its effects.

It is to be hoped that the spiritual exercises prescribed for our correspondent by his defunct master do not grow in strength – or that he finds an acceptable mentorial substitute to advise him on further action: in case the exercises were not originally intended to go on for ever. Whatever good they may have done, I am tempted to reflect, they do not seem to have exorcised his ill-temper. Perhaps they have implanted a desire to write letters, since he sends me quite a few, including copies of letters which he writes to other people, on all manner of subjects. In a way I am copying him, by making this copy of my reply to him: or perhaps the exercises are so strong that he is transferring the epistolatory compulsion to me.

Sincerity and Truth

Q: *Can you comment upon the function of sincerity and truthfulness in the work, having regard to what you have already said about the relativity of truth? I realise that this is a question where religion must fall back on dogma, where politics must, as you say, 'positively affirm' in the name of the organisation, and where modern philosophy has outrun itself.*

A: I shall give you something to think about. The philosopher says that he does not know what truth is. The theologian says that truth is what he is saying. The politician says that there cannot be any other truth than he sees. There is, nevertheless, a search for truth. Man seeks truth, wants truth. I have already said once that you must accept what seems to be true or what you *know* to be true.

Knowing is something which is not open to discussion, like the statement that H_2O is a formula for water. I shall therefore exclude this aspect, since the question is not concerned with it. Sincerity and truth are usually associated with religious systems. When people have doubts or become atheists, there is a reaction upon their idea of truth. They must replace it, attach it to something else. They attach, it, say, to general 'doing good'.

Now the conflict in most people's minds is due to the fact that they want to give up the doctrinaire approach to religion, but do not want sincerity or truth, which they feel to be necessary to them. They have a sense of guilt, and this is 'carried over' into their new attachment.

We start at an earlier stage, as we do with most things. Sincerity is the attachment to a cause, recognising one's own involvement. By this I mean that there is no need for altruism. There is a conflict when people start to ask themselves: 'Am I alleviating pain in others merely because I am afraid of pain myself?' They do not realise that they are involved and that it is one and the same thing. This is because they cannot see a great many things as a whole, being trained or adapted to studying fragments.

People who will become sincere are those who strive towards sincerity, not those who think they have it and that it is something which they are using or profiting by. You must fill a jug before you can pour out of it. The prayer 'This is my sincere belief' can be blasphemy unless one knows one's own sincerity. But in that case the word itself would not be used. Stop thinking of sincerity as a palpable quality and you will be nearer to it. Truth means saying what seems to you to be true, when you are engaged in this work. You can attain to real truth, as it happens, by striving to behave in what seems to be a true manner. Not telling lies is one way. Truth is not, at your level, something which you can buy in a pint pot, or tap into like an electrical circuit. If you did, it would kill you, like a million volts.

Eastward Journeys

Q: *I have often felt that the only way to find out how the people of the East have solved the religious and psychological problems is myself to go to the East. I can see that the history of the West is the failure of religion and, that psychology is still in its infancy here. Where should I start on such a journey, because I realise that one can spend one's whole life in journeying, and never meet the correct teacher?*

A: My dear friend, you are a prisoner of a certain way of thinking. Let me try to dissipate this by means of analogies easily grasped by you.

Assume that you are a missionary, trained to speak a foreign tongue in Rome, and sent out to bring Catholicism to the people of some remote African territory. You start to talk to the people, as soon as you arrive. They say to you: 'This sounds interesting. Where do you come from?' You answer: 'I come from Rome, the seat of our teaching and study.'

'Very well,' say the locals, 'we will journey to Rome, to the source and fountainhead of your teaching.'

You tell them: 'First, you speak no Latin, no Italian, none of the languages of the countries through which you would have to journey. Furthermore, you have not the wherewithal to make the trip. Your customs and way of thinking at the moment are unacceptable to the people of Rome, where none will understand you. It is for this reason that I have spent many years in studying your language and your ways, having been especially equipped for the task which brings me here. Can you not see that I am an instrument, fashioned for the purpose of making possible your learning which would be impossible otherwise?'

In a similar way you must realise your own capacity. Such journeys to the East or West, are for the man who is ready for such a journey. If you do not even know that you are in the situation of the remote tribesman, you are less than likely to be ready for a trip to a place and among people who are, in fact, unable to communicate with you except through the instruments of their own fashioning.

Ask yourself whether you are asking this question from self-pride, thinking that you are ready for such a journey. Or are you perhaps asking it not because you are satisfied that there is something to be found, but because you want additional proofs? If you seek them in some distant and romantic place, seek them through the thirst of your emotions, you will never find them at all. Study the story of Nasrudin and the lost ring. He dropped it in his house, but looked for it in the public square because there was more light there.

The Magic Potion of Onkink

There was once a man who wished with all his heart that he might be able to transform himself into some other kind of creature, to understand what it understood, and to learn what it might know, and to see things that it could see.

He spent a good deal of his time wondering how to achieve this aim, and enquiring from experts of all sorts the way in which it might be done.

Some people, of course, laughed at him; some could not see the point of his ambition, and others simply thought that it was impossible. But the man did not give up. He was often deceived by people who offered him charms and talismans, advice and rituals, which they said would produce the effects which he desired: but all to no avail. He read books, joined cults, practised strange rites, adopted fads. None of them worked.

Then, one day, as he was walking along a street, deep in thought, he came across a bottle lying on the ground. Something made him pick it up and put it in his pocket. When he got home, he saw that there was a label on the bottle, which said:

> Open this, place three drops on your tongue, and make a wish. You will then be able to do whatever you want to. Simply ask how to do it when you have taken the elixir.

This was his chance! With trembling fingers, the man uncorked the container, measured out three drops onto a spoon, and put the liquid on his tongue.

After a moment, he had a strange feeling; for the first time he felt that he could, indeed, do anything he wished.

Now it so happened that the bottle was indeed full of a magical fluid: and so the man, in the twinkling of an eye, heard a voice say, 'What is your desire?' Naturally, he automatically answered, 'I wish to become another kind of creature.' Looking up into the sky, he saw a skein of grey geese flying south on their winter migration. He added, 'I want to become a giant grey goose.'

The voice instantly answered: 'Repeat the word "OINK", and you will become the finest goose that ever lived. When you want to change back again, or to become something else, say the word "INK".'

No sooner had he said 'OINK', than he found that he had been transformed into a large and beautiful grey goose. What was more, he felt wonderful. He knew everything that migratory grey geese knew, and could observe his own thoughts as a goose, while retaining his thinking capacity as a man.

This was really amazing. Now, he thought, he would try something else: he would become a man of wisdom. The magic word, he remembered, was 'INK', and so he began to articulate it. Strange, he thought, nothing was happening. He tried again, and realised that, instead of saying 'INK', he was saying 'OINK' every time he tried. And that, of course, was because this is the sound which grey geese make. There is no goose, grey or otherwise, which can make the sound 'INK'.

And so, as you have already guessed, the man who became a grey goose had to remain a grey goose, spending the rest of his life trying to say 'INK', but never managing to say any more than 'OINK'...

Knock Quietly

Assumptions haunt people, much more than they know. People generally deal with situations by means of assumptions.

This habit is useful, it can mean that you do not have to think. If you see a man in a blue uniform you can assume he is a policeman. That is why admirals are regularly mistaken for ticket-collectors on railway stations.

Do not make assumptions all the time, and do not let your life be ruled by assumptions.

Remember the sad case of a sign-writer who lost a commission because he made a wrong assumption.

A lady asked him to paint a notice about the dog to put at her front door. He lost the job because he produced one saying:

'Beware of the Dog.'

'You stupid man,' said the lady, 'the notice I wanted was "Don't wake the dog".'

Clockwise

Q: *You say that things in the thinking of the ordinary person are reversed. If this trend is perceptible in mental things, is it not there in physical ones? By this I mean the things which we do or make in physical life? If so, can I have an example?*

A: You can have an example, but please note that it is up to *you* to find such things, not me. I merely point the trend.

Here is your example: you could call 'clockwise' the rotary movement from left to right. Look at your clock, from the clock's position. The hands, for it, are actually revolving in the opposite direction: anti-clockwise. What you call 'clockwise' is in fact not clockwise at all. It should be described, if one were to give things their proper connotations, thus: 'The seeming movement of the hands of a clock, etc. when viewed from a laterally reversed position facing the mechanism, etc.'

Haven't you noticed yet that when you stand facing a person, his left is your right, and vice-versa? What do you see in your looking-glass? Is the image which is transmitted into your eyes not projected there upside-down? There is no state of right and left, or of a thousand other things. There is no absolute sleep and wakefulness known to most people.

Meaning of Words and Experiences

Q: *Surely material reality is true and we can understand things from sight, description and experience. Information is reliable. The significance of words standing for events must be standard. If I see a statue, I know what it represents: especially if it has a halo on it. When I come to see you, the airline people weigh my luggage to prevent overloading. When I see a headline: 'Motorway Disaster' I know that cars have crashed. And so on.*

You seem so often to claim that people don't know what is happening or why something came into being or what things mean. But I know that facts are facts.

A: Facts are useful for some purposes. For others, they are extremely misleading. I will take your facts one at a time. 'Disaster' may mean a crash to you, but etymologically it means 'a bad aspect of the stars', and it meant at one time, something caused by astrological influences. So much for what words for events mean: they mean what successive people want them to mean. Even a motorway disaster does not mean a car crash to everyone. It may mean a bridge fallen onto a truck. As for a statue: you may or may not know what it means. Anthropologists and archaeologists do not know what the oldest human figures mean, but assume that they are idols or votive offerings. Everyone thinks that he knows that the statue which stands in Piccadilly Circus in London represents 'Cupid, God of Love'. In fact, it was sculpted by Alfred Gilbert to symbolise 'Christian Charity', and commemorates the Earl of Shaftesbury. I wonder, by the way, if when you see a halo attached to a statue you know that these were, in ancient times, placed there to collect bird-droppings and thus prevent the disfigurement of the face of the statue? Or did you perhaps think that they 'represent a nimbus' as people now think, because they looked at the halo shape and not at the function?

When the airline checking people weigh your baggage, whether it is to come to see me or otherwise, they allow you 44 lbs (20 kg.) of luggage. It may be imagined that this weight has been fixed because of what the aircraft can carry. You may be interested to know, since you are concerned with secondary things, that this 'wasn't the finely calculated allowance designed

155

for the jet age which the airlines proclaimed it to be, but a rule instituted by Wells Fargo in the 1880s to ensure that stage-coaches were not overloaded, and adopted wholesale by IATA (International Air Transport Association)'.★

Perhaps the approximate and ever-changing meaning of 'facts' may enable you to understand why so many people have for so long sought for something more reliable. Facts are useful up to a point. This is what has led people to imagine, un-reflectingly, that they must be of absolute value, or useful for all kinds of things to which they are not suited. Your facts, as we have seen, can be shown to have different 'meanings' by means of yet other facts. Facts, therefore, are not what they are assumed to be. Facts are only relatively true. Those who are interested in ultimate truth cannot regard material reality as more than transitory.

Things You Cannot Say

Q: *I get glimpses of things, and of ideas. I find them impossible to put into words. I cannot say them. And I have no words for them. Often they come as a result of things you have said, a sort of 'recognition of truth'. I wish I could get closer to this.*

A: I suppose this is a question. These 'glimpses' of something you cannot formulate are like that because they cannot be formulated by the ways you are used to using. If you try to say them they will disappear. You wish you could get closer than this. This closeness comes when you find one of these things, or a group of them, joining with another, or with another group. But you have to be at the stage when you can come and ask for the method. As long as you keep struggling you won't get any

★ *Business Traveller*, 'Travelog', London: Summer 1978, page 27, col. 2

further, because you cannot get closer with your present apparatus. People who tell you that you can do so, tell you that for one of two simple reasons, which I will give you:-

(1) Because they know that they have to tire, evade or exhaust your 'intellectualising' capacity before you will accept the existence of another faculty.

(2) Because they are deliberate or unconscious imitators whose teachings are derived from parroting the above stage, having been repetitiously transmitted from this early stage at some distance.

The Rich Man's State

A millionaire decided to visit a Sufi, to obtain his blessing.

He made a long journey, accompanied by a glittering retinue, and arrived at last at the sage's home.

'O Illuminated One!' the rich man cried as he entered the presence, 'Teacher whose invocations are always answered, say a prayer for me!'

The Sufi asked, 'What prayer would you have me say?'

'Ask,' requested the man of wealth, 'that I should never fall to a lower state than I am now in.'

The Sufi agreed, and the prayer was said.

Some years later, the Sufi entered a miserable caravanserai to find a beggar, dressed in rags, who at once attacked him.

'I am that magnate whom you prayed for, you false and villainous so-called Sufi!' he screamed.

The Sufi said, 'What, more precisely, is your complaint?'

'Complaint? Look at me, begging and unhappy...'

'Your prayer,' the Sufi told him, 'was indeed answered. Your state was greed and insecurity, and you are still powerfully in its grasp.'

Car Keys

Q: *Do people in the West really imagine that their imitations of the shallow or obsessed Sufi imitators of the East is really worthwhile? I constantly see television programmes featuring European and American so-called Sufis, who are as absurd as they appear numerous.*

A: You are writing from the East. This imitative phenomenon can easily be understood by looking at equally superficial behaviour in your own country. After all, these Western unfortunates have learnt their antics from spurious or self-deceived 'Sufis' of the East. Just look out of your window and you will see hordes of imitators of the West, believing that by dressing in denim or talking or behaving in a certain way, they have become Western in some way. Go to any Middle Eastern airport and look at the hordes of people jingling car keys when they have no cars, and trying to look as if they are about to board aircraft. You should realise that, although imagining themselves to be 'spiritual', these Western imitators are in reality only 'jingling car keys'.

SECTION V

Eight Analogies

There are several extremely important analogies, which can be put in the form of anecdotes, which enable one to isolate for study and benefit, characteristics, mistakes, which block higher perceptions.

The first is concerned with assumptions, especially the assumption that people who have a certain repute must have the flexibility to advise one on every necessary emphasis of study.

It is often used to describe the condition of pedantic and formula-thinking scholars, whose expertise may even stand in the way of enlightenment, however useful it may be in the secondary field known as learning.

This version concerns a woman whose son had gone away to study medicine. She heard that he had graduated, and was therefore overjoyed when she received a letter from him.

Unfortunately, however, his handwriting had become the scribble which is often associated with medical men. She decided to take it to a chemist, knowing how experienced they are at reading doctors' writing.

She took the paper to her local pharmacist. He looked at it, whipped out a bottle, and said: 'There you are. Take two spoonfuls three times a day.'

Another mistake is to assume that a formula, or a piece of instructional material, is exclusive and unvarying. The tale attached to this tells of an engineer who was one day found staring at a lion in a zoo.

Someone said:

'You seem very interested in that animal.'

The engineer replied:

'So I should be – it has infringed the patent on my new shock-absorber!'

The random or partial adoption of techniques or ideas is reflected in the third anecdote, dealing, too, with the tinkering tendency of psychologists and supposedly spiritual people alike.

161

A man went to visit a friend who was in a mental institution.

He said to the psychiatrist in charge:

'Is he any better?'

'Better? I should say he is,' said the doctor. 'He used to think he was Louis XIV. Now he only thinks that he is Louis V.'

Sometimes the narratives can be put into guru–disciple terms, as in the following one, which deals with the absence of real perception in the general populace as to the spiritual and the imitative:

A guru once related, so goes the tale, how he became a spiritual mentor.

'I was sitting by the roadside wondering what to do, when a man came and squatted opposite me. We carried on all sorts of chants and exercises.

'After some weeks, I said:

"Tell me, what shall I do next, Master?"

'The other man replied:

"But I thought that *you* were the master!"

The behaviour of disciples is often noted to be somewhat less infused with common sense than that of the general public; something which has been observed as a fact for centuries. One esoteric teacher tells this story to impress on learners that they have to think clearly as well as to follow blindly:

'What,' asked a teacher to his pupil 'will people think of you, buying meatballs from a street-vendor five times a day?'

'That's all right,' answered his follower, 'I tell everyone that they are for you!'

Again in this vein, but referring to 'idolatry' is the tale of the man who went to a far-off land to study metaphysics under one or other of the great teachers who abounded there.

He visited one after another and, although all seemed

willing to accept him, they always ordered a dog to be killed for dinner.

Finally, he found one who served the meal without any sign of this – to him – distressing tradition.

He studied under this man for years and finally said:

'I chose you, you know, Reverend Sir, because you did not have a dog killed for our supper.'

'Perish the thought!' answered the sage. 'We do not kill dogs here: that is a barbaric habit. For our meals, we wait until they have died of something.'

The idolatry, of course, is the attachment to literalism.

Seventh is the story of the man who went to a genuine spiritual teacher and said:

'I have come to you because after being the disciple of such-and-such a supposed teacher for seven years, I realised that he was not a spiritual man.'

The true mentor answered: 'You remind me of the man who was asked why he had left his house after living there for seven years. He replied: "Because I found that it had no bathroom!"'

Finally, illustrating the need to have common sense at all times, is the graffito reportedly chalked on a wall by a desperate would-be disciple, which starkly shows that he was in no condition to learn anything:

'I shall,' it ran, 'leave all my money to whoever can give me immortality!'

The Need to Understand Restrictive Roles

There is plenty of talk about archetypes and roles. People have learned, through discussion of these subjects, to look for archetypal individuals or experiences. By looking for them they may have found them. They have yet to realise that if you assign a significance to a limited array of factors you are in trouble if it happens that there are other factors which you haven't heard of. If you think all soup has lumps in it you will fail to recognise soup without them. A similar difficulty exists with roles. People expect others to fill one of various predetermined roles. This means that covertly they are asking themselves what the role of the person they are dealing with really is. This means that they lose something if they find someone fulfilling a role they don't know about; or if they have miscast him. All this is quite apart from understanding their own roles: are you, for instance, a Chief or an Indian?

Now if you talk about these things, you may be sure that it will provoke rejection or discussion. This is only because, at this time, the conception is new and therefore not welcomed. Better to stand back and look at whether people's talk and behaviour really does accord with what I am saying. You will, I think, be surprised by what you observe.

In contemporary Western society people will take a lead only from certain well-established types of figure. They want to know if you are an educator (which means something like an academic), or an artist or similar, or an artisan or a priest/guru. Not only have they only these categories to work with: they are also landed with endowing inadequate ranges with certain defined functions, limiting them in their scope, authority and importance. It is when this rigidity of thinking is made more flexible that progress towards learning something more becomes possible.

It is useful, too, to note that nobody is objecting to others limiting themselves to these categories within which they approach learning. But when they try to approach our subject through these restrictions, it is for us to speak out.

Work

Q: *My difficulty is to understand what I am doing. I realise that I cannot really do anything unless I understand it. Until that understanding comes I feel myself to be at a standstill. Can I be helped to understand more of the Work, so that I can progress in it?*

A: You are not as alone as you have assumed. Things which you do have an effect. This effect is not the simple effect that you may think they have. In every action there is a 'work' content, which will contribute towards your progress whether you know it or not. This factor has been forgotten, or may be concealed by someone who wants you, for specific and limited periods, to consider yourself on your own, or something of the sort. What you are talking about is something emerging from an individual's situation; it can never be a rule. It depends upon 'time and place', upon 'occasion and necessity'.

When, however, you understand the deeper areas, dimensions, of what you are doing, then you will benefit from the very same action several fold. You put in effort, work. You gain muscles. You may not have noticed that at the same time you were earning money. When you learn about money, then you can take the money into your use and pay for things with it.

You cannot learn more until you can learn more.

This word 'Work':- it is not being used in its real sense. In Arabic 'work' is another word for religion. In alchemy the 'Opus' is the Great Work, the transmutation. To the Sufis 'Wazifa' or 'duty' is another word for a duty carried out under instructions. There are numerous other possible examples.

165

The kind of work in which we are interested is work which contains many dimensions. Each of these functions of Work is there, whether consciously understood or not. Their value, their yield, however, only becomes operative when the situation is ripe for this. And Work can only be carried out with a chance of this *yield* coming when it is deliberately planned and launched as a part of a programme demanded by the origin of the teaching; the permanent and timeless call as we term it.

Frozen Attention

Q: *What is the greatest barrier to learning?*

A: Preconceptions and concentration upon things which one thinks one wants to learn, but which may not be one's real needs. This causes part of the attention capacity to become locked onto the preconception, assumption or query.

I gave a lecture in a Middle Eastern country nearly thirty years ago. When I had finished and asked for questions, someone stood up and asked:

'What is foam?'

I said: 'Why do you want to know?'

He answered: 'Because I have always wanted to know what foam is!'

More recently, in fact three days ago, I spoke to someone on this problem for two hours, insisting that there was no value for him in being so keen on obtaining random facts, when what he needed was the kind of information which would enable him to decide what facts to seek.

I asked him if he understood.

'Perfectly,' he said, and thanked me.

166

So I showed him to the door. As I was opening it, he said:

'By the way, can you give me some information about the Kabbala?'

Now this is a very long-standing and characteristic problem in teaching, and there is a famous Indian story which illustrates it.

A certain teacher was explaining something to a disciple, who at the same time was watching a mouse wriggling into a hole.

Ultimately the teacher said, 'Now, is it all in?'

'Yes,' said the student, 'all except the tail.'

This may seem a small matter. In fact it is one of the biggest, because failure to obtain the flexibility of mind to switch attention off one's preoccupations onto what else there is to study makes that study impossible. And, surely, this is a very big matter indeed.

Heedlessness

Q: *Could I have an example of heedlessness, as the Sufis call it, in the form of not keeping alert to our studies?*

A: Recently I had a request, from a group of people who had been studying my books for some years, for fresh material. I knew that they did not need fresh material, and that they had only taken from the existing books the things that amused or interested them, not the material that was there. I therefore paraphrased several dozen passages from these books, and put them in a slightly different form. After typing, these were sent to the group. Their reaction was almost to weep with delight at this 'new and exciting, really marvellous stuff'. They had already had several hundred times as much material of this quality; they also had this identical material in paraphrase, but this they believed to be 'new'.

This is heedlessness in the form you mention. These people do not deserve more because they are plainly incapable of dealing with what they have; they are liable – if we are not careful – to take up time which we could give to others who do bother to learn and to stay alert. And, of course, we have to remember that there are many people (though these are statistically small) who do respond to the materials we give them by keeping alert to it and using it, instead of merely crying out for more, like idiots who have not looked at what they have already got.

Revealing His True Nature

There was once a disciple who complained to his Sufi teacher that he was not being initiated into the secret teachings of the folk, in spite of his having faithfully studied and worked under his master for a number of years.

The Sufi told him, 'It is not a matter of years or of the intensity of your study: it is a matter of the results.'

'But,' said the disciple, 'what may be visible to you, in my shortcomings and the means to redress them, is invisible to me and to the other disciples. Is it therefore essential that you alone should be able to diagnose my condition and prescribe for it?'

'The work of the teacher is indeed that,' said the master, 'but there are opportunities for disciples to observe at least an equivalence of someone's condition, and we shall make an opportunity to display this.'

One day not long afterwards, the Sufi was walking to his assembly-hall when he called to the cook to prepare some stew, and then signalled to the complaining disciple to accompany him. They entered the hall, where the rest of the students were collected. The master sat down with the disciple beside him and told everyone to pay close attention.

'This man, who is a merchant, is well-known to all of you,' he said, 'and he expects that his inwardness shall have been transformed in accordance with his work on his outwardness. We propose to see whether this is the case.'

Now the proceedings were suddenly interrupted by the entry of a messenger, who asked permission to inform the merchant that some of his ships had returned from afar, bringing great profits, and asking for urgent instructions. The merchant gave him his orders, and then the Sufi said:

'Since you have gained such good fortune, would you not perhaps like to contribute something towards the upkeep of the community, for you have not been able to give much these many years, no doubt through poverty...'

'I think that I should attend to that at a more appropriate time,' said the disciple, 'if you will remind me.'

The Sufi agreed.

Then came another interruption, this time by an officer of the court, who asked whether he could have a private interview with the disciple. The Sufi took them both into his study.

The officer reported that the merchant had been granted a piece of land about which he had been in litigation, worth a great deal of money.

When the man had delivered his papers and withdrawn, the Sufi said:

'That is an enormous tract of land. Will you give us a piece, so that we may grow crops for the upkeep of the community?'

'You have always said,' replied the merchant, 'that poverty is preferable to riches, and I do not propose to offer you any unless you really press me.'

'Would you not offer it, and give me the opportunity to refuse?' asked the master.

'Putting temptation in another's way is equal to committing a sin,' said the merchant sententiously.

Time passed, and the merchant heard that his fate was favouring him more and more. A gold mine was discovered on his property: but when the Sufi visited him and asked that he give some of the gold for the poor, he only said that he would attend to it at a later date.

Then the King was short of money to wage a war, and he borrowed large sums of money from the merchant, making him Prime Minister in exchange. This time the Sufi asked him to intervene with the King to remove oppressive laws against the Sufis, and the merchant promised that he would help, but did nothing.

Finally, when the King died, the merchant-disciple was elected in his place. After the coronation, the Sufi asked:

'Now that your Majesty has all power in this realm, will you give us the material help which you had promised, for we need these things in order to organize our work?'

The King replied: 'I really have had enough of the importunings of useless Sufis – begone, before I give orders that you and your community be banished from my realm!'

'In that case,' said the master, 'your Majesty can continue with ruling your own kingdom – and we shall eat the stew!'

The merchant looked around and saw that he was back in the assembly-hall of the dervishes, and that only an hour or so had passed since he entered it with the Sufi teacher. By the power of *limiyya* (hypnosis) the master had made the man believe that all those things had happened to him, and he, together with the disciples, had watched his reactions as a rich man, as a powerful one, and as a king.

'Now,' said the master, 'we have shown your true nature. As with material things, so with spiritual. You must be worthy of promotion, otherwise you will act in a way which is against the interests of the spiritual world, and at best your experiences will be wasted.'

Hypocrisy

Q: *Why should a spiritual master be treated with respect and thought of with awe and humility?*

A: Not for him, but for ourselves. It is the posture of mind which accompanies the feeling of respect which attunes us to reality and banishes self-satisfaction. Just as when people mourn the dead they are doing so because of themselves – the dead are unaffected by it – so, too, when people are too self-centred they cannot learn. They have to think of others as more important than themselves.

People sometimes become too man-worshipping, however, and think too much of their spiritual teacher. It is because of the need to balance the attitude to get it just right that this story of the sanctimonious Dervish is told:

There was once a religious man, who liked to think of himself as a true dervish. He liked, too, to abide by all the rules of the divine and secular laws, and because he felt pride at this he became, like so many other people before and since, an unconscious hypocrite. This state, quite naturally, prevented him making any real progress on the spiritual path, and an angel decided to help him out of his difficulty.

One day, therefore, when the Dervish was looking at a condemned man being led past his house, and feeling how right it was that the miscreant should suffer, the angel appeared before him.

The apparition said:

'For imagining sanctimoniousness to be real piety, you are condemned to wander the face of the earth, without hope of salvation, until buds shall appear and blossom on a dead branch!'

The Dervish was at first indignant, and thought that the angel must be an impostor. Then, as events forced him from his home and onto the public streets, he realized that there might be some truth in the matter.

There was an old blasted oak tree at the top of a hill, which seemed completely dead, and the allegedly pious man used to go to look at this, pondering his fate and wondering about his potential.

One day he ran into a barber on the road. The barber said, 'If I do not keep in practice, I shall not be able to get a job when I get to my destination. May I shave you?'

The semi-Dervish at first felt affronted that his reverend beard should be assailed; but suddenly the thought struck him that he was, after all, a fraud, and there was no point in keeping a beard if the man behind it had not attained perfection. So he agreed, and the barber shaved his beard off.

It was at that moment that the roots of the tree started to take in moisture and nutrition.

Then the Dervish saw a very poor man walking along the road, without a rag to cover him. 'All I have myself,' he said to himself, 'is this patched dervish cloak . . .' Then he remembered that the sign of the patched cloak was to indicate his state, and yet his state was one of outward show while he wore it. So he took the cloak off and shared it with the poor wayfarer.

Then it was the sap began to rise in to the trunk of the tree on the top of the hill.

Not long afterwards the Dervish was sitting under the tree when two seekers-after-truth came along. Seeing this devout-looking figure before them, they asked him to teach them something. He said:

'What I can teach you is that whenever you see anyone who looks devout, who wears a beard, who is glad to teach you, who allows people to address him by religious titles; you are probably dealing with a fraud!'

At that moment buds appeared on the branches of the tree, and almost immediately afterwards, they burst into flower.

Missed the Point . . .

A very distinguished religious figure was here today.

I asked him how he dealt with the fact that many of his ancient traditions were completely unacceptable to the people of today.

'That is easy enough,' he said, 'because I simply do not mention such things. There are plenty of beliefs, other than those you mention, which we can work upon.'

'But,' I went on, 'how can you manage when people insist upon discussing matters which contemporary knowledge finds anachronistic?'

'I simply say,' he told me, 'that these are minor points, and that they are worrying too much about them . . .'

All this reminds me of a tale. Read it and decide whether our prelate is not doing much the same as the cook in the story:

IRRELEVANT

There was once a cook who was surprised by his mistress while straining soup through one of her husband's socks.

'Whatever are you doing with the Master's socks?' she cried out, in alarm.

'Nothing to worry about, mistress,' said the cook 'as they are not his clean ones!'

Personally, I prefer the retort of Dr. Samuel Johnson, when asked by a lady why he had defined the word 'pastern' as 'a horse's knee'. 'Sheer ignorance, Madam,' he said.

Black and Blue

One of the most interesting – and little-known – facts about higher knowledge is that its pursuit is as much dependent upon exclusion as inclusion. It is as important to exclude certain elements as it is to include others. You may think that all you have to do is to find the right formulae of belief, ritual, exercise: but if you do not at the same time avoid doing or thinking or practising certain things, these unexcluded things can – often do – act as contaminants to your efforts. This is one of the functions of real teachers: to tell you what to avoid as well as what to do. Equally, of course, you can tell who is a real teacher and who is not, as often as not, by whether the teacher is merely giving you a bundle of instructions (prayers, meditations, fasting, concentration, and so on) and hence not excluding, or whether he is also telling you what should be avoided. The latter admonitions will deal with the time and places, the company and the response to reactions, which are part of the authentic knowledge of the real teacher.

In one story which is used as an analogy of this, a woman tells her husband to go to a reputed teacher, and to obey him in every particular. He is, in fact, to repeat everything that the teacher says. When the man arrives at the sage's house, the venerable one says: 'Who are you?'

'Who are you?' repeats the man.

'What do you mean?' continues the teacher, and the would-be student echoes, 'What do you mean?'

After a few exchanges of this kind, the sage orders the man to be beaten and thrown out. When he arrives home, the wife asks how he got on. 'Well enough,' says the husband, 'but I don't know how much more of this I can stand: they have beaten me black and blue, and this is only my first lesson!'

Slavish imitation, as the story tries to inform us, results in nothing, and may even be harmful. None of this is helped by the ordinary human mimetic habit, in which people very often copy the manners, acts and even dress of those whom they esteem.

The Barriers

A man is anxious to free himself from a prison, and yet he strengthens the bars. Will he escape? These bars are the habits of depending only upon the secondary self, the desire for emotional stimulus and greed.

Supposing someone were to want to rise above the surface of the water but persisted in holding on to stones at the bottom of the sea. What would happen to him and what would you call him? These are the attachments to outworn and irrelevant systems, ideas and slogans.

Suppose someone were to want to grow taller, but kept himself in a box which dwarfed his growth? This box is the reliance upon cults and organisations which dwarf people's capacities.

Supposing, again, that someone were to think that he wanted to travel, but yet placed great weights on his feet so that he could not walk or even move. What would you call such a person? Those weights are the desires for attention and for getting something before the time is right.

Supposing, yet again, that some people were to aver that they wanted to be better people, yet they constantly stole what belonged to others and told lies, working against being better in any way. What would you call such people? Those actions are paralleled by believing that one will get paid twice: once by feeling good after doing something good, and once in a future life.

Supposing, finally, that there were people who said that they wanted to see around them, yet who persisted in wearing blinkers, what would you call them? Those barriers are the habit of mixing attractive but useless formulae and totems with specific teachings.

Undigested

It is extremely important to absorb what one is taught, not just to taste it, or swallow it.

People generally are in such a hurry that they do not allow themselves to digest materials which, however, can be useful only if absorbed.

There is a parable about this, which helps to fix it in the memory; it is the story of the

PIECES OF GOLD

There was once a greedy miser who went to a king regularly and begged from him. Each time he went to the king, he came away with a piece of gold, which he had grabbed from the monarch's hand and stuffed into the recesses of his cloak.

As soon as he got home, he would drop the coin into a hole under the hearth.

One day the miser died, as we must all die.

When his money was found, it was noticed that on each coin was the name of the king, and all the treasure was returned to him.

Apricot Pies

There was once, in Afghanistan, an old woman who had been famous for thirty years for the deliciousness of her apricot pies. Everyone for miles around knew of the pies, and ate them whenever they could. Over the years, hundreds badgered her for the recipe.

She went on making the pies, in the soft-fruit season every

year: she handed out pies right and left – but she would not tell anyone the recipe.

One day, fearing that the woman might die with her secret untold, a rich man – who was also something of a miser as well as a lover of apricot pies – offered a reward of a hundred gold pieces for the secret.

He could find nobody who could bake pies like the old woman, although there were plenty of people who clamoured for the reward, pretending that they could. Finally, however, he was surprised to find the woman herself at his door, offering to sell the recipe.

'I thought you would never tell anyone,' he stammered.

'Ah,' said the ancient one, 'I wanted to find a sign of sincerity first.'

'But how do you know that I am sincere?' asked the miser.

'You,' said the lady, 'are a man in love with gold. To be prepared to part with *any* of it, let alone a hundred gold pieces, for anything shows, in your own terms at least, that you are sincere. That is the nearest to real sincerity that we can arrive at in this region, it seems – so I shall give you the secret.'

The rich man was beside himself with delight. He took up a pen and a piece of paper and asked the woman to dictate.

'You won't need pen and paper,' she said; 'since there is nothing much to tell. I pick apricots, free, from charitable people's trees. Then I add water and a little honey – and that's all there is to it.'

'But that's how *everyone else* makes apricot pie!' shouted the man; 'I'm certainly not going to give you a hundred ashrafis for telling me that.'

'Take it or leave it,' said the woman.

'It's a lot of nonsense,' said the miser; 'but if the secret is not in the contents, it must be in the pie-crust. How do you make that?'

She smiled. 'I don't make it at all. I go to the village baker and ask him for some left-over pastry, cover the dish with it, and have him put it in his oven with the bread he bakes, and there you are.'

177

'But there must be something special about the pies,' said the man; 'and I want to find out what it is.'

'Very well,' she said, 'follow me and do as I do, and we'll see how you manage. We'll see whether you know what a recipe is.'

Together they went on a tour of the local apricot orchards. The old woman, as is the custom in those parts, was admitted free of charge, while the miser had to pay a copper coin before being allowed to pick as many apricots as he wished.

They took their dishes to the baker, and had him put some of his left-over pastry on the tops. Then they settled down to wait, until the pies were ready.

When the pies were cooked and had cooled, they tasted them. The old woman's one was delicious. But the pie made from the fruit collected by the miser was very ordinary indeed.

He shook his head in perplexity, and then started to berate the woman, calling her a fraud who had introduced some secret ingredient, then a fool who would not give the secret out, and finally a witch in contact with evil powers.

When he had exhausted himself, and was sitting on a bench outside the bakery, the old woman smiled again. 'After your huffing and puffing, after your superior airs and reliance upon money, after all that nonsense rooted in the disappointment of false expectations,' she said, 'I'll tell you where you went wrong.

'As you know, poor people are allowed to collect as much fruit as they wish from our orchards. In appreciation of this, I have never picked the ripe and perfect fruit for my pies, because the farmer is entitled to keep the best fruit, to sell so that he can support his family.

'So I have always chosen the unripe and the over-ripe apricots, blended together, for my pies. That is the secret of their wonderful taste. You, on the other hand, are so greedy, for perfection and for gain, that you – like everyone else who has sought my secret – always picked the most attractive fruit.

'The result was ordinary apricot pies.'

With these words, she tucked the bag of gold pieces in her belt, and went on her way.

The greed, anxiety and compulsion to compare Sufi teachings with prior assumptions, conspicuous in the reactions of many students, causes parsimony of all kinds, produces barriers to understanding and blinds people to things which are perfectly obvious to those who approach the teachings in a simpler manner.

Loading and Unloading

When someone learns something from someone else, and starts to teach what he has learned, a situation exists which we should look at very carefully, because most people do not understand what is happening.

Forget for the moment that it is 'teaching' that we are talking about. The human being, at a far more basic level, 'gets' something from someone else. This thing may be a blow, information, money, the idea that he has had an experience.

As soon as this thing is 'got' or believed to be 'got', the next, automatic move, of the human being is to try to pass it on. This is because the human is a communicator, or operates as such.

It is only at a later stage (even if this stage comes after only 2 seconds) that the individual decides that he has 'got' knowledge which he must communicate BECAUSE IT IS KNOWLEDGE. Because he is unaware of this characteristic, he will imagine that it is the fact that it is knowledge which prompted him to want to communicate it.

A certain, brief, verification of this is to be found in watching small children. They try to communicate. They try to get, and to give to others, any sort of object. And they seek a response.

Because of the socially-determined ethic, of course, this getting and giving often reaps the richest rewards. A person getting a lot of money and giving most of it away will earn plaudits and honours.

Another important part of the getting-giving process is when ideas are offered to people. You often find that people who have ideas to communicate (whether these are of any value or not) will spurn or refuse to entertain other ideas. This is often because they are already 'getting' their ideas from somewhere, or have got them, and their giving-out process is at work.

We are all familiar with the situation of people wanting to hold forth on some subject and refusing to listen to anything else. This is exactly what happens when a person is being interrupted during his 'unloading' phase. This helps us to understand why people are sometimes bigoted. They are to all appearances intractable, but in fact what they are saying is: 'I am operating my unloading phase, do not interrupt it'. This comes out as 'Smith's ideas are of no importance'; or 'that is irrelevant to our theme', and so on.

Ignorance of the existence and operation of this phenomenon causes people almost to live in a dream: because they are wondering why Smith's ideas are of no importance, or why this or that is irrelevant. They should instead realise that they should not be interrupting an unloading process.

Diet of Grapes

Once upon a time, in the days of long ago, there was a wise and powerful prince, who lived within a walled estate. His palace was surrounded by orchards and gardens, and he was generally thought, because he did not explain his actions, to be uncaring of the people's interests, and neglectful of his duty to strive to improve himself. Those people who were considered wise were unable to understand him, and spoke against him. Those who knew little about him thought that he was bereft of qualities. Those who wished to curry favour praised him: but since such people are generally superficialists, this did not extend his repute far.

Now the territory in which this prince lived was, as is the way of life, attacked by barbarians, who successively reduced the neighbouring principalities until they were fast approaching his own. Time and again the prince sent messages to the other rulers, asking them to ally themselves with him against the invaders, but such was their arrogance, their ignorance of him, or their other tendencies that they took no heed.

This behaviour on the part of his neighbours did not seem to distress the prince. All he said was, 'The burden of wisdom is almost too much to bear. I have, as a truthful man, been forced to tell them that I have to be their leader if the war is to be won in co-operation with them. Naturally they will not accept such a condition. Therefore the only option is to wait until the Second Stage.'

The barbarians continued to advance, until those who had been opposing them, in ever-increasing numbers, fell back upon the domain of our prince to make a last stand. They were the remnants of the knights and soldiers of every one of the vanquished princes.

Thus it was that one day when the prince was resting his minister approached him and, after making the customary obeisance, said:

'O Point towards which the Compass turns: we have been unable to prevent the remnants of the defending armies from climbing the walls of the Domain, in their flight. They are now huddled in the vineyards, covered in mud and blood, in the last stages of exhaustion.'

The prince raised his head. 'And what else?' he asked.

'And,' continued the minister, 'they are too exhausted even to eat or to attend to their wounds. They are now lying fast asleep, like dead men, while the enemy masses without.'

'Very well,' said the prince; 'now you have made your report, you may withdraw. Return to me the day after tomorrow, to describe conditions then.'

The minister, though knowing that his master was possessed

of wisdom, wondered why the prince did not take some action to defend the domain, but, like a good servant, made his salutation and withdrew.

Two days later he again approached the prince and said: 'Lord of Princeliness! I have come as instructed.'

'Give your report,' answered the prince.

'The exhausted warriors,' said the minister, 'have now slept for two days.'

'And what are they doing?' the prince asked.

'May your life be extended!' said the minister, 'they are now so famished that they are devouring grass, leaves and raw grapes.'

'Very good,' said the prince. 'Return in a further day and give me an account of conditions.'

The next day the minister announced: 'High Presence! The lords, warriors and ordinary people who fled to our domain are now eating the ripe grapes, having restored themselves somewhat.'

'Continue your report tomorrow, at midday,' said his master.

The day after, the minister said, 'May your Shadow never grow less! The refugees are now selecting the best grapes and eating them'.

'Excellent,' said the prince. 'Now call them to me, and I shall prepare them for the victory against the barbarians, for they are ready. Before this, they were in no condition to struggle, and had to get what nutrition they could from us. If we leave it any later, they will be so sated that they will start to argue among themselves, and will not listen to us. Prepare for victory!'

And that is the tale of the wise prince whose actions nobody understood. When the final battle came, and the barbarians were slaughtered, the victorious army fell out with one another. Returning to their own lands, their historians wrote conflicting accounts of what had passed. All accounts had this in common: they misunderstood the prince.

Attention

A teaching Dervish was once asked why it was that the questioner found it so hard to keep awake: to remember the things which he had read or been told. In reply the Dervish gave this lesson:

'There was once a Dervish who used to lecture regularly before a group of people among whom were an old man accompanied by his grandson, a small boy.

'And, regularly as clockwork, the ancient one used to fall asleep as soon as the Dervish had got into his stride.

'One day the Dervish had an idea. After the meeting he took the boy aside and said, "I'll give you a silver piece if you jog your grandfather awake every time he falls asleep during my lectures." The boy accepted.

'For three meetings in succession, the old man was nudged every time his eyes closed, and the Dervish was pleased.

'On the fourth week, however, the grandfather fell fast asleep, just as before.

'Taking the boy aside after that meeting, the Dervish said, "I thought you were going to keep the old man awake for a silver piece?"

'"That's right," said the boy, "but when I told him, he offered me three silver pieces not to do it."

'And,' continued the Dervish who was telling the tale, 'the single silver piece is your desire to pay attention. The three are your natural laziness, your habits and your unobserved opposition to the truth.'

When is Learning Not Indoctrination?

Indoctrination may be called 'the instilling of attitudes without the saving grace of digesting them'. Indoctrination is not what some people claim, that is to say the more rapid accomplishment of something which ordinarily takes a culture many years to achieve.

What makes a 'digested' system more acceptable than an imposed one?

Two things. First, a greater time-scale and conditions of freedom give an opportunity for rejection. Second, where there is a time-scale measured in years – and where there is opportunity for dissent and discussion, there is room for modification.

Inducing people to believe things – and then, usually, turning around and saying that this belief, because it is belief, is sacred or even inevitable – is the hallmark of indoctrination.

Putting ideas forward, and giving people information which enables them to test these (including testing them against other ideas) spells freedom and education, both of which are distorted or abolished by indoctrinators.

Two things prevent the foregoing being widely known at the present time:-

1. The discovery, certainly in the 'West' and the modern world, is recent. It will take time to percolate.
2. When the facts are presented, they are an embarrassment to those who, examining their own attitudes, realise that, in certain areas, they are themselves victims of indoctrination.

Connection Between the Traditions

Q: *What is the connection, if any, between the various metaphysical traditions?*

A: There are, in your terms, numerous connections. The important ones to note are:

1. The world is littered with the remnants of genuine traditions, whose action has become vitiated or repetitious.
2. It is a natural law that teaching be renewed in conformity with the place, time, people involved and needs of the process.

Q: *What form does the renewal take?*

A: Simply this. A Teacher, dedicated to a certain kind of function, organises and presents the teaching in a manner suitable to the conditions just cited.

Q: *Does this mean that traditional teachings which we find represented in various countries are not now of any real function, because they represent survivals from a period when they enshrined real 'work'?*

A: That is so.

Q: *But how much reality or function do such organisations now have?*

A: In your terms, these spiritual, psychological and other systems have three main components:-

1. The component of reality, which is ultimate truth, which is more or less locked in by the human formulator.
2. The component of decay, which is what has crept in at the point where the effort ceased to act truly, perhaps on the death of the formulator.
3. The component of outside appearance, which becomes

after a time, unwittingly, the main interest of the participants. This is the least useful but most attractive component.

Q: *How is it known to the participants of such a group as to how accurate or meaningful their 'work' is?*

A: There are no two ways about it. Either it is known to their teacher, if one still exists, in which case he will remedy defects, and they will not be perpetuated. Or it is totally repetitious, and the effort has become an *administrative* one. This happens when there has been no true succession of teaching, so that there is nobody at the top sufficiently developed to be able to diagnose the situation. In this case the group has become to a greater or lesser degree a prisoner of the automatism of the formal world.

Q: *Does a teacher appear in a group which already exists, or does he not?*

A: He may or he may not. He comes to fulfil a law. He may revalidate the working bases of a derelict group.

Q: *Why does he do this?*

A: In response to an inexorable need.

Q: *Does the group always recognise him?*

A: Certain people generally do. It will depend upon the apparatus of perception which they have. The onus on him is not primarily to preach, but to make himself available to the perception of the people.

Q: *Does he need the support of such groups?*

A: Both parties can benefit, because there is no such thing as solitary work. Even a derelict group can be producing semi-consciously a quantity of necessary force ('substance') which we might say goes to waste unless it is correctly used.

Q: *How can we account for the dramatic rise of teachers who purport to have been 'called' to bring, for instance, spirituality to mankind?*

A: Do not generalise about this. One form is the result of

186

physical laws. A group of people can engender necessary force (substance) already mentioned. They do not know what to do with it; they may not even really know what it is. An individual, who has another development analogous to their own, may contact this force (distance has no relevance here) and make use of it. Now we have the amusing and also tragic situation in which (a) force is raised by a certain group, (b) it is perceived and employed by someone else, (c) this temporarily reinforces, through vampirism, the 'teacher' who becomes prominent, (d) because of the similarity of this person with their own defective tradition, the victim group think that he is their teacher, (e) they join him, not realising that he seems to be like them because he is using their own nutrition!

What you call a movement is part of an organic, natural development. It takes on a local colour because of the culture in which it grows. It cannot be imported together with the local colouring. It may attain a certain degree of necessary force in its location, but its spread into other areas is conditional upon two vital factors:

(1) That it takes root naturally and becomes naturalised in the fresh culture.
(2) That there is a need for it in the new culture.

The latter condition is operative only when there is a teacher, adequately commissioned to provide a formulation in that area.

Q: *So there is no point in travelling to seek knowledge, since it seems that one must wait until a teaching is offered to one?*

This is not what I meant. In your terms, the process is something like this. Certain individuals may be 'called' to make journeys, in order to acquire certain capacities. This call which you have too easily assumed to be an act of personal volition, is the result of natural conditions. Such people are attracted, we might almost say, 'imported', to be a centre of teaching when this is necessary, in order to fit them for their task. There are different varieties of such individuals. They are 'called' from one cultural area to another precisely when it is necessary for the teaching to be projected in an area of similar cultural background to their own. They become the instrument of the transmission of the teaching into a fresh culture.

Q: *Will this process be described by the teacher to his followers?*

The teacher will describe to his followers exactly what is necessary for them to know in order to attain a development which it is his duty to assist. His task is not to provide geographical, biographical or mysterious stimulation except for a multiple purpose. Remember that what he does is itself conditioned by necessity and is largely in a realm which is not perceived by the unregenerate.

Q: *What form does the teaching take?*

A: It may take many forms. The first step is to attain a stabilisation of mentation which will enable the student to learn. We do not start with an unwarranted assumption that the individual is capable of learning. He may have to learn how to learn.

Because of veneration of tradition and lack of understanding of essentials, deteriorated systems concentrate upon the repetition of certain mental and/or physical techniques which provide only a partially-balanced individual. The real teaching covers a very wide range. These include 'undertakings' (tasks) given in order to awaken certain functions which are needed to connect with certain other ones. They may be mental and physical movements, music and special exercises.

Q: *Are there any special factors which we in the West do not understand, which might be said to play an important part in the real teaching?*

A: There are many. Here is one. You are accustomed to assuming that you can be taught something provided that you have the capacity and the conditions. This can be nonsense. People are trying to learn things without realising the simple little fact that certain things can be studied only at certain times. These times are not measured by clock-time. They are known to the teacher through inner cognition, and unless he teaches at those times, all the books or exercises in the world will have next to no effect.

Q: *I notice that you are not using technical terms very much. Why is this?*

A: Because you are accustomed to the use of technical terms associated with a fragmentary tradition. If I use a term you recognise, you will immediately associate it with past experiences and incomplete formulation. It will be handled by your intellect and not correctly used. Further, the terms which are used in one phase of the work are not necessarily those which apply to another. Remember always that if you are using two-thousand year old terms you may be trying to 'work' in a role suited to the people of 2,000 years ago. This is where 'tradition' becomes a trap.

Q: *But surely there is a system?*

A: You do not know what a 'system' is. The work is really systematised at a level much higher than intellect as you know it. Any apparent systematisation is merely a working frame, concocted for the purpose of bringing the teaching a little nearer to you. It does not have universal validity. The system is known by the teacher and equally developed people, just as you know something so well that you act in accordance with it inevitably. This work is natural, organic and changes form, not content, in accordance with the needs of the people, the work and the teacher. What serves as a system in one phase of the work is not a system in another.

Q: *You mentioned exercises and music. Can you tell me something about music and dancing?*

A: Very little that you will understand. However, what we call 'dance' is sometimes a developmental exercise, sometimes for communication of various kinds, sometimes for accumulating something and holding it, sometimes symbolic. Based on principles which have to be known in an inner sense, the dance is one of the most vital things, but it has deteriorated in cultural and even religious use, into mere repetition.

Music has many functions, all dependant upon the

environment, the participants, the instruments used, the stage which the work has reached in a certain community, and so on.

Q: *And prayer?*

A: Prayer depends upon knowing how to pray and what it is for. The usual idea of prayer is merely emotional, and performs a conditioning function.

Q: *So contemporary religious beliefs and action are not real?*

A: They are composite. There are some fossilised remnants of real things; some functions for the ordinary man, so that he may continue to behave in a certain way, some elements of mis-understanding, some built-in personal quirks of individuals who have sought to organise without understanding.

Q: *Can a person who has not got a comprehensive view of these factors teach anything in your way?*

A: Very little. He can be given a task, but this he will have to fulfil for himself. He will bring his own distortions to others if he tries to teach. He may be allowed to try to teach, or to organise, but unless his own teacher is available to correct his excesses he will do more harm than good.

Q: *What is the position of a repetitious organisation, carrying on in the belief or the hope that they will achieve something?*

A: This will depend upon the organisation. In general it may be said that such an entity is merely a self-perpetuating entity, not a teaching one. The more it tries to teach, the more the defects which will be transmitted. The blind cannot lead the blind. Generally such organisations become soaked in self-esteem and lose humility. Few Christian leaders today would accept Jesus, for instance, if they met him. Instead of really knowing any-thing, they feed upon self-esteem, which develops into what we call the 'Commanding Self'. It is very terrible, because this is diametrically opposed to their real possible destiny.

Q: *Do you test people who are interested in what you are doing?*

A: We do, indeed. All too often they do not know that they are being tested. They expect some crude, obvious test that they are willing to go through. They have little idea of the subtlety of the means available to us. What do you do in the case of people who have a great deal of self-pride and not enough conscience?

We do not deal in theoretical instances quite in the terms of this question. But it may be said that we make available to them, in a manner which they do not intellectually grasp, a communication or spark of truth, to enable their inner reality, their *Dhat* (essential factor) to receive our signals. This operates, when the 'mirror is not too rusty' by letting them really feel something of the danger they are in, so that their conscience is stirred.

Q: *Does this sometimes lead to paradoxical behaviour on the part of the teacher?*

A: Certainly. Nothing is more revealing than to meet someone who thinks that he or she has some degree of perception, and yet who cannot pick up one's 'signals' when transmitted on a non-verbal or non-intellectual level.

'Barbarians'

The assumptions of the polite society which we have erected for ourselves in various familiar human communities most effectively prevent the development of real understanding, mostly because the cultural systems erected by men in general are patchy and incomplete; patchy because not comprehensive, incomplete because they do not exist in depth.

Here is an example:-

You look at an object, and judge it by the associations which it conjures up. You may like it or not. The reasons for liking it are seldom reasonable at all. A person may, legitimately, like a flower. He likes the colour, shape, total impact, smell and so on.

But he has no conception of any deeper meaning of the flower. By this I do not mean the airy-fairy feeling 'that this must really mean something'. Such an idea is far too imprecise and primitive. The flower has a meaning and a value which I call the deeper meaning. *Meaning* here signifies the real relationship between the flower, the individual and the group, as well as its real function in relation to the totality of life. Some philosophers and poets *talk* and *think* about these things. Almost none participates in them.

From this way of thinking, from what we call the perception of what, say, a flower really signifies, those who are absorbed in the aesthetics of the flower are 'barbarians', confined to sensory impacts and their mental processing.

Here is an analogy. You get the value, the real value, of a present given by a good person, if you receive it in the right spirit. The greedy person sees only the value of the present as cash, goods, status, emotion, and so on. There is a form of human cultivation far higher than the ordinary aesthetic, artistic or socially conscious and well-behaved person imagines. And this cultivation conveys specific not woolly-minded, scope for further development.

The Refined Barbarian

It is difficult for many people to credit that, though they may be in one sense refined, this is only a refinement of certain branches of their thinking or even of small parts of their observational capacity. A cultivated man may be a barbarian in many ways, even if only because he has not had his attention drawn to the additional material contained in life which he and his predecessors have not bothered to look for or to give value to.

Ancient science has for millenia used diagrams and symbols

for actual developmental and evolutionary purposes. The superficial man – our modern barbarian – sees in certain relics of the past only pretty designs, or art-forms. He may think that they are derived from natural objects, because these are what they suggest to him. At best, he generally sees them as having as functions only the effects which they have upon him, or upon the mind of the early or previous people as he thinks they thought.

He is holding a mirror to himself, and thinking that the image which he sees is the real meaning of the symbol or the meaning which others have invested it with.

The Western scholar does precisely this, and has taught many Eastern scholars to do the same. This is erudition of the 'barbaric' kind. Worse still, the scholar of the type we mention restlessly searches for evidence to support his own interpretation of these phenomena. He may seek this so-called evidence on the spot. He travels to countries of ancient culture and observes followers of a deteriorated form of a lapsed tradition; real – though not obvious to him – 'barbarism', using the materials in this crude way, as representation, for intellectual or emotional stimulus. He accordingly concludes that this is the original use or intention of the materials. Now why is this so undesirable?

Because when basic attention is fixed on a wrong idea, the mind is incapable of profiting by the internal force for development of that of which the idea as studied is a travesty.

Analogy: While a man believes that the earth is flat, he will not be able to circumnavigate the globe in a planned manner. He cannot profit by the fact of sphericity deliberately or consciously, and remains at a low level of attainment as a result.

How to Measure Human Development

Q: *Can you give me any information on how your developments can be given a statistical basis? Much research is being done in an attempt to show the possibilities of super-normal communication or cognition. All the tests are always subjected to statistical analysis.*

A: Such efforts as you mention will be unsuccessful in discovering anything of real importance, because what we are involved in has a series-system and a periodicity different in kind from the statistics which you mention. It is useful, however, to look at the innocence of the assumption that everything, in order to be significant, must obey a certain set of time and measuring laws. You can measure, by statistics, the occurrence only of those things which come within the limited range of statistics as you know them – a minor part of the possibilities of calculation, even in this sphere, the sphere of happenings. Make a careful note of the fact that something which 'obeys' a stimulus which you apply to it, in a certain rhythm, is not itself working purposefully. The rhythm which it has initiated does not obey your stimuli – neither does it manifest itself in your arena by symptoms which you can measure by your statistics. Are you capable of conceiving such a parallel periodicity outside your own scope?

Q: *I am just able to conceive the possibility but the idea is completely new to me. Can you elaborate?*

A: In so far as we can discuss it at this level, I can draw your attention to the fact that your statistics are based upon a very limited pattern. So we would call it primitive. You have been reared to observe things moving in accordance with a certain sort of regularity or irregularity. You refine this as much as you can, and then *assume* that nothing has reality unless it can be encompassed within this narrow limit. Now do you see what I mean?

Q: *Yes, I do, but it must be a devil of a job getting into another system, with all our associations with familiar statistics.*

A: That is the point. It is the *getting* into the system, not the talking about it theoretically, which is important. This can happen only by experience and participation in a thing, not by wondering about it.

Laws and the Teacher

Remark to someone who mentioned that a system should be applied systematically, otherwise it is no system at all.

If a system has to be applied at all, presumably it should be applied systematically, though this does not necessarily follow from the fact that it is a system.

It is all very well to take developmental principles and apply them ruthlessly. If you do so in a doctrinaire manner, you merely get an automaton as the result. Take mechanicality. To draw attention to it is one thing. To know which parts of it are truly mechanical and which are necessary, correctly absorbed developmental factors, is another. This knowledge comes from an overall perception not from the mere application of dogma.

You will see that we have dealt with two points, both of overwhelming importance, yet seldom in practice taken advantage of. The first is:-

> The rigid application of an inflexible principle, considered as an inflexible law, produces an equal image; a belief in the rigidity of the principle.

The second is:-

> Even principles cannot be actually applied by anyone who is not correctly designated, harmonised, operating as a teacher. It is one thing to study principles; another to attempt to apply them.

Above all there must be that discrimination of the situation, the individual and the needs which brings to the consciousness the many dimensions of such a principle as 'Man is a mechanical contrivance.'

Read what has been written by people who have tried only to study principles such as this. You will see that they have fallen into the error of trying to teach while believing that they are studying. Even in this narrow range their discrimination is, in our phrase, 'barbarian'.

Therefore, systematisation has to follow the rules of flexibility, otherwise it is the true antithesis of what we are working with: evolution partly determined by environment and impact, partly by individual determination, partly by factors which seek to preserve inviolate their diversity and subtlety.

Upper Class

A lady writes that she is religious, and that reading our books it seems to her that they are put in rather an 'upper class' way.

Now this goes to show how opinions can conflict. People, you see, often accuse us of being 'low class' in our attitudes.

For myself, I would think this to be somewhat closer to the truth. After all, from the top end of the social scale, is it very upper class to go about telling people that they are doing things wrongly, and that they should change?

Traditionally, 'upper class' people don't criticise or recommend change – they just give orders: and far more specific ones than trying to change or to reform.

I would call this effort to change people rather a 'lower middle class' occupation, if we must put a label to it. It is, too, a common occupation of proletarian activists.

The more 'upper' you are, the less you *do*, and the more you *are*, or feel that you are.

The king, in fables, is advised by peasants and even by beggars, and often by Wise Men. Do kings ever advise Wise Men, or even beggars?

'Upper class' people, or those who think that they are such, concentrate upon imitating kings and the like, who are the real 'upper upper' people.

That is the traditional picture, and things have not changed very much, if at all. There is still an 'upper class' in all countries. The higher you go, the less interest (as distinct from lip-service) you find in learning.

Of course, there are a lot of lower-class ignoramuses. And it is they, I fancy, who are deluded by the wordy and supposed 'upper class' (I mean the literate and vocal writers, teachers, academics, artists and similar communicators) into thinking that this motley crew is the 'upper class'.

But why worry? Remember the saying: 'The Upper Class on earth is hardly ever equivalent to the lowest class in Heaven'. After all, our correspondent writes that she is 'religious', and can therefore probably take comfort from the quotation.

Justification

Q: *How can you justify influencing people against their wishes? Can any good ever come from deception?*

A: I don't know anything about influencing people against their wishes, and you have to be very sure that you know what you mean by deception.

Taking the second point first: you could call deception doing something without the knowledge of another person. Well, what about secret charity? What about helping someone while pretending not to? Your idea of deception is likely to be flawed, to say the least; people use these catch-phrases without thinking about them.

Now, about influencing people against their wishes, listen to a story:

THE MAN WHO WOULD NOT HAVE MEDICINE

There was once a man who went to a doctor and said, 'I know that medicine will not help my disease: both because of my experience with doctors and through my own beliefs. I want you to cure me, if you are as wise as they say, without the use of medicines.'

The doctor gave him a stick, and said, 'Take this stick, and use it for a three-mile hike every day for twenty days, and then return to me.'

When he returned, the man was cured. The doctor said, 'You did not believe in medication; so I put a powdered medicament on the handle of the stick. When your hand sweated, the powder acted on your tissues.'

Now, as for acting against wishes, which WAS the patient's real wish: to be cured or to avoid medication? I advise you to avoid the confused thinking which results from accepting second-hand ideas, and do some thinking yourself.

The Machine

The other day I was talking to an eminent scientist who is also an inventor. He was explaining a new labour-saving device to me.

I said: 'Yes, it is marvellous, but the machine needs looking after. Couldn't you automate it so that the housewife did not have to carry out various operations every time the bell rings? It will surely break up her time.'

He said: 'This machine is a "hybrid" of technology and psychology. We have discovered by testing that the human being will buy and like a machine if he thinks it *can't* work without him.'

This frightened creature is the lord of creation: twentieth-century man – the real one, not the mythical one he pretends to be.

Translations

I heard you say that you have read several of my books in translation and that the translation is no good.

Ever since my first book was translated, some thirty years ago, people have been saying this.

In fact, they have been saying it, writing about it, even stopping me in the street to draw my attention to it.

They are never satisfied: that is their chief characteristic.

How do I know this, and believe it rather than believe that such people are being helpful and acting from the best of motives?

Two things: first experience, second experimentation.

The experience tells me if the individual is acting from goodwill or malice. The experiment can produce the most hilarious results.

For instance, when I have sent the complainant off to tackle the translator, they almost come to blows. Often neither will yield, with the result that nobody knows what IS the right translation. Sometimes, again, the newcomer will persuade the translator that he was wrong: but in so doing he is not always right. I have seen cases where a correct translation was contested by some busybody, who got the translator to retract it – and I have found that there was no reason to do this, other than that the critic had a stronger personality, and had intimidated the translator!

For these and other reasons, therefore, I have avoided this subject for years.

SECTION VI

Questions

Q: *I have read a lot of your answers to questions; but I am bound to say that I do not find amongst them the sort of questions which I would ask. Why is it that you do not get more intelligent questions asked from you?*

A: This is one of the most important questions one could be asked, and I have done some research on the matter. The fact is that people constantly stand up or write and say that they don't like our questions, and that they could do better themselves, or ask different ones, at any rate.

Now, the interesting thing is that when this has happened, I have invariably answered, as I do now:

> 'If you want to ask more representative, profounder or more interesting questions, then you are at liberty to do so and I shall answer them.'

I have never received any questions at all from such enquirers which are (a) voted by others present to be more interesting or profound; (b) not already covered in the questions received and already answered; (c) not answered because they already appear in a slightly different form.

So the answer must be one of two things:

1. You have an unreliable idea of the intelligence of the questions, or
2. People, when challenged to supply questions, are so vain that they are afraid that their queries may be thought trivial, and will not expose themselves to such assessment.

So either you are wrong or you are vain. If you are wrong, there is nothing wrong with our questions, and your question needs no answer. If you are vain, there is nothing that *I* can do about it. If vanity stands in the way of intelligence, that is after all only what Sufis have been saying for a long time now.

Anyone who takes the responsibility of asking a question will always have it considered. But if it is already, in some form, covered by answers already given, it may not be answered again. If the person asking the question wishes to present an intelligent one, I can only say that I would be delighted.

Negligence

It is related that a visitor once gained admittance to the presence of a dervish by a pretext. When he had entered the assembly he said:

'Why do you spend your time with these unworthy ones?' – for he was annoyed that he had not been welcomed with any sign of favour.

The dervish immediately ran forward, kissed his hand – and threw him out of the house.

After this the dervish changed his circle of disciples frequently. When he was asked the reason for his strange behaviour with the haughty man, he said:

'I changed my ways because the reproach was right. I kissed the man's hand in recognition of this. But though the criticism was right, the *man* was wrong – and I made a start by removing him from the assembly of the wise.'

Cyclic

Q: *Don't you get a large number of interruptions to your work; people calling, useless letters, cranks and people who want interviews, people who want information that they could very well get elsewhere, that kind of thing?*

A: Yes.

Q: *How do you deal with them? If you ignore letters people may get annoyed; if you spend time on callers, essential work may be interrupted, if you tell people what they are really like they won't, surely, accept it, if they haven't learnt already?*

A: Well, I admit that I am always telling people what I'm telling you – that this sort of pressure is common to anyone that the public gets interested in, or who has a lot of work to do.

Q: *Yes, but they have ulcers, flocks of secretaries or filtering-out systems of one kind or another...*

A: The most important single thing to realise after you've registered that many other people have this problem is that it is cyclic. If you get many letters, callers, crises and so on, you find that they appear to come in cycles, and can profitably be treated as if they did. People, for instance, who are indignant tend to appear to act as if they are being indignant in batches, in bunches, at recurring times. This means that you can plan your behaviour to obtain the best results by looking at these cycles. The same is true of visitors: there are times when you can, through experience, say, 'Here they come!' and you are flooded with visitors for a week or two. Then the thing slacks off. Take enthusiasm and support. Same thing again.

One of the other great advantages of identifying such a cycle is that it enables you to avoid thinking that you are on the crest of a wave, or in a trap, or anything like that. You are simply in a cycle. And since this is not *your* cycle, particularly, but belongs chiefly to other people or to situations that they have created, you cannot become personally involved to the extent that you damage yourself – with ulcers or anything else – or become inefficient through introspection or self-consciousness linked to these cycles.

Q: *But how can you be 'sure' that this really is the case?*

A: It would be a brave man who failed to take advantage of something that worked over a long period of years, gave consistently good results, enabled work to be done, and harmed nobody.

Why Questions are Asked

Q: *Why do people ask questions?*

A: One important reason is because they need experience. Answers are nothing. Experience is everything. But the answer gives you the wherewithal to acquire experience. This is why teachers insist upon humility. But it must be a constructive humility, not the artificial 'veiling' (rationalising) kind which is just assumed, or unctuousness.

Q: *But you once said that the very fact that a person asked a certain question often showed that he was incapable of understanding the answer.*

A: Exactly. Incapable of answering his own question within him, so he externalises it. Incapable, too, of understanding the answer merely by mulling over the words which he receives back. The answer must be used as a starting-place to feed his ability to *live* or experience the answer. A question is asked because the answer is difficult. It has to be absorbed. As Mulla Nasrudin says: 'People don't ask whether it is possible to drink water.' This is because they are so thoroughly permeated by the experience of drinking water that they drink water without needing any problem about it resolved.

Q: *What is the limit to the number of questions which can be asked – because I have so many?*

A: You can have two reactions to this question as sufficient for the present.

The first is that many of the questions which I am asked are the same question in different forms. Some people never ask more than the one question, even though it takes many different forms to them.

The second observation is that the asking and answering of questions, among other things, follows the rule of saturation. If you get too many answers you will not be able to absorb them.

Not be able, that is, to work on the question, make the answer 'your own property'; attain a permanent increase of cognition through experiencing the answer.

Ponder questions and answers, because there is no short-cut to the *process* of which they are a part. If you do not digest the question and the answer, you will ask it again in another form and so we will go on until 'the penny drops'.

Many questions are only asked in order to win attention.

Why People Ask Questions

Q: *Why can some questions not be answered?*

A: Because the fact that a person can ask a question does not mean that he can understand the answer. The question may be wrongly put. For instance, a child can ask the question 'Why is cheese cheese?' Or the person cannot understand the answer at all: 'Tell me all about nuclear physics'. The assumption that a mechanism capable of putting a question is capable of understanding both it and the answer, and that there is an answer in a certain form, is one of the most ludicrous of all.

Questions do not differ in terms of importance, so far as their answerability is concerned. They differ in subtlety and nuance and in other ways. This fact is so repellent to the scientist and scholastic because it implies that he must equip himself to operate in different dimensions when he prefers the safety of assumptions, his 'psychological nest or fortress'. So, like the villain in the Nasrudin story, he trains himself and everyone else to deal in crude assumptions and attempts to fashion a world around them. There is no wonder that unresolved factors keep popping up and plaguing people. I say 'plaguing' because the inconvenient factors are generally labelled 'aberrations' and so on. Something does not fit into your lovely plan. This makes it opposed to you. Hence the assumption that such and such a thing is 'opposed to reason', 'unscientific', and so on. Theology has tried to capitalise upon this by taking the odds and ends which protrude from the bundle and labelling them 'mysteries'. So the theologian sits on a number of these and derives his ascendancy from them.

This is like the man who hands out fire in a primitive community. He is divine because he is the only man who can make fire. The theologian and ecclesiastic performs a less useful service: he does not even hand out fire. Generally he hands out reassurance, alternating with threats. He is like the witch doctor who said 'Look at this fire! You can't understand it. It will burn you.' Then he says: 'Look at this fire! It produces warmth and cooks food.' The fire happens to be a deep deposit of oil which is on fire, and the priest merely has squatter's rights: plus agility of mind: 'Hurry, hurry, hurry: The greatest flame on earth!'

Reverting to questions, people ask questions about the fire based on (1) their assumptions about it; and (2) what the priest tells them about it. One or the other, they feel, must be the correct question. This is the sort of thing they ask: 'Why is the great god of the flame angry with me?' or 'When is the great flame going to devour the earth?' or even 'How can I serve this flame, because, knowing that it is divine, I know that my destiny must be to serve it.'

Is your question really necessary? Is it true? How and why was it formulated? How long will it continue to be valid for you? Nasrudin was asked: 'What is the greatest question in life?' He said: 'How am I going to get my donkey to market tomorrow?'

Answer

Q: *Why do Sufis so seldom answer letters? I do not, in fact, know of a single instance when a letter to a Sufi actually was answered!*

A: Well, you may have heard of a saying of Rumi's, 'no answer is in itself an answer'. For my own part, I have never known a sensible letter to a Sufi not to be answered. The assumption in the question is very interesting. It is that the letter is bound to be worthy of an answer. Very much to the contrary, in my experience, most letters received by Sufis are not only not worthy of an answer: they should not be answered at all, since this silence will in suitable cases cause the writer to reconsider what he has written, and help him to try again. If the letter is in fact answered, it will always, you may be assured, cause an unsuitable effect, since the need for the original writer to reconsider what he has written will not be there nearly as strongly as if the reply is 'reconsider what you have written'. The assumption that any letter to a Sufi is of the kind which can and should be answered only serves to show that the questioner does not yet understand that there are different kinds of letter; just as there are different kinds of statement. For instance, both 'the Moon is yellow', and 'two and two are four' are statements; but they are not of the same kind, they only appear to be so because they are statements. This elementary kind of understanding is something which should be at the disposal of the writer before he writes a letter. Certainly, it is no part of a Sufi's work to teach it; though, if he has time, he may do so, since it is not teaching but simply ordinary sense.

No Answer

Q: *I wrote to you in great detail a month ago, enclosing a stamped envelope for your reply. All I have received so far is a list of books. What is your answer to my questions and request to see you soon?*

A: A personal letter to this individual would in fact have been useless, as we can see from his own words. He wants to learn, but he does not want to accept our response – our answer is only a list of books. In his judgment, this is not interesting enough, perhaps not enough of anything. Certainly we have annoyed, depressed or perplexed him by not answering his questions, in spite of the stamp which he enclosed for this service. Well, for the stamp he got the list of books. When will he ask himself as to whose judgment is correct in these matters, his or ours? Whether he needs the list of books or a letter containing answers to his questions?

But just as 'no answer is in itself an answer', so, too, an answer which the person cannot understand or profit from is no answer either. So we do not answer his questions. They have shown us that he needs books first.

But if he is not registering that he needs books, and in fact writes again quite baffled or annoyed, what is the use of sending him book lists or sending him silence?

Simply this, that there is always a chance that he will review his letter and your booklist, and realise his real situation and what you are in fact saying to him through the silence and booklist. If he does this, he will have carried out the first correct self-observation exercise, and should be able to go on from there.

Letters and Answers

Q: *There is a large pile of letters over there which does not seem to have been opened. Do you not answer letters?*

A: I certainly do answer them. That pile is from people who are currently writing to me every day, or sometimes more than once a day. From time to time, like many other people, I get shoals of letters, sometimes running to 24 pages, from the same person. Now, can you imagine what would happen to one's correspondence if one were to react automatically – like a machine –

to this flood of letters? There would be no time to do anything else. Because I was responding to the letter-writing compulsion of a few people (and, often, answering them often makes the malaise worse, resulting in more letters, and more) I would be preventing all the other correspondents from getting an answer, more likely than not.

Q: *But do those letters which are written 'compulsively' not contain anything of value?*

A: All letters contain something of value. The question is, is it fair to give some people more than their share of one's time, one's services?

Q: *Then what criterion do you adopt in dealing with this phenomenon?*

A: The same one anyone would apply in a similar situation. First, if people ask questions that have already been answered in printed material, they do not rate an answer. Secondly, if they have not taken advantage of the training available at school and by reading in their public library how to form their thoughts, they need this study in coherence, which it is not our place to give. Thirdly, if they are not thoughtful enough to realize that there are other people in the world, with pressing letters to have answered, preference should be given to those who do realise this, and who act upon it by thinking before they write, and keep their letters short. These are the sort of criteria adopted.

Q: *If people get no answer from you, how can they obtain any advantage from writing?*

A: I cannot do better than quote Rumi on this: 'no answer is in itself an answer'.

Q: *Does this mean that people who get no answer are rejected?*

A: It means that only to paranoids and neurotics. If people cannot try to assess their shortcomings by normal methods, we have no authority to operate a psychotherapeutic clinic for them. You should note that a very large number of people *do* read their answers carefully; many *do* frame their letters carefully; very many *do* re-assess their approaches, and so on. These are the people to whom we owe the first debt. It is a matter of priorities. You serve first the people whom you can work with. Those who may be casualties of the social processes and so on are the first priority of the psychotherapeutic organisations.

Q: *How would you put this in a catchy aphorism?*

A: I would say: 'Don't apply to us for psychotherapy – the clinics don't offer our insights: we don't take their customers away!'

Rhetoric

Q: *If there is so much wisdom in the East, why are the people there in such a mess?*

Q: *If Eastern knowledge is so important, why is it so hard to learn?*

Q: *Why does this knowledge not exist in a WESTERN form?*

A: First we should ask ourselves whether any or all of these questions are rhetorical or not. I am inclined to think that they are. After all, a moment's reflection would enable anyone at all to provide possible answers to any or all of the questions.

We ask this because we have no therapeutic responsibility to deal with the rhetoricists. On the contrary, in the interests of any real students present, we have something of a duty to identify and exclude them, so that they may find their therapy as soon as possible wherever it is available.

So, before attempting to answer questions, we have to study the students. They may need remedial training or exclusion. Or their rhetoric, as is often discovered, may be rooted in in-effective thinking-patterns. Directing a sensible part of their mind towards our subject might be all they need: though it might take some time for them to relearn how to do it.

Helpful in leading towards this sorting-out process is spending time with these people, studying them in group activities, and testing their reactions to various written and other materials and situations. It can also be useful to inform them about a true analogy on the physico-mental level:

In some diets there is a deficiency of nicotinamide, a B-vitamin also known as niacin. This lack is known to cause a mental condition characterized by a suspicion that people are plotting against the sufferer. They can become very wild, violent and obsessional indeed. But the irony of it all is that when you offer the remedy (vitamin pills or even only B-vitamin-rich bread) the victim takes this as proof that you are trying to poison him or to send him out of his mind...

Idealism

Idealism should never exclude a desire to know the truth. If it does, it will destroy the much more valuable thing of which idealism is only a manifestation. Idealists must always be ready to find answers, must never imagine that they know all the answers already. The so-called idealists who want things done which are not solutions at all are not idealists, but the destroyers of good. Idealists who lack necessary basic information about their field are extremely harmful to the human race.

Here are examples:

Professor Ward Edwards has shown that man tends to reach conclusions rationally by using all available information. So far, so good. But he has also established that conclusions reached on insufficient evidence are likely to be stubbornly clung to, even when contradicted by subsequent superior evidence.

This means that there is more than a danger that people are incapable of changing their minds when they should do so.

He also discovered, by careful tests, that more than one person in three tested were unable to make accurate decisions because they were 'befogged by superstition, biases and logical incoherence'.

The ordinary idealist will want to reject this evidence, perhaps because by a wider-based humanitarian test he is not an idealist at all. An idealist would be someone anxious to understand and to serve, especially humanity. But the self-styled idealist whom we most often meet, faced by such facts as these on decision difficulties, will turn out to be someone who has made up his mind that man is always already potentially logical, resolute and capable of forming sound opinions and making the best use of whatever data is provided to him, whenever it is given in a reasonable manner. Now, if this type of idealist is right, then Professor Edwards is wrong. And there would be only one way of proving him wrong: to conduct tests which provided different results from the Professor's.

The idealists to whom I have so far submitted the above facts, however, have all reacted in another way: they have employed flat denial instead of reason or experiment. In my opinion, therefore, they are not idealists at all, but people who imagine that they are idealists and may induce others to believe so too. It seems that the idealist himself may fall into Professor Edwards' category of people who cannot change their minds.

One is almost tempted to say that it would not be logical to continue to accept self-estimations of people as idealists if their decision-making and opinion-altering capacities had not been tested to determine whether such people were deluded and unconsciously trying to involve others in what might be discovered to be a deluded system of belief.

This whole problem, of course, does not rest upon Professor Edwards' work alone. Ever since it was discovered, it has been frequently verified that what was formerly regarded as true, altruistic belief could be produced, or apparently duplicated, by indoctrination and conditioning.

Even before this, it had been uneasily noted that people of very different, even mutually exclusive, ideas could apparently regard themselves and be regarded as humanitarian idealists. That is to say, once the principle had been accepted that two people could hold, equally sincerely, totally opposing views, it was only a matter of time before it would become necessary to test the ways in which opinions are formed and what lies behind 'believing in good'.

The relativity of 'good' – the fact that something might be good under one set of circumstances and bad under another – could be concealed or have little or no effect upon human thought only while people lived in exclusive societies, often competing or mutually hostile, and where there was very little interchange between them.

The keeping of one society distinct from another, the avoiding of 'cultural contamination' from one to another, has even been defended on the principle of 'not rocking the boat'. Modern communications have rendered such a possibility obsolete.

Remembering Conversations

Q: *I find it difficult to remember your conversations, even though I sometimes go away and try to write them down. Why is this?*

A: It is not always necessary to remember conversations. Some of them take such a shape as to defy the kind of memory which we are accustomed to using. There is, however, another point, more relevant to your individual case, and also to that of several others present here this afternoon. People can get into the habit of coming and listening to talk. They surrender themselves to what they think the atmosphere is. This is a form of autohypnosis or it may be laziness. They are not taking the essence of the conversation, but simply riding along on the sound.

Too Vague

Q: *I have a sense that the goal is before me, like a challenge, and that I must respond to it. I feel that I am getting nearer to it. I have spent twenty years in studying spiritual things, from the time I was in a seminary. Then I went into all sorts of occultism and metaphysics. I believe that the result of this will gradually provide the source of the illumination which must come.*

A: Do you? Well, I would just carry on then. You did come to me for reassurance and to put your own feelings, didn't you? If, at any time, you have a sense of:

> what the goal is,
> where you stand,
> how you have changed,
> what is the nature of the new experience which you have had –
> come back to me, if I am still here.

Prisons of Thought

People think they are being spiritual, when their thought is so polluted by subjective psychological motives that they have lost all sense of what is really spiritual.

There are three major 'prisons' of thought which manipulate people, instead of their being on top of them:-

* Demanding sequentialism in everything; there has to be timing and stimuli within periods of time stipulated by the 'prisoner';
* Expecting reward and punishment connected with

spiritual ideas, irrespective of whether they are really involved;

* Thinking in terms of contract: 'give me this and I'll give you that'.

If you escape these, then there follows, closely behind, the curse of needing either the familiar or the unfamiliar. People seek the familiar for comfort or verification; the unfamiliar for emotional stimulus or excitement...

Discouraging

Q: *Why do Sufis constantly discourage people from doing things; for example, I have been told that there was no point in my writing a book on Sufis. At another point I was not encouraged to make a film about Sufi teachers. Someone I know wanted to form a Sufi society, and Sufis said that this was not indicated. I want to know when I can use my talents to bring out something of the Sufi heritage and its value...*

A: The only people discouraged by Sufis from 'doing things' are those who are trying to run before they can walk. Making films, writing books, forming societies may all be useful, providing that whoever is doing it knows enough of the timing and methods in which such things are done in the Sufi field. Experience in other areas may not be enough. At the worst, people who are always trying to do such things may be above themselves; at the best they are often people who have not got to the point where they know certain essentials: such as, for instance, that there is a special timing which has to be adopted, as well as relevant selection and attunement of materials and activities.

We are invited, by the question, to explain the Sufis' attitudes. What is more important here is to note that the questioner seems to have little idea that the encouragement or discouragement by the Sufi is a *response*. If the approach is right, the response *must* be encouraging. If it is not right, the response *must* be negative. It is far less to do with the Sufi than with the other individual and the circumstances.

The Importance of Intention

In comparison to more ancient times, people of today are in an excellent position to examine their actions from the point of view of intention. The basic reason for this is that there is now a strong awareness that people may do things because of unconscious motives: being themselves unaware of the wellsprings of their actions.

Traditionally, of course, it has been realised by many cultures that 'a man may be kicked by a superior and as a consequence kicks his donkey'. The intention is not to hurt the donkey, or even to get the donkey to move. This is a case of motivation taking the place of intention: 'false intention' it might be termed. An observer, of course, will often attribute an intention to an action which he has witnessed, because of the desire to account for an action: 'He kicked the donkey, therefore the donkey had done something wrong'; or: 'His intention was evidently to get the donkey to move'.

But, for whole populations, thoughts, words and actions are the result of internalised ideology: frozen intention, not of the individual or group but of the inspirer, instructor and trainer (or training system or organisation) of the group.

In the religious field there is in general only a feeble appreciation of the role of 'crystallised intention' in the acts of the believers. Lip-service may be paid to the need to have a right intention, and not to profit personally from a thought or action. But it can easily enough be demonstrated in many cases that people will – say – proselytise others because of the emotionally satisfying quality of the act. The intention, then, overtly and as far as the individual is concerned, being to serve the community and to help the proselyte, is nothing other than to provide an emotional satisfaction for the missionary.

Those who oppose this view often turn out, on close inspection, to be people who are in fact receiving such 'substitute satisfactions'.

It is vital, however, for the real intention of an action to be known. If it is for emotional satisfaction, then there is no harm, providing that there is a need for this and providing, too, that it is not mistaken for something else – piety, for instance. This is because there is an area of the individual where real intention resides, beyond personal satisfaction. If this is not developed, the individual, however pious, is living an illusion.

Nature

A certain scorpion, wanting to cross a river was scuttling about on the bank, looking for a means of getting to the other side. Seeing his problem, a tortoise offered to carry him across.

The scorpion thanked the tortoise, and climbed on his back. As soon as the tortoise had finished his swim and unloaded the scorpion, the scorpion gave him a really powerful sting.

'How can you do such a thing to me?' cried the tortoise. 'My nature is to be helpful, and I have used it to help you. Now I get stung!'

'My friend,' said the scorpion, 'your nature is to be helpful, and you were. Mine is to sting, and I have. Why, therefore, do you seek to transform your nature into virtue and mine into villainy?'

The Boat

Q: *It is hard to know, from reading Sufi materials, whether it is better to have patience or to concentrate upon work. The same holds, it seems to me, with all systems of knowledge and spirituality. Sometimes they speak of service and activity, sometimes of quietism and patience. How does one choose between these?*

A: Sufi activity, like all spiritual paths, is a preparation. It is not a matter of what you are doing alone, but how it is done, and why.

This is why there are Sufi instructors, who monitor progress.

Activity and patience are equally good and equally useless, according to the degree of their efficaciousness towards the goal.

There is a proverb:

> The fast and the slow both meet at the ferry-boat.

Do they know where they are going? Have they the fare and provisions for the journey? Or have they just been worrying whether they are fast or slow in getting to the embarkation-point?

Superficial Reading

People read books, which affect them in various ways. They will admit that they cannot get the best out of a book if, say, they are too young or inexperienced to know the words, or to understand what the author is talking about. But once they are adult, and accustomed to reading books, they will assume that they must be able to profit by the text in exactly the way in which the author intended. This is not borne out by experience, and it is even unsound otherwise, being based upon an assumption for which there is no proof.

The way in which some books are written, and the purpose for which they are written, is only half understood by most people. The idea, for instance, that a book is designed to be read under certain circumstances, or at different stages of development, is not well known to current cultures. If a book appears to be understandable, the reader will take it that it means just what he or she has been able to deduce it means. This is not, of course, a correct assumption. Books of real developmental value can be read only under their own conditions. The teacher explains the way in which the book is to be read, and other things necessary for the current position of the student. People very often recommend books to each other to read, without knowing about the inner content of the book or the fact that the book may in fact be a highly technical contrivance, simply looking like an ordinary book. A book of abstruse philosophy, and in the East we have many, may merely cloak directions for carrying on various essential exercises, which are infinitely more precious than the intellectual content of the book. Again, people who are recommended books not infrequently are greatly moved by them emotionally.

Experiment will readily show that a book on religion, given to someone who does not know how to read it for its specific directions, will merely move that person emotionally; either because the words or phrases are such as to evoke emotion, or because of the person who gave them the book or the recommendation. These reactions are superficial, though they may appear to the unregenerate reader to be deep.

Since the Middle Ages, when books minus the knowledge of how to use them became more plentiful, this problem has existed, and become more acute. The amusing thing is that we now have millions of books, in some of whose texts there is lurking the knowledge, the *real* knowledge, which the academician does not suspect.

It is as if we had a rhymed telephone directory, thinking that the rhyme was the point, without knowing that at a certain time and place this book is of inestimable other, practical, value.

Writing

Q: *I recall that Feroz Shamshiri, the great Sufi of Tashkent, used to live there but seldom held meetings of his disciples. He always communicated with them in writing. Why was this?*

A: If you have any experience of spiritual groups, you will know that too many people focus their attention on the teacher and not on the teaching. Indeed, this is such a frequent abuse that some people become completely fixated on a teacher, whether true or false.

Even in the East, people mistake this phenomenon for sanctity, or for religious experience.

Knowing this, many Sufis do not teach directly at all; much will depend upon the condition of their followers.

It is therefore not uncommon for teachers to write or dictate teachings, which are then read or read out.

When, however, individuals or groups of learners are able to concentrate upon the essence and not on the appearance or the presence of the teacher, meetings do take place.

It is only recently in the West that psychological workers have discovered that the actual presence of someone supposed to be teaching produces a sense of awe, significance or religious devotion which is, of course, not the same as perceiving what really is there.

The Shade Without the Tree

'There is a learning which is not in books. There are experiences which cannot be described in words. There is a direct perception of Reality which I believe humanity was intended for: that is what I seek . . .'

This yearning, yet confident, series of statements is repeated again and again in the letters which I receive and in the mouths of those who come to see me.

For twenty years I have answered it with a series of questions, designed to elicit whatever real conception there may be about Reality, behind these words.

The questions have usually been in this vein, naturally following the classical Sufi model:-

'Do you know how to recognise this non-verbal learning?'
'Do you now know that the "learning not in books" may be elicited by books, in their instrumental function: making books necessary?'
'Have you not thought that when your perceptions have developed, you will then have the means to understand some books: so that the prior need for them in providing frameworks for thought is recognised?'
'Have you thought of, or heard of, or even suspected, the functional role of books and words, which lies behind their intellectual, factual or emotionally stimulative use?'

Nothing tells us so much about someone, in a book-oriented society, in respect to his or her potential and actual progress, as the attitude towards literature.

223

The fact is that less than one person in fifty has had any conception of the 'real use' of the word. Jalaluddin Rumi spoke of 'one in a thousand' among the Moslems of his time, so perhaps the contemporary picture is brighter. But the crude attitude towards the word which is the result of the superficiality of current society's beliefs about it will undoubtedly be seen in the future as comically barbaric.

Remember, virtually all the great classical Sufis worked with words. Ask yourself: why was that?

You may be looking for shade and dislike the sun which creates it. Very well. But you need the sun, and also the tree to provide the shade.

Dervish Literature

Q: *Can you tell me something about the dervish literature which is available in English? Which books should one read?*

A: Many books have been translated. In order to profit by them, even the translation, you have to know something about them which is rarely expressed; and you also have to be in the correct state. The thing you have to know is that they are often not literature at all as commonly understood in other spheres. They are constructed to fulfil a multiple purpose. Academicians have treated them as literature, source material for facts, expositions of doctrine. This can really only be done by people who know what and when to extract from them. As to the timing of their study, the nourishment depends upon the situation of the learner.

The only way to get to grips with this literature and to profit by it in a useful sense is to study it as it is intended to be studied; as a part of a comprehensive plan, in ways, at times and under conditions suited to its study. Otherwise it might be likened to seeing a colour television transmission on a black and white screen. You get some impression, useful in some ways, varying in impact according to the extent to which the monochrome can reproduce what is originally intended to be in full colour. Some people have soaked themselves in this literature; they have profited more or less, but always remember that it is possible to profit less, as well as to profit more, through the effort exercised. You can even lose by such an enterprise.

Meaning of Biographies

Q: *I am deeply interested in the lives of teachers and guides of all kinds. Which of the books which are available in the shops are useful reading? Usually the people who write these books, it seems to me, are at a much lower level than the teacher whom they are writing about. They are convinced that the person they are writing about is real, or important, and so on. But it seems to me that the snag is that they are only pious observers of something which they do not take a full part in.*

A: A biography of a teacher, or a description of his doings and sayings, written by someone who has no objective (real, complete or meaningful as we call it) perception of that person's mission, is generally useless except to keep 'mystery' and 'wonder' alive: if you can call that useful. Such a work is probably only a product which draws crude, undifferentiated attention to things said or done, not to real meaningfulness. I say 'generally' because there is a form of literature which is deliberately ingenuous, dissimulative, designed to produce a certain preparatory climate in the mind of the reader or to inform those who are not able to understand the total implications of a person's function. These books have a value which is not

225

immediately obvious, but which is useful in many ways: they sort people out. They show which people become 'idolatrously' attached to the book or the personality portrayed. Such people have themselves applied a 'stop' to their development; a point probably adequate to them, perhaps on the other hand, short of their potentiality. Those who are prepared to see the 'wave as an aspect of the sea' can learn that the book, a part of its content, is a stepping-stone to something else.

In cases where the function of the teacher is real, there is a possibility that even the useless biographer may be able to transmit something, almost unconsciously, which shall be of use. This is known as the doctrine of 'The canal does not drink, yet may conduct the water to the thirsty land'. Some books are intended for special communities, or to operate for a limited period of time.

I might add that the particular book which you came here thinking about, is of the superficial sort, recommending itself to sheer, undifferentiated emotion, although it is indistinguishable to most people from 'profundity'. This is *your* answer: the answer to the unasked question which your overt question conceals. I have taken this opportunity of giving a general interpretation. It may not have occurred to you that bafflement has distorted what the authors are trying to portray. This is so in the case of the book which you have in mind.

Q: *What are the various levels on which the published teachings of the great Masters can be appreciated?*

A: The generally available material on the teachings of such Masters is not a source adequate for studying their teachings on various levels. This is because such material records sayings, doings and teachings without regard for time, place, the need for special formulations, distinguishing between allegory and fact, or even what levels are being dealt with.

In most cases material recorded at various levels and for different purposes has been accumulated and edited. The levels can be distinguished only by someone who has access to these levels, in which case he has little need for the literature, unless it be his need to project his teaching, *the* teaching, within the cultural framework of the people whom he is addressing, which will consist of these vitiated traditions. If he is a mere learner, he cannot learn direct from the material, because he has no real access to the levels. Hence, for most people, the material is useless. For the others, it is garbled, and the task of re-projecting it in a true form is thankless. Hence, one reason for the capacity and need for reformulation. Because of the last two remarks, the question is really invalid. Scholastics and other comparatively superficial workers, of course, are obliged to assume, as the questioner has, that there is a useful content in this material; that it is accessible, that it can be unravelled by academic or logical methods. But the scholastic is not right, he is merely claiming the use of materials (like the potter uses clay) because he cannot operate without using them in his own particular way.

SECTION VII

Religious or Sufi Presentation

Q: *What is the difference between the harangue of the revivalist or religious enthusiast and the lecture or intense presentation of the Sufi? They both seem the same to me. Surely the Sufi is working his audience up to a pitch of excitement, just as the tub-thumper is doing?*

A: The difference is that the enthusiast is increasing excitement, tension and concern. The Sufi is aiming to increase potentiality and the ability to learn. The one is indoctrination, attempting to induce a desire for repentance, action, commitment. The other is attempting to help to provide the atmosphere in which first learning and then understanding can take place. The former insists that you cannot understand, must only trust. The latter is insisting that you have to learn, and when you understand you will know what trust is. The religionist believes that belief is the greatest thing there is. The Sufi asserts that belief is a substitute for knowledge: 'If you know, you do not have to believe. A fact needs no conversion mechanism.' Hence the indoctrinator needs people who can be manipulated; the Sufi needs only people who will give a minimum amount of attention: the same quantity that is needed to learn, not the amount required to absorb other people's beliefs.

The 'unsung hero' is the one who does something because of the knowledge that it is the thing to do, the one who gets no publicity. The acclaimed one is whoever does something because of a deeply implanted belief. The interesting thing is that the implanter does not trust belief: he has to induce it. He cannot believe that people can be or do anything from knowledge: they have to be made to do or be something. And the mechanism of effecting this is an assault upon their minds.

Which Is Which?

It has been said that Sufism is a form of religion: and also that 'Religion is a form of Sufism.'

While the first statement may seem more likely, it is only by looking at both assertions that we can see what the Sufis say that Sufism is.

Sufism, in some of its aspects, undoubtedly helps us to see what many forms of religion really are.

The Sufis, for instance, like contemporary social scientists, have for many centuries correctly described certain forms of religion as social and tribal phenomena, with emotional and intellectual mainsprings, rather than detectable spiritual content.

They do not necessarily condemn such activity, but they often insist upon it being seen for what it is.

This is because the Sufis are outstanding analysts and describers of human behaviour. As with any system which purports to describe, the Sufi method not only points to limitations but also to possibilities.

Those who fail to note this (and there are many) will always imagine that the Sufis are trying to reduce the value of something. The Sufis, and others, however, easily sustain the argument that being descriptive is not the same as being critical. If, in the process, paranoid or over-sensitive reactions are elicited from others, this becomes a medico-psychological problem. As such, it passes out of Sufi competence at this point, and Sufis are clearly entitled to detach from controversy there and then.

Indeed, failure to observe the arrival at this point will plainly distinguish the Sufi from the imitator, superficialist or impostor.

If you have a piece of rusty metal, there may be two stages in its rehabilitation: the first is to remove the rust; then comes the polishing. Finally, there may even be the rustproofing. Those who know nothing (or little) of the process will appear absurd to those who do. To outsiders, however, their insistence upon perfecting before polishing, or treating rust before anything else will always seem to be unnecessary, inexplicable or even unacceptable.

Sufi work is essentially constructive. But if you dig soil to prepare it for seeds, there will always be someone who insists that you are disturbing something.

This all means, of course, that not only must rust-removal be done, or tilling before sowing: it also means that the theoretical basis of such activity must be conveyed and understood.

It is only because the theoretical basis is not communicated that confusion can occur.

But it must be clearly understood that the communication of the theoretical basis does not depend upon the existence and activity of the communicator. If there are people who do not really want the communication, virtually nothing can be done.

The most common communications problem is when people invite communication but prove not to be listening after all.

The 'listening', in this sense, is nowadays made relatively easily possible by the provision of abundant literature which forms the ground and context of communication.

It is thus of the greatest possible interest to note that those who are not in fact interested in communication like to take refuge in the statement 'I do not want to read books...'

Invincible Ignorance

When you get supply-and-demand, people asking for their teacher to fill a certain role, and when you get a teacher who feels equally pleased in filling it, you may get education. But if you look around you, you will see that more often than not you are getting what is nothing more than the formation of a new tribe, or a business, trading one thing for another.

This transactionalism has its uses. If, for instance, someone gets pleasure from giving orders and others derive acceptable pleasure from obeying them, there you may have the makings of a constructive or a destructive enterprise. Most human activities are modelled upon this pattern. The limitations of this process, however, mean that only those things can be projected and carried through which afford acceptable stimuli to a certain range of people at a given time.

Let us postulate a community which needed, say, a certain medicine or piece of information or knowledge of a skill. Before any of these could be effectively introduced and maintained, it would be necessary for the factor, object, teaching or whatever it was to be presented in an acceptable way, by someone who was liked and perhaps respected, and also in such a way as to afford the kind of stimuli expected by the audience, readership, community and so on.

There is always a great deal of talk about restrictive societies; but one point worth considering is that all societies, until one exists which grasps this point, are self-restricting by the very nature of their assumption that someone or something is only acceptable to the extent to which it (or he or she) pleases the members of that society, or some of them.

Today I got a request from a publisher for an introduction to one of my books. This is a collection of stories designed to cause a certain effect upon the reader, which effect depends upon such a reader having no preconceptions as to what the story might 'do' to him or her. But the would-be publisher asks me to provide an introduction which shall inform the reader of the intended effect of the stories!

Quite recently, too, I had a conversation with another publisher. He said, 'I know that you have said that your materials simply *must* be presented in the way in which they are: but, without asking you to write a general theory about the whole corpus of your materials, I would like you to do me a book which contains, shall we say...'

He paused, without having anything further to say. I said, 'How about a general theory?'

'Exactly,' he answered.

It so happens that publishers are involved in these examples because they tend to have to articulate what their readers want but cannot formulate so plainly. They even have a phrase for it, 'the creative side of publishing'. The only thing wrong with this approach is – it means that the publisher will only accept something which accords with his preconception of what he and the reader should have.

On a certain radio programme, when I was invited to discuss one of my books, the very distinguished reviewer who was presiding over the programme had a question. The book was one containing Sufi stories. He felt that it was odd that, in these tales, the Sufi always came out on top. It staggered me to realise that this very competent and intelligent man had failed to observe that this was a book of examples. Would he have advanced a similar criticism in the case of a book of mathematical tables: 'Why do the equations always come out right?'

This problem, of nearly invincible ignorance, is not made any easier to understand when one takes into consideration the fact that the malaise is by no means universal. Although it is very safe to say that of all extant cultures of which one has any knowledge, every single one is hampered by a similar blindness: yet one constantly comes across people who can and do approach problems, including Sufi materials, without any hint of that obtuseness. So we can hardly say that the human being is essentially someone who narrows his vision to such an extent that he cannot see, or that he is someone whose culture is bound to blind him to alternative ways of looking at things.

But it is equally plain that we live in the world we live in precisely because it is much easier to think in small circles based on transactionalism.

And experience teaches that the way out of that bind is to refuse to dilute, to abstain from popularising, to deny oneself the satisfaction of compromising, when dealing with materials which unless absorbed in the manner which yields results turn into something else: into entertainment.

I once gave a lecture to several hundred people in the United States. I spoke for a long time about the sterility of ritual and the meaninglessness of 'metaphysical exercises' since they were the mechanical relics of formerly instrumental and specially-calculated impacts.

At the end of the lecture I had difficulty getting off the platform. This was because I was besieged by people pleading for rituals and metaphysical exercises...

Once mechanicality has taken root, as it were, in the human mind, you need not fear that anything will easily disturb it.

I once presented a collection of very important and entirely comprehensive materials, in published form, to a certain widely-respected man whose repute as a spiritual teacher in some circles was impressive.

He looked at me. 'Yes, this is all very well,' he said; 'but (and here he adopted a confidential, almost conspiratorial, tone and dug me in the ribs), what we really want is something which has *not* been published.'

Obviously, the sense of something secret, restricted, unpublished was greater than the presentation of something which actually was useful.

So marked is this thirst for the outlandish, whether it is useful or not, that in the West people adopt Eastern names before they try to teach their fellows; they claim to have visited remote mountain fastnesses, to have been commissioned by mysterious Orientals to take messages; they invoke the names and writings of people about whom they understand little, they adopt foreign customs and diets, clothes and exercises. When I mentioned to an interviewer that certain Eastern gurus exulted in this and simply fed these Western people what they asked for, there was a howl of protest from the imitation Orientals and their followers which still rings in my ears.

'We have scoured this planet, end to end,' one of my remote ancestors is reputed to have said, 'but we have found nobody to whom to entrust our knowledge.' But I am sure that he found plenty of people who would have taken it if it had been crazy enough.

Sufis and Cultists

The effect of the deliberately mysterious and sometimes out-rageous behaviour of the adventurers who flood into the West from Asia is often to paralyse their pupils' critical faculties. Even their common sense is distorted or held in abeyance; but their imaginative credulity is proportionately increased.

Sufis sometimes use action-teaching to illustrate this condition, as practically the only therapy for it.

In one documented instance of this, an Indian mystic in England was surrounded for decades by a band of loyal and totally unquestioning disciples, who never assessed his usually puerile vapourings.

Desirous of showing him up in a way which would give the captives some chance of seeing how low they had sunk, a certain Sufi planned an illustrative incident.

He had himself carried, on a stretcher, to a meeting being held by the guru, and lay on it throughout the proceedings.

When the lecture and ritual prostrations of the faithful were at an end, the Sufi stood up and began to leave the hall.

The 'miracle' had not passed unnoticed.

As he had expected, one of the guru's followers stopped him, and asked, 'Are you not going to testify that you have been miraculously healed by the Master?' The two were, of course, surrounded by eager disciples.

The Sufi said, 'Not unless you want everyone to know that I was not sick at all, but only wanted to be comfortable while listening, to avoid sitting in the over-crowded conditions which your Guru forces everyone to endure!'

Conditioning

All systems, cults, metaphysical groups and almost all human organisations, practise conditioning. That is to say, they instil into people a limited range of beliefs and require certain automatic practices. Unknowingly, the people concerned (which can include the instillers) become 'servants' of the system.

Some systems are what we can call non-comprehensive. These would include those which do not have a world-view, and which function effectively enough within well-understood and accepted limits. A group of people associated together for the purpose of playing a game, carrying out a business or pursuing a limited objective could be called non-comprehensive.

'Comprehensive' systems are those with a world-view, or with an outlook which causes their members to act as if they had a world-view. Such systems are those which require (deliberately or in practice) their members to act with regard to a comprehensive set of beliefs which cover all, or most, eventualities.

It will be noted that the 'Comprehensive' type of system seems to include virtually all major religious systems. This is not, however, to say that the original form or understanding of the system was comprehensive in the sense of being regarded as immutable. Certain principles may have been held to be unchangeable: but others, some of them fundamental, can be seen as having been absorbed, over the years and centuries, into the kind of strait-jacket thinking which is a common feature of systems of belief. Understanding is replaced by dogma. The origin of the dogma, and the stage at which it became crystallised, are easily forgotten.

The importance of understanding this phenomenon, the dogmatisation of the flexible, is great. Because so many beliefs and practices are taken for granted as central or essential to a whole belief-system, people in general (in any culture) tend to think in strait-jacket terms about a wide range of things.

Consequently, they find it hard or impossible to absorb new – or unfamiliar – knowledge.

A further complication is that most extant human systems are currently projected by people who fail to make any distinction between spiritual feelings and socio-psychological ones; or between emotion and spirituality.

Until comparatively recently this was not a problem for such people. Most peoples lived in mutually exclusive communities, isolated from one another. Social science and psychology were in their infancy or excluded, and in general, multicultural communities had little access to single-culture ones, which latter effectively dominated the world.

But a new situation, unprecedented in its spread and urgency, arose with the discovery and wide publication of the phenomena of conditioning and indoctrination. When confronted with this knowledge, few extant cultures could explain why conditioning was necessary, or why so many well-established belief-systems were indistinguishable from 'brainwashing' ones.

Looking at the history and development of belief-systems, it is not hard to perceive that they always deteriorate in their flexibility and capacity to understand. They also, and as a consequence, tend to rely more and more upon authority and over-simplification. None can be said to have guarded effectively against conditioning. The Sufis, as the published record over the centuries shows, have worked against the mechanicality of conditioning, but have until recently lacked appropriate conditions under which to insist that this factor be taken into consideration.

The Sufi contention is that, traditionally, there was a clear-cut method, widely if not universally applied by 'those who know'. This involved (1) indoctrination of the people (or some of them) to remove superseded ideas which had begun to operate as blinkers; (2) removal of the indoctrination to restore flexibility of viewpoint and consequent enlightenment; and then (3) application of stimuli to help make this enlightenment effective in the ordinary world.

There are fairly close parallels in the mundane educational

process. If, for example, everyone believed firmly in alchemy, it would be hard to liberate from it the science of chemistry. The fixation on the alchemical goal would have to be weakened in certain people before they could profit from chemistry.

This perception of conditioning and flexibility, can be used to examine virtually every human system of thought or action in the spiritual field. Indeed, until it can be applied by someone it is not possible to hold a meaningful discussion with him or her.

Nowadays, few people contest the importance of knowing about conditioning in order to examine belief-systems. Why, therefore, is it so difficult to communicate with so many people along these lines? The answer is very simple. We are at a stage in understanding human behaviour analogous to that which obtained when people began to try to talk of chemistry to those who were fixated upon the hope of untold wealth (or, sometimes, spiritual enlightenment) through alchemy. Like the alchemist or those who want easy riches, people want dramatic inputs (emotional stimuli, excitement, reassurance, authority-figures and the rest) rather than knowledge.

It is only when the desire for knowledge and understanding becomes as effective as the craving for emotional stimulus that the individual becomes accessible to change, to knowledge, to more than a very little understanding.

So learning must be preceded by the capacity to learn. THAT, in turn, comes about at least in part by right attitude. And THAT, again, is where the would-be learner has to exercise effort.

Deception

A scholar said to a Sufi:
'Will you not admit that you Sufis deal in deception?'

'I will, indeed,' said the Sufi. 'And I will do more, explaining to you why this *must be*.

'Everyone seeks his own advantage, everyone is greedy for gain without effort and advantage disproportionate to contribution.

'Nobody is attracted to anything unless there is a promise therein.

'People are attracted to scholarly activity, your own métier, because learning gives people a flattering reputation. How many scholars are there who do not glory in their learning?'

The Sufi's words and deeds appear to the neophyte, too, to promise much: power, secrets, salvation, safety and attainment greater than any other pursuit on earth. So such a person, like the would-be scholar, is attracted to the Sufis.

What is the difference?

The difference is that whereas members of other groups increase the deception by self-pride and flattery of one another and pretence before the world, the Sufis make it their first concern to disabuse any entrant of his likely chances of getting something easily. And they do not exactly massage the False Self, either...

Gods and Demons

Q: *How can people be expected to believe the Sufis, when they say that they are in touch with the unknown, that they see a thread in life which others do not, and they are able to bring this into human education?*

A: Before I can answer that, I must ask you whether you believe in the gods and demons, the sacrifices and the incense, the sacred robes and the relics, of the religion of your people?

Q: Yes, I do believe in them.

A: Very well. Let me tell you a tale. There was once a man who was threatened by a powerful opponent. This man struck his head against a bough while walking under a tree, and was knocked unconscious. As it happened, his enemy was passing at the time, and stopped to see what the result was. The oppressed man, when he revived, saw his opportunity. He immediately said to the other: 'I have been dead, and visited, in the twinkling of an eye, the Other World. I actually met your family there.'

The oppressor believed him, for some reason, probably due to curiosity and superstition. He said, 'And how are they faring?'

'Not well', said the other man. 'Your ancestors have the most menial jobs, everyone laughs at them, and they are as miserable as anyone could be.'

'But what can I do for them?' asked the unhappy recipient of this news.

'There is nothing that you can do while you are alive, except to look after me. I have also learned that when I am dead I will be able to put in a good word for you, if I live to a great age, and I'll not tell anyone of your family's disgrace,' said the former victim.

And so it was that he escaped from the captivity of his opponent, using his weakness against himself ... Now, how does that appeal to you?

Q: *I do not see why the oppressor should believe that the trickster had been to heaven or wherever it was supposed to be; I don't see how anyone could believe it . . .*

A: But you do not know how or why it is that anyone can believe what you assert you believe, which, to those not brought up in your particular tradition, seems equally implausible. Both truth and lies, as well as imagination, seem true to some, and untrue to others.

Prayer

Q: *If one small prayer can bring comfort, as we know it does, does continuous prayer, as practised by some ascetics, not give even more?*

A: There was once a poor old half-blind woman. She stumbled in a crowded street market, and her iron-tipped stick tore the hem of the robe of a courtier who had paused beside a shop.

A crowd gathered as the nobleman's servants berated the old lady.

But the aristocrat was kindly, compassionate. Saying, 'Accidents will happen, Mother', he gave the woman a gold piece and went on his way.

It happened that there was an idiot in the crowd. 'A gold piece for a tear in a robe!' he exclaimed to himself. 'This really is something to follow up.'

As idiots will, he made his plans, based on his own conception of the situation.

The next time he saw the rich man in the market, the idiot ran up to him, tore off the brocade robe and, ripping it to pieces, cried, 'Torn ten times! You owe me ten pieces of gold...'

The old lady had been innocent and contrite; the idiot was foolish and greedy. What you do not see may be the determining factor in an occasion or other matter. Effects will depend upon your own inner state just as much as upon anything else.

The purpose of Sufic preparation is to become attuned to higher, subtler things: not to try to impose formulas upon a mind which still contains too much greed and also mistakes it for legitimate aspiration.

Demons

Q: *Primitive peoples, who undoubtedly include members of advanced societies only a few years ago, attribute psychological oddnesses, quirks and barriers to demons and delinquency. Nowadays, with so much psychological knowledge, it must surely be easier for Sufis to get their point across?*

A: Nowadays, when people say, 'I cannot accept this', or 'I don't understand that', or 'I want this or that', they can indeed be seen by some as suffering from inhibitions and so on and not as possessed by devils. There are two problems, however, which many people have not yet learned to deal with. The first is that having reservations may be a protective factor, and can indeed help people to avoid being exploited. The second is that raising the barriers without being able to see the situation can deprive people of progress. Rumi's tale of the lion who could not drink because he was afraid of his reflection in the pool of water is an illustration of that.

Modern psychology has pointed out the barriers, but has not yet developed any methods of dealing with them, except in clinical situations. But the social situation is far more extensive and common. You have to look at unpolluted Sufi literature to see how the matter has been dealt with. Few people do so, because the Sufis, for whatever reason, were virtually alone in pointing out these facts among ancient commentators. They shed the demonic explanation centuries before anyone else: and certainly well before this conception appeared in the modern world. This statement in itself sometimes raises the barrier of disbelief which is part of the malaise we are discussing. So the only therapy is to see if we can make sure that the objectors familiarise themselves with what the Sufis have done over the centuries.

Hero or Ignoramus?

The major difference between Sufis and 'believers' is that belief is conviction, certainty without proof, while Sufi knowledge is factual. This is often disputed by theologians because they regularly confuse knowledge with belief. This is easy to demonstrate. If I *know* that it is ten past ten in the morning, or that there is a fly on the wall, it is absolutely unnecessary, lunatic, even, to describe this as a belief. On the other hand, the people who believe that something is true do not know it in anything like the same way. Why? Because if they knew it as a positive, objective fact they would not manifest any emotion about it: neither would they be so keen to make others believe. All human experience shows that it is only things about which there is doubt which are believed in this characteristic manner. Facts, true ones, are not subject to either emotion or proselytization. The theologically-centred people, then, are not wrong or deluded, they are feebly informed as to the difference between, say, 'I know that this is a pencil', and 'I know that there are spiritual beings, because I have felt that it is true.'

A useful illustration of this is seen in a certain tale. There were once three men in an aircraft which was losing height, and the pilot asked one of them to jump out to lighten it so that it could land safely. 'I cannot jump,' said the scholar, 'because I am too valuable to risk my life, as the instrument of education'.

'I shall jump,' said the priest, 'because I have faith that I shall be saved.'

'There is only one parachute left,' said the Sufi, 'and I shall use it, because I know that the pilot will ask for another volunteer in a minute, and I shall land safely.'

'But,' said the scholar, 'was the priest not a hero for believing that he would land safely?'

'He was more than that,' said the Sufi. 'He picked up your rucksack, instead of the parachute, and strapped it on...'

245

Publicity

Q: *How would you describe the people who publicise their claims to being Teachers of the Way, who make musical and vocal advertising of their claims, and who operate retreats for disciples, in the manner of so many mechanical and emotional religionists?*

A: They have not changed at all through the centuries. I need add nothing to what the classical Masters have said about them. The pity of it is that people do not study these admonitions. If they did, they would not have to ask questions like this. It is as if, in algebra, people continually asked whether there were such things as equations, when the books are overflowing with them.

If you want an example, look at the story in Rumi's *Mathnavi* about Dalqak the jackanapes and the Sayed who was Sultan of Tirmid.

The Sayed had given out that he would reward anyone who could go to Samarqand and carry out some urgent transaction for him in three or four days.

As soon as he heard this, being in the country, Dalqak leapt upon a horse and travelled as fast as he could to the Sultan. Such was the urgency of his flight that two horses dropped dead under him, and the people were thrown into confusion and fear by his headlong progress. They imagined that some dreadful enemy, perhaps, was about to attack the realm.

When admitted to the Sayed's presence, the jackanapes paused to get his breath while everyone was agog for his news. Finally he told the King that he had heard of the offer, but had come to explain that he could not fulfil the task!

This is an analogy of the confusion and doubt sown by these supposed 'Sufi teachers', who are in fact engaged in nothing else than flurry and scurry, in agitation and causing tumult – even when they are supposedly proclaiming stillness and meditation.

Rumi himself uses this story as an example of the actions and true role of just such people as you are describing. What need is there for me to do any further defining?

246

The People of God

A Mongol conqueror sent spies disguised as merchants into a country to bring him back information about its government.

This was their report:

'In that country they have not one ruler, but two. The first one is called the King, and his employees are well-dressed, well-fed and enjoy their lives. The other ruler is called God. The people who follow him are garbed in dull clothes, have long faces and are under-nourished.

'We have not been able to discover the reason for the institution of the two rulers over one country, but we know which one, given an equal opportunity, any newcomer would prefer.'

Easier...

There was once a Dervish who was a barber. One of his customers was a religious fanatic, a Mulla with a great bushy beard which he decided to get trimmed, as it was beginning to grow into his mouth. As he was a greedy eater, the beard had started to get in the way of his meals.

The first time the Dervish trimmed the beard, he asked his customer: 'How do you feel about infidels?'

The second time the Mulla settled down for his beard-trim, the Dervish-barber again said, 'Are the infidels getting stronger these days?'

And again, the third time the Mulla came for his trim, the Dervish who was a barber said, 'Let's talk about infidels...'

The Mulla rounded on him and shouted: 'Why can't you talk about something more wholesome? Every time I come here you want to talk about infidels. It strikes me that you have degenerate tastes, and yet you are supposed to be a Dervish...'

The Dervish laughed. 'It's nothing to do with *my* tastes,' he said, 'it's just that whenever you hear the word "infidel", your beard bristles so much that it is easier to cut.'

Idiot

People who are conventionally religious are usually admirers of things which their associative mentality tells them are 'holy' or 'good' or 'devotional'. They obtain emotional satisfactions from hearing the familiar or from seeing people do things which have been established as devout. Because this has become their source of personal pleasure, they fail to notice that it is often of no other value whatever. Hence such people delight in seeing others at prayer, or at producing 'spiritual' reactions which they have been taught denote something higher than they really do. In the process, really spiritual sensations are lost. The cruder emotion has driven them out.

Hence the tale of the parrot and the priest.

There was once a priest who went into a pet shop and asked if they had anything that might interest him.

The lady who worked there produced a parrot.

'This is sure to please you,' she said. 'If you pull this leg on the bird, he says a prayer, and if you pull the other one, it will sing a hymn.'

The priest was delighted, and felt a sense of holy joy suffusing him at such a familiarly devout observance.

'And,' he beamed, 'what will happen if I pull both its legs at once?'

The parrot shouted out, 'I'll fall on my face, you idiot!'

248

Distress

Q: *Is distress the way to God, as so many Sufis have averred?*

A: I have no knowledge of any real Sufi who has stated this. Indeed, if it were true, all the people whom you see around you who have been distressed are or may be on the way to God. A lot of emotionalist dervishes, who have over-concentrated upon distress have imagined that this is some sort of a religious path. This you can find in print and repeated by misguided people. Sensible people, however, those who have given the matter some study, will at once tell you that it is not the distress but the response to distress which can improve or deteriorate a person. If a person needs distress and can handle it, it will improve him or her. Otherwise, no. You really have to beware of these over-simplifications based on imagining that there are simple formulas which give you things. Remember, if you will, the definition once given of the difference between a dervish and a Sufi: 'A dervish tries to be holy – the Sufi does not need to try!'

Displacement Activity

Displacement activity, sometimes called 'exchange symptoms', forms a most important part of human behaviour.

As an example, people who claim that they have no interest in metaphysics are often over-reacting against just such a curiosity.

On the other hand, people who fervently claim that they are deeply concerned about such things are seldom in the right state to profit from them. Their excitement is used as a means of preventing them from going further.

Their anxiety paralyses them: but this may well be inwardly intentional.

You can see this, on a very ordinary level, when you look at agitated believers in all sorts of cults and systems. Because they 'have belief' they do not believe in learning. They use belief, in fact, to prevent learning. This is partly because the urgent 'desire to learn' is a low-level, emotional activity, a form of pleasurable agitation, a displacement.

'Believers', too, hold onto beliefs and do not allow them to be modified easily, certainly not by experience, because they really seek a systematic formula to make themselves feel stable. The space in their minds is there for system, not for truth. It is such people who imagine that there has been a great change in them when they merely exchange one belief-system for another. They are not believers in the sense understood by a genuine belief-system, merely temporarily stabilised.

Emergency

Q: *What do people from other cultures think about the style of preaching which is used in the West?*

A: Well, of course there are many styles of preaching. But some of them, quite obviously, are not so much preaching as an outlet for the excess energy of the preacher.

I remember I once took a Sufi to a lecture given by a very famous spiritual man in a Western country, to observe the Sufi's reactions.

The religious propagandist stood in a pulpit, and as he was small in height, he was almost completely dwarfed by it and looked as if he was boxed in.

As he warmed to his theme, he got hotter and hotter, and waved his arms and spoke in the most alarmingly ferocious manner.

At the height of the discourse, when the histrionics were in full flood, the Sufi turned to me and whispered:

'What do they do in this country to protect the public when these people escape?'

What They Respond To

Q: *People who attract really large audiences bring them together by a combination of things. There are the words and the actions and the appearance of the event. Sufis, on the other hand, traditionally do not make displays, except for imitators who delight in beards and robes and the rest. What do you feel about this?*

A: It is a matter of whether you are primarily teaching or entertaining. You can choose, by your display or lack of it, appropriate kinds of people. I once asked a priest why he had incense and vestments and invocations and so on. He said that he had worked out that it was because of the problem which was faced and solved by a man at a busy road junction.

This man's house was so situated that cars roared past, endangering his family. He put up notices begging people to be careful, but they had no effect.

Finally, he hit on a solution. The next day all the cars were crawling past, as soon as their drivers spotted his new notice.

It was a large placard, which read: 'Motorists! Nudists crossing...'

Levitation

Q: *How do you account for the fact that a large number of people can experience, or believe that they experience, quite extraordinary sensations which seem to be of a spiritual nature, and that these are often so similar that they, surely must be real?*

A: Real spiritual experiences, and by that I mean not low-level, tentative ones that people are always talking about, cannot be described in words. They occur in a different area from the verbal. Again, some of these may be real, and others not. Therefore it is not possible to generalise about such matters, which belong to specific instances.

But you should remember that few people realise how easy it is to believe, or to make others believe, that something exceptional has happened to them. Let us take only one example, out of many:

The astronomer Patrick Moore announced one day on the BBC that an unusual planetary condition was about to occur. The consequence of this, he went on, would be that the force of gravity would have less effect than usual upon people on this planet. He suggested that, at the time when the planet Pluto was causing this effect – at 9.47 a.m. on that day, people should test the loss of gravity by jumping. They should feel as if they were floating.

Hundreds of people rang the BBC to report that they had indeed jumped, and that they had felt the floating effect. Since studies have shown that, even with very exciting experiences, less than one per cent of people telephone the BBC programme concerned, this must mean that many thousands of people had been convinced of this gravity negation effect.

They had all forgotten, of course, that Moore made his announcement on April 1st, the day for hoaxes.

Need I say more?

Blinding Them with Science

People constantly come to me and say that, although they at first obtained satisfactions and even what they are pleased to term spiritual experiences from following this or that spiritual system, the effect wore off and they found themselves as far away as ever from what they desired.

They stick to the claim that there is something in what they have been doing, and expect one to explain things in such a way as to enable them to retain the element which they feel was satisfactory in the former teaching.

Their difficulty is that they are not objective observers of what has happened to them – with the result that there is, effectively, nothing that you can do for them in that state.

There is an analogy in the story of the man who had fleas in his bed. He first put out the light, so that the insects could not see to bite. This man was making assumptions which were logical enough, but which did not work since he did not know how to structure his experience. When someone told him that fleas could bite in the dark, he still couldn't learn. He installed floodlights to blind the fleas. This seemed to work, wonder of wonders; but presently he found that he could feel them biting again.

How did the floodlights 'work'? The fact is, of course, that the light so dazzled *him*, that his attention was drawn from the fleas, giving him the impression that they were not biting him any longer. When he got used to the brightness, he began to feel the fleas again.

He still feels, we are told, that success lies somewhere along the road of floodlights. And he prizes his few brief hours of freedom from bites.

The Two-Thirty

Someone asked me how it is that so many unfunny comedians manage to develop such excellent reputations that people laugh at the mere sight of them. The enquirer, quite rightly, pointed out that very many of these performers are not funny at all, yet pull down unbelievably huge salaries.

I was not sure, but soon afterwards I saw a demonstration which told me. Not by a comedian, but by a preacher who had the reputation of answering every question, no matter how difficult, to the satisfaction of almost everyone in his audience.

I realised that it is done by means of what amounts to a trick, seldom seen through by the audience. If you care to observe such people, you will see it done again and again, as I have. Even the newspaper correspondents who attend such events have not spotted it yet.

The 'trick' is connected with a human peculiarity. People, unless they are careful, forget exactly what the question was, and are carried away by the fact that it *seems* as if the speaker is answering the question. The confidence in his voice bluffs them into imagining that he has in fact answered relevantly.

On this occasion I went to a meeting because the speaker, I was assured by several otherwise sane people, 'had the answer to everything'.

When we got there an unruly member of the audience called out to the 'man who knew everything':

'Well, then, tell us what's going to win the two-thirty at Doncaster tomorrow!'

The magical man of faith, without a second's hesitation, started a flow which went on for fifteen minutes, with the following words:

'I am glad you asked that question, because it gives me an opportunity to talk about the most important problem of our time, materialism...'

When we poured out of the hall, people were excitedly saying to one another, 'He *does* know, you know...'

The People Who Impress Us

You have asked me, firstly, how a teaching which has no intrinsic merit can impress so many people, including yourselves. You have asked, secondly, how it is that amazing and even miraculous things can be done by people who are quite ordinary. Do such people, you ask, not merit attention and respect? You have asked, thirdly, why the impression which such people make cannot be of great value to you, and why they should not be regarded as teachers.

Now, as you may imagine, these questions have been asked and answered over and over again: and the fact that you are asking them is an evidence of your lack of information, not of the need to ask them. People have looked at raw dates and thought that they would ripen when they would not. They have regarded their wells, which had run dry, as having been miraculously filled with water: when there was another reason for the presence of the water. The questions have been asked, too, by those who rejoiced in their children, though they might have had less cause to do so than they believed.

This story, which is a very old one, is one of those which have traditionally been used to answer your questions:

THE TREE, THE WELL AND THE SON

There was once a man whose date-tree stopped bearing, and whose well ran dry. He feared that he would starve, as these were his means of support, and so he went to a reputed wonder-worker for help.

'I can certainly help you,' said the miracle-man, 'but you must pay me a hundred gold coins if the tree is to be made to bear again.' He added, 'And you must keep away from the tree at night.'

The man paid, and the magician – in the night – took some green dates and stuck them in bunches onto the tree, making it look as if real fruit had suddenly sprouted.

255

His client was delighted, and asked if the magician would help him with the dry well.

'Certainly,' he said, 'but you must pay two hundred gold pieces, and avoid the well at night, when my captive spirits will do the work.'

The bargain was struck, and in the night the villain had had the well replenished by accomplices, who carried numerous goatskins full of water and threw them in.

The delighted man, when he saw the well brimful again, said to the magician:

'My wife is barren, and we want a child.'

The magic-man again promised to help: this time for five hundred gold pieces, and providing that the man kept away from his wife for many nights.

The well dried up again, of course; and the dates withered on the tree. But, some months later, the wife was delivered of a child. The birth of the baby so enraptured the husband that the two other disappointments were, in his mind, fully compensated for. After all, the magician had managed to achieve what others could not do, had he not?

Valuable Secrets

Three eminent individuals – one a businessman and industrialist of note, another a senior government official and the last a prominent figure in the world of scholarship – have been calling, sending people to see me, writing letters and telephoning me a great deal for the past three years.

They insist upon getting in touch with me because, they say, they were given secret admonitions and private instructions years ago by some mysterious but important spiritual person or being, which they now feel impelled to discuss with me.

My difficulty, which I find up to the present moment imposs-ible to convey to them, is that we have no relevance in our tradition for such communications. If you have special and high functions which stem from some experience with esotericist or higher areas, according to us what you now have to do is to get on with it, not bombard other people with missives designed to arrange a meeting to talk about it!

It appears, too, and very unfortunately, that the 'people who locked the door did not provide the key'; that is to say, the source of all this important stuff failed to let our friends know how to act, what to do, and how – if it is so vitally necessary – they could induce us to answer their letters hinting at secrets, answer the telephone when we are told about how valuable it could be for us, and so on.

Piety

Q: *Why do Sufis decry the efforts of pious people, who carry on spiritual exercises, dress in a certain manner, follow ritual prescriptions and generally act as they have been recommended by high religious authority?*

A: My friend, I assure you that you will not find any Sufi, today or yesterday, on the surface of this earth, who does what you say they do. Your question therefore comes into the category of the notorious one: 'Have you stopped beating your wife yet?'

But what the Sufis are against is the profession of piety without the action, and the carrying on of ritual without content.

You may care to hear this anecdote from Saadi's *Bostan*:

Saadi and some companions visited, in a distant part of Turkey, a man who had a reputation for being good and pious. He received them kindly, and treated them with respect. And he spent the night in prayer, while the visitors remained hungry, although their host was a man of means.

One of Saadi's friends, at length, said: 'Give us some food rather than being attentive to us. Instead of touching my shoes in respect, put your own foot upon my head, and give me something to eat!'

If you find that these pious, spiritual, robed and ritual-minded people behave with generosity and thoughtfulness, treat others well and refrain from calumnies, you will have found truly decent and religious people. If, however, they cause others – anyone else – to feel sadness, sorrow, deprivation or dislike, you will know that you have found those of whom the Sufis speak.

Believing

Q: *Is it not useful to be quite sure about these matters before one makes any progress in them? I feel that we must 'believe' before we can understand.*

A: 'Being sure' and 'believing' each refers to various states of mind. Many people, for example, think that they are 'sure' when they are only obsessed. Others refer to their condition as 'believing' when they have merely been indoctrinated. Until quite recently, those who pointed this out were often regarded as agents of the Devil: which both indicates the aggressiveness which goes with obsession and conditioning of some kinds, and also illustrates the poverty of understanding of the victims.

So widespread is the false belief about believing, and about 'sureness', which is more likely to be cocksureness in a large number of cases, that this was recently tested, in relation to supposed ESP (extra-sensory perception).

There was an overwhelmingly negative correlation between

258

'believers' and ESP capacity among people who claimed to have such perceptive abilities. That is, people who claimed that they 'believed' generally had less ESP capacity than those who did not. Again, people who claimed to be 'sure' about their suitability for higher perceptive studies were found to be eight times *less* likely to understand these matters than the general population.

'Believing' before understanding is, as we found, for many people 'becoming indoctrinated so that one need not try to understand'. People who *want* to believe so that they can understand are therefore found in general to be people who want an inculcated belief, something which is not compatible with deeper understanding.

Real belief comes after understanding. Once a thing is understood, it *must* be believed, because it now has the status of a fact. If, however, we are talking about 'belief' as something which can take place without understanding or knowledge, this is really only a synonym for obsession, and belongs to a medical, rather than a spiritual or psychological, area.

Human Beliefs

If a large number of people believe something, do you imagine that it must be true? Probably not, unless you happen to be one of that number. If a large proportion of people believe something, then it is likely to be thought to be true. In most populations, there will not be very many dissentients.

Until fairly recently people did not move around much: large majorities of people would continue for generations believing things to be true without very much likelihood that such beliefs – true or otherwise – would be disturbed.

Although human mobility has increased, human assumptions have not kept pace. Human knowledge may have increased but human assumptions have remained fairly constant.

There has not been enough time for people to realise how much is now known about human thought and behaviour which could explain 'facts' in a quite different way.

Within the past few years, for instance, scientific and/or medical examination of certain problems have shown them to be very different from what they may seem to be.

Look at this example. A chemical, powdered bleach, was being moved from one place to another. Three workers at the factory concerned were affected by fumes: but no less than SIXTY were taken to hospital, because they had been found to be ill. On arrival, the fifty-seven people were discovered to be suffering from 'mass hysteria', and not sick at all.

In the absence of scientific tests, these people would undoubtedly have been considered poisoned. And nobody could have shifted that belief.

If nearly twenty times as many people can have hysterical illness than were really affected, can you imagine what this means in terms of human beliefs – and what people may think or do as a consequence of such beliefs?

No Better Proof...

Surely there is not, cannot be, any better proof of imagination confused with real experience, than something which happened to me during a tour of holy places in the Middle East.

I was with a party of very devout people belonging to a certain faith, we need not say which one. They were visiting places reputed for their spiritual history and atmosphere, mostly belonging to another religious tradition.

Their guide was new to the job. To help matters, he read in detail from a Michelin guide as we went from place to place. 'Here martyrs were killed ... Here is the site of the cell of a

certain holy monk ... Here such-and-such a person had a holy
vision...'

Every single time the devotees stood respectfully, showing
every sign of appreciating the deep spiritual feelings which
suffused the places...

Then, one day, we were taken to a site where the guide read
out about the horrors which had been perpetrated there, how a
certain tyrant had murdered scores of good men of God, and
how the whole area was reputed to be cursed. All shivered and
eagerly discussed how they felt the 'very essence of evil' sur-
rounding them.

They were still exchanging accounts of their own blood-
curdling experiences at the hotel that evening when the guide
shamefacedly called us together in the foyer and admitted that he
had been mistakenly reading from the wrong page. In spite of
the 'very essence of evil' which all had experienced, we had in
fact been standing in the middle of a burial-place of saints...

Spiritual Teachers

What do spiritual guides actually give to their followers?

People in the Middle East, and also in India, where the
following tale is current – and has been for centuries – have
given the matter some thought. After all, they have had the
opportunity of observing the question.

Three wandering holy men applied to the captain of a ship to
take them from Persia to Africa. 'As you are without money,'
said the Captain, 'what can you contribute to the journey?'

'My perceptions,' said the first, 'for I can see at such a great
distance that things invisible to the ordinary person are plain to
me.'

'My perceptions,' said the second holy man, 'for I can hear
things which are utterly inaudible to anyone else.'

261

The Captain agreed that they might be useful on his voyage, and agreed to take them. To the third he said: 'And what is your speciality?'

The third holy man said, 'I point out irrelevances, so that relevancies might remain.'

'That does not sound very interesting to me,' said the Captain, but he agreed to take the third holy man, out of the kindness of his heart, free of charge.

Since the first two holy men seemed to have greater endowments than the third, the Captain sat with them, repeating their invocations, while the ship sailed southwards, in the hope of gaining spiritual merit thereby.

Suddenly one of the holy ones cried out:

'I can see, away in the farthest distance, the daughter of the King of India, sewing at the window of her palace!'

The second holy man shouted:

'And *I* can hear that she has just dropped her needle, and it has struck the ground below her!'

The third holy man, who had been standing by, looked at the Captain, who was beginning to feel greatly impressed by these miracles. The Captain caught his eye, and remembered that he stood for the observing of irrelevancies.

'I think,' said the Captain to the third holy man, 'that the time has come for me to become *your* disciple, for I nearly failed to learn your lesson: which I need before I can benefit from information about the life of the Princess of India!'

But the ship's first officer, it is understood, was so impressed by the amazing powers of the two holy men that he became their follower. They were able to keep him attached to them for many years through the recitation of their truly astonishing powers.

What do people really want, and what do spiritual guides actually give their followers?

Gold Talks, Not Belief

Q: *Why do Sufis have to illustrate their teachings with actual events, while philosophers and psychologists simply enunciate theirs?*

A: Your assumptions are not entirely true, because some psychologists of the modern type are beginning to demonstrate, though they are still comparatively at the start of their understanding of this kind of instruction, which they often call 'therapy'.

It is necessary to get people to see themselves. To ask them what they are doing and why simply does not work. Have you not heard the anecdote of Jesus, related by Al-Ghazzali about nine hundred years ago, in the Third Book of his *Revival of Religious Sciences?*

JESUS AND THE GOLD

It is reported that a man once accompanied Jesus on a journey. After some time the two came to the bank of a river and sat down to eat. Between them they had three pieces of bread.

Each ate one piece of bread, leaving the third piece. Jesus stood up and went to get water from the river. When he came back, there was no sign of the bread.

'Who has eaten the bread?' he asked his companion.

'I do not know,' said the other man.

They continued on their way until they came upon a deer with two fawns. They caught one of them and ate its meat. Jesus said:

'With the permission of God, rise up!' And the deer was miraculously restored to life.

Then Jesus said:

'Tell me, by Him who did this miracle: what happened to the scrap of bread?'

'I do not know,' his companion answered.

They arrived at another river, and Jesus walked across it on the surface of the water. 'Tell me,' he said, 'By the One who displayed this power, who ate the bread?'

'I do not know,' said the other man.

Eventually they reached a place which was full of earth and stones.

Jesus collected sand and earth and said over it:

'With the permission of God, become gold!'

Immediately the rubbish was transformed into gold.

Jesus divided the metal into three portions. Then he said:

'One portion is for me, another is for you, and the third portion is for him who ate the third portion of that bread.'

His companion answered:

'It was I who ate it!'

So Jesus said to him:

'Then *all* three parts of the gold are for you.'

And he went on his way.

Now two other men had seen the gold, and they decided to steal it, after killing its owner. They made friends with him and suggested that he should go to the nearby town to buy food. He agreed, because his own idea was to poison them. He bought bread and put poison in it.

When he returned to the others, they fell upon him and killed him. Then they ate the poisoned bread, and they, too, died.

Jesus passed that way again, with some of his companions, saw what had happened to the three men, and said: 'This is the world, so fear the world.'

The Moth and The Soot

Q: *People talk about psychological and spiritual evolution. Is this misleading? If physical forms change in response to the interplay between inner and outer forces, how can this happen in more subtle areas? It seems to me as if we are talking about brain-washing and indoctrination if we work on the human mind in a way analogous to evolutionary processes.*

A: This is an interesting question, because it enables us to explain something which pin-points the *difference* (not the similarity) between mind-shaping and Sufi learning.

Let us begin with the currently very popular true story of the light grey *Biston betularia*, a common moth of Manchester, in England.

The body and wing colours of this insect were grey, a form of protective camouflage which enabled it to merge with its woodland surroundings and escape the birds which would otherwise have killed it. Some time after the great nineteenth-century industrialisation of Manchester, such was the prevalence of soot deposits on many surfaces that the moths began to show up against the grime. It was then observed that, by the interplay of its genetic characteristics with the darker environment, the moths began to grow darker. After half a century, the overwhelming majority of those born were black. This development also took place in many other industrialised areas throughout the world.

Now, in the social field, something very similar occurs. Put someone among people who wear different clothes, sing certain songs, carry out unfamiliar practices, and what do you get? This individual will either reject the new environment, will remain unaffected or will imitate it. It will depend upon where he (or she) finds most comfort and safety. In the case of people with a well-defined idea of their own identity, and with a community with which to identify, you may expect rejection or no effect. Among those who are uncertain, estranged, fearful, you will be most likely to find imitation. This 'convert' will have found what is imagined to be safety.

Intake

Q: *I am really revolted by all the occult mumbo-jumbo that I hear; and I really do dislike most of the people whom I meet who are involved in it. I think that something should be done about this contamination of our society. What are you doing about it?*

A: The effects of spurious systems and crazy ideas on society are not good. Many of the people who follow them are in some way sick, and therefore, like perhaps lepers, they can be revolting. Now, if something is revolting and the people who suffer from or through it are unpleasant, what does one do about it?

Leprosy needs understanding and treatment. In the case of the imaginedly spiritual people who are really only sick from an intake of bad ideas, we have to understand, first, that this is their condition.

Now there is the matter of treatment. The circulation of appropriate ideas is one of the therapies. There are others, and they are being applied by experts. Disliking something will not help to alleviate it. And remedies are only to be applied by those who know which remedies are indicated.

So far as the ordinary person is concerned, only 'hygiene' can be attempted: being normal oneself, being sympathetic to the sufferer, and helping to make basic and healthy ideas widely known.

Earth, Sun, Black Cats . . .

Q: *There has been a flood of new information released in the past few decades by Sufi sources in the East. A lot of this, although clearly authoritative, contradicts much-cherished ideas about Sufis and Sufism which have been held by writers and others for a large number of years.*

266

I have been a member of various supposedly Sufic groups which have actually dissolved because they were only held together by such practices as rhythmic movements, now seen to be prescriptive and not to be prescribed for everyone; by reading certain books, now revealed as tailored for past not present audiences; by hierarchies now shown to be mistaken in their assumptions about the Sufis.

My question is, simply: surely it would have been better for some people to be interested in and getting something from these ideas and practices, rather than providing materials which have robbed them of their chief support and interest in life?

A: You may answer the question yourself, if you transpose it into another framework: or, rather, a more familiar one. Many people felt that the bottom had dropped out of their world when it was revealed to them that the Earth was a satellite of the Sun, and not the other way about. Is that an argument for halting the spread of authentic information or education? If people might feel cheated if lucky black cats were found not to be lucky at all, or might not seek medication, should we leave them with their superstition? Your question assumes that false information is harmless, and can even do good. But suppressing truth in the way which you suggest can also prevent the useful action of truth itself. Is this what you want?

Warning

Narrow-minded religious enthusiasts and fanatics have always opposed Sufis, even though it is the Sufis who have done as much as anyone in maintaining spirituality.

This is well illustrated by a story. A humourless and sour religious pedant was coming out of his house one day, when he saw a Sufi standing in the street.

'Dog!' shouted the Sufi.

The cleric shook his fist at him, and cursed all Sufis.

At that moment the dog which he was being warned against rushed forward and bit him . . .

Travelling Tales

Due to a typing error, a tale which I had made up myself was described in one of my books as an ancient traditional narrative. This attribution, no doubt, gave some people the idea that if they copied it, and paraphrased, they could always say that they had obtained it from some other source than my work, or even from the same source as I did.

Within four years, the story had appeared as their own 'invention' in the books of two widely revered 'spiritual teachers' (from whom I extracted compensation for violation of copyright); was rewritten and published as a science-fiction story; was analysed and determined to be a 'nature myth dating from prehistoric times' by one scholar; was recited on the radio as having been heard in Asia from a monk by a traveller and seeker-after-truth, and had been worked up into a whole book by an enterprising and well-known contemporary author.

Evidences of its diffusion still come in. Not long ago I was sitting in a large publisher's office, when he said: 'Now the kind of story you ought to write is this, which my daughter heard in a sermon at college,' and he told me my own story. I doubt, however, whether I shall ever have a more full-circle experience with the tale than what happened just two weeks ago. Someone wrote to me, enclosing a manuscript of his own composition, asking for my help in getting it published. It was my own story, in a form which looked as if it had been read and then recited to someone, who had taken it down and rewritten it, imagining this process, perhaps, to constitute his 'own composition' . . .

Set against that, even the long disquisitions by literary critics on my story as 'revealing the ingenuity and the mind' of the novelist who made a book of it, seem less hilarious.

Miracles . . .

Q: *I know that you deride miracles, and seem to put them down to imposture. But why should we not accept that miracles do occur, especially when we have the testimony of many reputable people that they have happened?*

A: I am not denying that miracles occur. What you have to do is to be very sure that something *is* a miracle, and not the product of an imposture or a misunderstanding.

Q: *I don't see how a miracle can be seen as such through a misunderstanding...*

A: Don't you? I'll tell you about one in which I was, peripherally, involved. I was contacted by a multi-millionaire who was an adherent of a certain guru. He was a hard-headed financier who was converted by 'personally witnessing a miracle'.

The miracle took place at a gambling casino. A man had lost a fortune and went outside, fired a shot, fell to the ground covered in blood. While an ambulance was called, the manager of the casino, to prevent a scandal, put a large sum of money in the pockets of the recumbent man.

The financier was with a small group of people accompanying this guru, who happened to be passing. He said to the guru: 'If you are a miracle-man, give that corpse life again.' The guru raised his hands to the heavens – and the 'dead' man rose, wiped off some of the blood, and walked away!

Now the guru was perhaps sincere, wanted to revive the dead man and was convinced that he had in fact done so. The disciple was sincere, and was convinced that the dead man had been revived. After all, it was he who had asked for the miracle – the thing hadn't been staged by the guru!

So what was the answer? Simple. The 'dead' man had heard that when anyone committed suicide near that casino, the management always filled the deceased's pockets with money, so as not to be implicated as a cause of his death. The 'suicide' had faked his own death, in order to get the reward, which he did. There was an imposture, right enough, and that was it. But the misunderstanding was on the part of the guru and his disciple. That is what I mean.

Names

Some – but of course not all – mullas are really stupid. And such people, as is their way, become infuriated when they are called fools.

Forgetting this, a Dervish one day, in conversation with a certain Mulla, called him an ass.

The Dervish was immediately taken before the local judge, accused of defamation.

He admitted the offence, and the Judge said, 'You are let off with a caution, this time. But don't do it again.'

'Respected Judge,' said the Dervish, 'would it be all right if I were to call an ass a Mulla?'

'That would depend,' said the Judge, 'whether any Mulla laid a complaint before me about it. You had better go on your way, and watch your step.'

'Thank you, Judge,' answered the Dervish. To the Mulla he said, 'And I can see that you are a Mulla, Mulla!'

Missionaries

Q: *What is your opinion about missionaries and about people changing their religions? If everyone needs a basis of belief and behaviour to stabilise his ordinary life before reaching for higher understanding, as is the Sufi principle, what is the difference between the various forms of belief and action which one can choose?*

A: As the Sufis have pointed out for centuries, it is not a matter of changing your religion: it is a question of whether you really have got a religion at all. You may call yourself a member of a certain religion, while in your thoughts and actions you are an infidel or idol-worshipper.

A Christian missionary from India told me recently that he had lived and taught there for many years. One day he said to an Indian:

'Would you not like to become a Christian?'

'Yes, indeed,' said the Indian, 'providing only that you yourself truly become one at the same time. I have heard you preach, and I have watched what you do, and I cannot agree that you are yet a Christian.'

The missionary said that he was so ashamed that he left the country and 'had never dared to call himself a witness to Christianity again'.

I believe that your question can be answered so as to have reality, only when we are agreed whether we are talking about believers or propagandists. Believers are those who act in accordance with their alleged beliefs, propagandists are those who tell others what to believe or to do.

Rice

India has been celebrated for generations as a great missionary field. Various denominations have competed for the souls of the starving millions.

The tale is told of how one dervish, a penniless wanderer, became what is known as a Rice Christian.

'I went to the Protestants, and they offered me a sack of rice, a "rehabilitation allowance", if I joined them. Then I visited the Catholics, and told them what had happened. They suggested that they might be able to provide double: two sacks of rice.'

One of his fellow-dervishes, to whom he was reporting his adventures, interrupted: 'But I understand that you accepted the Protestant offer. Why was that?'

'Because it was obvious to me that the Protestants were less corrupt!'

SECTION VIII

SECTION VII

Sacred Rituals, Dances, Ceremonials

If you want to cause a certain effect, you use whatever you have. A light can be made to 'vary in colour' by interposing between the source and the eye a coloured filter. Deprived of suitable light-sources and coloured filters, one may try to approximate or duplicate these effects by other means. If you can't find suitable technical apparatus, you may, in order to let a person see a certain range of colours, dress up twenty people in coloured costumes, covered with designs perhaps, and have them move across the range of vision of that person. You would perhaps then have a 'ritual dance'. Anthropologists would come along, note affinities with, shall we say, peacock colouring, and conclude that this is connected with a peacock cult. You might, for functional reasons, build this series of movements into a dramatic performance. The participants might be unconscious of the light-impact function which they fulfilled, for themselves or others. They would imagine all sorts of roles for themselves (like being great actors) based on what they thought they understood of the medium in which they were working. How would they know that their ideas were secondary to the original intention?

What was known as the Doctrine of Signatures (like affects like), now much derided by science, is still with us. It takes a slightly different form, that is all. In this form, the modern researcher assumes that because something looks like, shall we say, a fertility dance, it must be a fertility dance. That there is an earlier or deeper meaning, or a more subtle reality of which this is a grotesque simulacrum, he is not yet cultivated enough to perceive.

'Togetherness'

Nothing highlights the non-spiritual but very social character of many relationships so much as the need for contact, association, relationship. People feel that they should be near someone of sanctity; that they should impart their blessing to others; that some sort of frequent or constant contact has some spiritual dimension.

The fact is, of course, that there are times and places where it is more important for people with mutual spiritual interests to be apart rather than together. Those who understand this and have experienced it are the spiritual people. Those who have not, are part of a sociological phenomenon: herding.

The origin of this desire to herd together is not far to seek. Those who lead the herding are inadequate: they feel doubts and discomforts when they are not in contact with like-minded people. Those who flock at the behest of the 'herders' are equally inadequate. But, in their case, there is more hope that they can be taken to a position where they no longer have to be dependent upon others; where their inadequacy is cured, rather than being reaffirmed by herding.

Deterioration of Costumes

Being asked a question about matters which are susceptible of superficial explanation, and being asked to choose one or other alternative provided by the questioner, has curious facets to it.

Someone asks: 'Is it a good idea to adopt the dress of certain people, in order to create atmosphere in oneself or others?'

I ask what this means.

'Well, the sacerdotal vestments of priesthoods are always

important, and contain symbols which perpetuate certain beliefs or feelings . . .' And a lot more besides, all leading to the assumption which is accepted without hesitation that robes, costumes and so on, are either mimes or symbols of something, or have a content which is to be explained in historical terms. Now this may be true in superficial or vitiated traditions. A man may wear a lion-skin in order to make himself appear or feel brave. He may wear one for another, more fundamental purpose. But within one generation or less, imitators are wearing the skin because it makes them feel or look brave, or because they or others have assumed that this was the original function of this garb. As an instance, I may wear a lion-skin because I like lion-skins, or because dogs are afraid of the smell of lions, and I want to frighten dogs. Someone comes up to me and asks: 'You are wearing that lion-skin because you belong to the lion-society, I suppose?' I say, 'Yes' – and the tradition is established. Many other possibilities in this sort of direction will present themselves to you, if you think a little.

Since the majority of people cannot perceive any real, objective or absolute meaning in dress, costume, regalia, ceremony and so on, they assume that they can interpret it through (1) history; (2) associations or (3) what they are told by people who may have no reason in the world to pander to their curiosity.

I will add no more than that if you are looking for a meaning of clothing and so on in association or impact, you are operating on a level and in a field which is so limited, crude and blind that you should stay there, and not concern yourself with the inner things of life. This crude interest belongs in the field of miscellaneous information, sheer curiosity, emotional influencing and crude admiration-impact.

These are forms of savagery, even though they are found in the shape of alleged refinement. The esoteric function of clothes, regalia and ceremony belong to a sphere completely removed from any familiar one.

To be Present

Q: *What is the use of attending meetings at which one cannot understand some of the matters discussed? Is there any advantage in being a member of a study group if one is not interested in theory or in explanations in words?*

A: The answer to both of these questions is the same. It lies in the fact that all these materials have many levels of action. Something which is expressed in philosophical form, or in complicated terminology, also has another side. This side can operate when one is not following what appears to be the main trend of the thought.

The rest of the answer is that the group is so formed as to help make possible a communication between members, between the teaching and the individuals, and between the teacher and the students by a process of which the words are only one of the outer shapes.

That is why, in more traditional terminology, we always say: Simply to be present at an assembly of wisdom is more effective than any other study, practical or otherwise, carried out outside of one.

Further, attendance at a teaching session is the manner in which people, through an inner development and not through using words, arrive at the stage where it is possible to achieve direct communication with them.

These peculiarities of real teaching groups, and not any need nor desire to group people for ease of lecturing, lie at the root of the group system. This is why all true teaching is at least partly carried out in large and small groups. It is for the sake of improving this system still further that sub-groups are formed.

The Mystics

Q: *How do people of various religious attitudes differ in their usage of money?*

A: This is too big a question for a short answer. There is one version, however, which I have heard as descriptive of some of their transactions:

They say that a man died and his friends, a group of mystics, gathered around his open coffin at the funeral. In that country, the custom was to put money into the coffin.

It is related that:

> The Yogi, who charged for his lessons, put in $5;
> The Monk, who had his monastery's charity-box to rely on, put in $10;
> The Sufi, who did not believe in waste, took the $15 out and put in a cheque for $100;
> The Zen master was the undertaker. He took the cheque and cashed it!

But, seriously, I do not take this as a pattern of how such people really do behave. The pattern which I see in the story is that the first man is the one who puts in something from what he has earned; the second is one who adds to it from what he has been given; the third is he who is able to make use of what others waste; and the last man is the one who takes away what is not intended for him. And what is put in, or taken out is, in this analogy, *baraka*, spiritual force. You should only take the labels – the Monk, Zen master, and so on – as irrelevant additions to make the story more colourful.

Yoga and Illumination

Q: *Some people say that Yoga is not connected with religion, while reference books say that it is Hindu mysticism. Can people become illuminated if they carry out Yogic exercises?*

A: There is a story current in India itself:

A man who had been carrying out Yogic practices and meditations, diet and so on in India decided that he needed real knowledge. He travelled to remote places and after many years found an ascetic in a forest and became his disciple.

Eventually he glimpsed Reality and realised that all seeming reality was an illusion. He cried out:

'I have been illuminated. This is true Yoga!'

The guru answered:

'Yes, you seem to be making progress, even if you are a little impetuous. But tell me – what is this "Yoga" you talk about?'

The 'Work Situation'

As in an ordinary enterprise, the 'Work' situation has certain minimum requirements. If we want to make a table, we must have wood, nails, work and expertise.

Supposing that a man wanted to furnish a house, and had materials and helpers, but house-furnishing was locally unknown. Suppose, again, that it was either inconvenient or impossible for him to explain the whole project to the people who were with him. The people are willing to help him, and he conveys to them that they, too, will benefit. What does this man do?

He collects, or has collected, the materials. These he adapts or has adapted to the purpose which he has in mind. When four legs and a table top are ready, he makes marks on the wood and says 'Drive in nails here, fixing these pieces of wood to this other piece of wood.' When this has been done, the table is complete. It is then seen to be an object whose use can be demonstrated. Its relationship with other objects, such as chairs, also becomes apparent in one of several ways.

Our man is a carpenter, whose objective is not carpentry but furnishing a house. The only way to do it in this case is to have his assistants work as carpenters.

To the beginner, the whole enterprise is confusing and difficult to understand. When he is told to take a piece of wood and smooth it, he does not see the point. He wants to see the table first. He has to be assured that in smoothing his piece of wood (which is to become something in the end), he is taking part in a work. He is in fact, in a work-situation; but wants it described to him. Describing might lose the time available for the completion of the whole task.

When a comprehensive activity is being organised, it is inevitable that the would-be carpenters work in the dark. The great Afghan teacher Rumi, once used this allegory. When a tent is being made, he said, some work on the ropes, some on the panels, some on the pegs. For each, his task is important. When each has completed his task, lo, a tent.

In our task we must remember always that we are in a work-situation. Individual comprehension of its meaning is less important – indeed, less possible – than the effective carrying out of tasks. It is to provide a plausible or even a mysterious format for the carrying out of work of this kind that innumerable organisations have come into being, of which only the husks remain.

To be lured by appearances is a bad sign in a person.

The 'Work' Situation II

The human mind, when it does become attuned to the possibility of purposeful action or organisation, tends to start to follow the groove of automatism. People see, for instance, someone doing something, and they all want to do it. They see someone rich – they all want to be rich. Or they see someone respected – they want to be respected. It is this factor which has made it possible for people to function in the mass as cogs in a machine, content very often to be slaves while they can maintain the illusion that they can move upwards in a pyramid.

Similarly, in a 'Work' situation, people will assume that if furniture is to be made, everyone has to become a master carpenter. The truth is more effective, more complex, more important than this.

What happens is that in an activity, as it progresses, some will find their expression and role in some aspects of the activity, some in others. Some will find that they have to acquire a certain expertise; others, other faculties.

There has been a perennial confusion due to the fact that the ordinary person prefers to believe that life is a road along which everyone is going, and that everyone must reach – or should reach – a similar stage and go through a similar stage. Again, the truth is much more refined than this. It may be said that people who think in this manner are automatically showing the absence, at least for the moment, of a capacity to think in inner terms. They merely think on superficialities generalised from experience in very ordinary, irrelevant fields.

In actual fact, the work-situation is closely allied with what we call 'function'. Function here means that you can only progress to the extent of which you are capable, and to the extent needed by the work, at any given time.

Some people are content to work, and expect to be told what to do. This they consider to be enough. They have to learn that submission to a work is not correct if it is done without a certain attunement. Without this, they can even be useless to the work.

Others demand a certain amount of knowledge as their price for being prepared to do any more. These fall an easy prey to people who specialise in providing a mere *sensation* of experience. Such people might, at the time in question, have first to retrieve the capacity to be passive in a special sort of way. Both have to earn something. They cannot assume that their assessment of the situation is right.

Ancient Monuments

Q: *What can we get out of the temples and wonders of the past?*

A: There are several things. Most people know next to nothing about these things. It is necessary to realise, if the individual is to benefit by the great works of the past, that they contain valuable elements greatly in excess of what the 'barbarian' mind can perceive. In order to convey something of this, I will point out factors which are probably strange to you. Temples and monuments – of China, Greece, Egypt, South America – had many functions. The least of these was to impress, to create 'atmosphere', to play upon the emotions. Because these places were used for certain purposes, they acquired a quality which in some cases still remains with them. Only those who understand the Work can make use of this substance, which is sometimes called *Baraka*.

Casual and fixated people who think that they have experienced the wonders of these places are generally only 'sophisticated barbarians'. They have been emotionally moved by the Taj Mahal in the moonlight. Or they are the victims of 'conditioning', have been told so much about the shrine of the Buddha's Tooth that they feel, entirely subjectively, that they have experienced something transcendental when they went there. With such people we are dealing only with emotionalists.

The dimensions and siting of certain buildings is another matter. A building is sited in a certain way for many reasons, of which the aesthetic effect may be considered to be the least important for our viewpoint. Again, the dynamic function in our sense of a building may have been discharged, as in the case of most Greek buildings, many centuries ago. It has been superseded by something else, elsewhere, suited to another time. What remains is the shell, which provides the emotional, intellectual, mathematical or other stimuli which mislead the refined barbarian into thinking of it as a wonder. It may, however, now have no meaningful function for the Work and as far as Wisdom is concerned.

These very important matters are seldom suspected by those who cannot perceive them directly.

Those who have only heard about them have too often spread imaginative and inaccurate theories, further misleading people.

Special Meanings in Service

Q: *Can you comment upon the principle of service as applied to human development?*

A: Here is an aspect of it:–

One person may serve another because he or she has to do so. This 'having to do so' generally stems from selfishness. '*I* am doing this because *I* will get something out of it.' The motive remains selfish even if the thing aimed for is acquiring merit, or going to Heaven, as the religious context has it. If service of another or of a cause is done because there is a need for this service, this too can be undesirable. In modern psychological terms such motivation may be called masochistic.

What is the service which is really performed, not from fear of punishment, nor of desire for reward, nor for temporary pleasure? In our tradition such people as Rabia and Hujwiri have stressed the fact that there is a finer conception which must be acquired. When this is operating, and not before, the individual and the effort as a whole is benefitting by the service correctly.

In general, people assume that service *can* only fall into one of the three categories which I have mentioned. In making this assumption they are defeating the possibilities of refinement in perception, mistaking an incoherent mass of material which they do not analyze for something which cannot be analyzed further than the crude sorting which they themselves have applied to it.

What is the result?

The result includes:-

1. For the psychologist, a faulty, partial and therefore limited understanding of human thought and actions;
2. For the outside observer, assumptions that all service is merely mechanical or emotional and depends upon the domination of one person by another, or of a corporate body by an individual, or of an individual by a corporate body; or of a person by an idea;
3. For the person who is involved in religious, political or other activities, an attachment – a blind attachment – to people and things or even to ideas, without any *real* conception of correct duty or the developmental function of 'service'.

How is real 'service' learned? Not from people who merely propagate mechanical or emotional service, which are in fact servitude. These include the majority of spiritual and other teachers, so-called, because they themselves have not broken through the outer, crude conception of service. They perpetuate servitude and demand it, sometimes actually thinking that it really is a part of man's devotional duty. It is learned only from such people as can see why, where and what service of an individual and a group does, can and should mean in any given situation, such situations being seen as a part of the whole of the human evolutionary situation.

Symbols, especially the Enneagon

Q: *I have been trying to trace the usage and meanings of symbolic figures for many years, and I am particularly interested in the nine-pointed figure, or enneagram. Why is it that I have not been able to find a version of this figure in occult and similar literature? And what, if anything, does it signify?*

A: You have asked a great many questions in two seemingly short ones, opening a large question which I shall answer in as fragmentary way as it is put, for we have not time nor opportunity to deal fully with the matter here, as you will soon see. Memorise, therefore, this information, for it is of the greatest importance. The Enneagon, or nine-pointed figure, is by no means unknown in 'occult' circles in the West. I remember a drawing of it from a manuscript in the Library of Grenoble, for instance. You have not looked far enough. It came to Europe with the Kabbala, based on the quite well-known mathematical work of the ancient Arab philosopher Ibn el-Laith, and this fact is mentioned in the *Legacy of Islam*, in the chapter on mathematics. It was thus by no means unknown in medieval circles.

But you should know something very important; that the nine-pointed figure is represented in many ways. One example is the ninefold decoration in the form of a door in the Tour Hasan (Hasan Tower) near Rabat, in Morocco. Another element most vital to remember is that the diagram and that which it represents is conveyed by one further remove in drawing. For instance, the eight-fold diagram which contains an extra space (made by superimposing two squares) in the centre is used as a code-form for the enneagon. It is, however, only if you are in harmony with the meaning of the enneagon (and the great diagram of which it is a part) that you can know what you are looking for. Merely to seek familiar representations for an enneagon which you can recognise by its shape as your 'enneagram' is ridiculous. Numbers and diagrams are meaningful to us only when we are associated with their reality. Otherwise it is like looking for, say, the idea or 'being' of a seed when you have only seen a grape-seed, and thinking that there is no 'seed' unless you see one of those.

Origin of Planetary Symbols

Q: *I have been a student of astrology for many years. Can you tell me anything about the origin of the signs used for the planets? It seems to be a mystery, but I think that they must have got their present forms during the Middle Ages. People have tried to relate them to Greek and other shapes, but not with complete success.*

A: The Sun and Moon are shown by pictograms – a disc and crescent respectively. Mars is a stylized form of the Arabic word (*Mirikh* – Mars), written upside down, probably through faulty transcription of Arabic manuscripts into Latin ones. Mercury is a stylized form of the Arabic word *Utarid*, (Mercury) standing sideways; the sign for Venus is the word Venus in Arabic, abbreviated into its initial and stylized. The same is true of the sign which you use for Saturn. The symbol for Jupiter is a shorthand contraction for the Arabic word for Jupiter – *Mush-tari*. No special significance attaches to any of these forms, though later pious imitators have invested them with some sort of sanctity – quite a common phenomenon of dereliction where something of unknown origin is concerned. As with many relics of the Middle Ages, only a fair knowledge of Arabic letters is enough to show the meaning; they were no part, for instance, of any code-system.

About Recognition . . .

I once saw a group of people who were camping in the country-side. There were six of them and, every morning and evening, one – and only one – was plagued by wild bees, which circled him as if looking for a flower in his hair or on his face.

Why did the bees not approach the five other people? Something about this man attracted them. It took a little time to find out. The bees were sensing the flower perfume which was in this man's shaving soap, because the scent was a genuine flower essence, and not a synthetic!

The bees knew real scent, but the other campers – who also used various fragrances – did not. To the humans, all the scents seemed equally 'genuine', equally perfumes. But the bees were the experts: their attunement was to the real thing, the attune-ment of the people was to the false.

It is true that the bees were not perfect, not to be preferred in any comprehensive way to the human beings; they could have been categorised, for example, as foolish, since they were unable to realise that scent did not have to mean flowers.

But if it had been necessary to distinguish between real and synthetic scent, it would have been useful to use bees, and useless to use humans.

For the humans, it may be argued, the synthetic sufficed for their purposes. Quite so. But if we look at the anecdote as an allegory, we must admit that the Real requires something which can perceive the Real. Even if the synthetic can be of some use. It all depends upon what we are really seeking.

Secret Meaning of Reincarnation Theory

'The Soul passes, from the Deity, into the gross material world. It then has to return to the Godhead by successively passing through six phases:

> Angels
> Demons
> Men
> Quadrupeds
> Birds
> Reptiles.'

This statement, found in traditional teachings, has been assumed by literalists and those without insight, to mean that members of the human race may 'inhabit' the literal physical body of one of the above-named six creatures.

The teaching, however, is in fact saying:

> The human being has six soul-states. Each one is symbolised by one of these creatures. (Although given in descending order, the Soul may proceed from any of these states to its perfection).

The debasement of the figurative, illustrative, into the literal is one of the most common degenerations of human thought. (Equally, of course, ignorant thought may achieve the opposite: the belief that the literal is only figurative).

The purpose of a real (enlightened) teacher is to reveal when necessary the true 'technology' and meaning of symbols. The greatest religious teachers have, therefore, always been known as 'reformers', rather than as creative innovators.

(The meaning of 'absorption into the Divinity, from which the Teacher returns in human shape to purge errors and teach the Path', is really quite clear, seen in the light of the foregoing).

Laboratory Experiments

Q: *How is it that laboratory experiments with extra-sensory perception do not seem to work, even though there is evidence that it does occur outside of the staged situation?*

A: For a similar reason to that which applies when you give boiling water to a hen, to make it 'lay boiled eggs'. The person who already knows how and why these things work will not attempt to structure the experiment in the way which is adopted by the ordinary experimenter.

We could almost believe that a certain old English rhyme was written to allude to this approach:

> Simple Simon went a-fishing
> For to catch a whale;
> But all the water he had got
> Was in his mother's pail.

Studying Here and Now

Q: *Might I know a major problem in making contact with the desires of the people? Is there a great division between what they need and what they think that they want?*

A: There is indeed a great division between what people think they need and what they actually do need. I have often referred to this. A major problem I would like at this moment to stress is, however, this one:-

We are living at the moment in a realm of distortion. This means that, in acting as one really should, one has to adapt, almost, the sense of direction to make use of what materials there are here and now. In other words, it is not true to say that there is a consistent, continuous line of progress between how the ordinary man thinks and how he could think. He has to refine this thought, and he has to do it without throwing overboard the present way of thinking, to which most of his life is geared. The result is that he must develop what seems to him to be new organs of perception.

You may call this life a parody of the 'life' towards which man should be aiming. The parody must be played out, like a play. And, also, the 'other life' or field of correct alignment or orientation, must be made a goal of endeavour.

There has never been any other true objective available to planetary man.

Dangers of Automatic Reasoning

Q: *I feel that if I carry on with my self-development long enough, I will arrive at the goal. I believe that the method is through application: like Bruce and the spider. I have studied a great many ways, and I see a general trend which I am sure I will be able to follow in the widest sense. I also believe that a person must find the way by himself. Can you comment on this?*

A: I not only can, but must. What you say about what you feel presupposes that you know certain things. One of these is that you are a stabilised individuality capable of making such a journey. Passing over this for the moment, it is necessary to say that there are other naive assumptions in the question. One of these preconceptions is a grave one. It is this:

You assume that what holds good for simpler (less complex) undertakings also holds good here. That is to say, you are familiar with effort and dedication. You have to walk, say, thirty miles. You tell yourself that providing you have enough discipline and enough experience (have walked to goals before) that you will get there. This feeling, by the mental phenomenon of 'carry-over' makes you apply the same reasoning automatically to your present case. It is less than adequate. In ordinary and familiar undertakings you have already done something of the kind before. You know what you are doing, in other words. In this case you do not. For example, you only talk about the general common denominators in this kind of quest. But you show no awareness of the relative importance of these factors.

In walking a distance, the problem is to take paces and walk a certain distance. In our field there are more dimensions. It is as if you had to walk one pace, skip seven and a half, then sing a song. You have no conception of this at all. This is the danger of automatic assumptions. The phrase that 'a man must find the way by himself' is good enough. But it does not mean to you what it should mean. You have to put in effort, but not blind effort.

You must find the way out of the wood, but in order to do so before you die of old age or give up through confusion, you must have something to go on. What you have to go on at the moment is assumptions which are not useful. We admire a man who wants to find his way through a trackless waste by himself. We do not admire him if he has no means, food, nor perceptions.

The method is by application: but this must be purposeful application. Do you know HOW? What you are saying in your statement is: 'I want to get up a mountain. I can lift my boots by the straps. Therefore I will put on the boots, grasp the straps, and pull myself up'. Try it sometime. To get anywhere you must have landmarks or instruments to arrive by observation or dead reckoning. You have neither of these. What you do have is a comfortable and tantalising sense of mystery. As yet you have no orientation. But you do not know it. Few people will tell you, either; for that is the way things are.

How I See You

Q: *I visualise you like one of the great teachers of antiquity, as you sit there surrounded by people and pointing out the stupidities of their opinions. There is some sort of uncanny flavour that attracts me. Is this the pull that makes people gather around every real teacher?*

A: If you were to see me also as someone who has walked into a garden where people can't grow potatoes because weeds are strangling the plants; and who walks among the plants plucking out the weeds; and who may or may not have something further to contribute, after the weeds have been plucked; but who has to do certain things in a certain order, even though impatient people are crying for potatoes when the plants have not even grown strong – then you might benefit me and my work.

'Warm your hands by the camp-fire of the dervishes' by all means: that is the minimum of their hospitality. But have your pound of steak ready for cooking on that fire, so that you may be fed. Remember the Sufi aphorism: 'he who tastes, knows'. You must eat those sausages, however attractive merely thinking about the general possibility of a meal may be to a hungry man or woman.

Dervishes on journeys gather around their fire for warmth and food. They may talk, sing and dance. Anyone who comes for warmth receives it. Similarly with other elements.

But only a moth dashes itself unreasoningly against a flame, again and again, until it dies.

Not For You

A Mulla who had not lived a good life – he was a hypocrite who always dressed as an ascetic – died and found himself in the nether regions.

A demon came up to him, looked briefly at a list, and then said, 'You are a 90% sinner, not a 100% one. That means that you get a choice of torments.'

'What does that mean?' asked the Mulla.

'It means,' said the demon, 'that you follow me and we inspect the various tortures and you take your pick.'

So saying, he led the Mulla down a long corridor, with doors on both sides. In the first room, whose door was opened, people were being fed red-hot coals; in the second, they were being branded with white-hot irons; in the third they were being torn limb from limb, and so on. 'There is bound to be a better one, somewhere,' thought the Mulla, and so he declined each and every one of the torments.

Then the demon opened another door. Inside *that* room the Mulla saw a man dressed as an ascetic, sitting at a table, gobbling down delicious-looking strawberries.

'Yes! That's the one! That's the torment I want!' shouted the Mulla.

The demon took out his list and consulted it. 'Room 599... No, I'm sorry, there has been a mistake. That's the room reserved for eternally torturing the strawberries!'

Preconditions . . .

Assumptions, the invisible contract: what a field for human study!

I see in a recently published book that the writer, a journalist, believes that newspaper and magazine offices are natural magnets for every kind of crazy person, people seeking attention, people who are convinced that they should be seen, talked to, heard, given attention.

But I have been told the same by local government officers,

especially those cowering behind the bandit-proof mesh in the social services offices. Bank managers and people working for building societies, too, think that they are singled out for special attention by people who, at any moment, may be irritated, violent even. 'Every shopkeeper,' a man told me the other day, 'has regular visitors who demand time, talk, and confirmation of their theories, loans, gifts, anything they can think of. Now I see why,' this director of a chain-store empire continued, 'why they have guards and police outside Buckingham Palace.'

It is the preconditions which interest me most. I am looking at a letter from a lady who both thinks that I know everything about the past, present and future – and also insists on seeing me to discuss her problems. Since long experience – not prescience – tells me that there would be no value in such a meeting, for either of us, I have written to her several times declining the honour. Still she insists.

What is striking about this lady – and many hundreds of others who follow the same behaviour-pattern – is that she will not accept the statements of the 'man who knows everything'. Last time she wrote, I, perhaps foolhardily, answered: 'Since I know everything, I know that a meeting would not benefit us.'

Never underestimate the ingenuity of the attention-seeker. Her reply says, 'I know that you know everything. But I also know that your refusing to see me is just a test of my dedication.'

When the attention-seekers started to come to the house, ringing the bell, pretending to be gas-meter men, calling out that I had better see them or they would make trouble for me, I sought the advice of my local police officer.

Would he think that I was some kind of crook, artfully laying down a story so that when some genuinely aggrieved unfortunate next assailed me I would be able to invoke his aid? Prescience did not tell me. So I went to his house, making no assumptions.

When I had poured out my story, he looked at me with infinite sadness. 'Well, Sir, all I have to say is that I would rather have *your* job than mine. Twenty people in three months? Why, I've had more than that since I opened shop this morning. And the doctor just opposite, he says that hardly anyone who calls or phones is really ill. They need attention, that's all . . .'

It's just as well I don't seem to need attention so urgently as to think that all these visitors are coming to see me because I am a man of great importance or something . . .

Telepathy

Q: *How can one develop telepathic powers, or how does one read the thoughts of others or perceive the future?*

A: The requirements for this are extremely well known among the Sufis. The question is generally not how to do it, but whether one can.

The human being is already perceptive of the things you mention. To say that he or she 'develops the capacity' is like saying that the Sun revolves around the Earth: it only seems like that.

The fact is that emotional tension, including that which is set up by wanting something, prevents the operation of these capacities.

Q: *Then why is it so often reported that people at times of emotional tension gain paranormal insights, and why do scientists, who are detached, not get results?*

A: People at times of emotional tension *never* have paranormal insights. They only get them (if they do under these circumstances) when they have worn out their emotional state, by over-running their emotions. At this point, they are temporarily without desires, and get flashes of perception. As for scientists, they get few or no results precisely because they are *not* detached: they want to produce results. This is important to them.

And so they inhibit the appearance of the function, and disturb it in others. Their experimental subjects, too, are similarly in states of emotion which have the same effect.

The process is described in the last book of Rumi's *Masnavi*, where he speaks of man's mind as a canal filled with rubbish, preventing him from reading thoughts. When the water has been cleansed, the reflection of what is beyond appears in it. 'Indulgence,' he says, 'is the simile of the pouring of defilements into the water.' These include fantasies and delusions, occupy the mind and prevent it from working properly.

Curiosity

A man came to see us today, bearing a large bundle of letters.

He explained that, for want of anything better to do, he had put a long-running advertisement in several papers and journals.

The words were: 'Thrilling Sufi Secrets! Write Box No...'

The response was huge. What interested him most, however, was the fact that not only a large number of eminent Hindu, Jewish, Christian and Moslem divines and prelates had sought 'secrets': but several figures claiming to be Sufi masters and teachers also – it seemed – needed to update their knowledge!

'If they are all trying to learn from me, and if I know nothing – I wonder what they *do* know themselves...' he said.

SECTION IX

A Little Anthropology

If you were to be asked, 'Which would you prefer – a little anthropology or a million dollars?' most people would, surely, say that they would take the million. Sociologists and others are nowadays aware, of course, that what people say is not necessarily what they would do: and a number of millions of dollars are not available for the test. But it has been noted that, when asked which newspaper they read, so many people said 'The Times' that had they spoken the truth, that newspaper would be selling – on extrapolated statistical analysis – several million copies every day. So it is not really unsafe to assume that most people would prefer the million to the anthropology, anthropologists included. Those who would not, might not only be statistically unimportant: they might very well be rather abnormal as well . . .

Why the choice of the money and not the learning? We have to go back a long way, perhaps via anthropology but certainly beyond it, to see; though when we do, we shall see clearly.

Take a human being, an animal, bird or reptile. He or she is moving along, doing nothing much in particular, in a territory, and life is humdrum. The creature is running, as it were, in bottom gear.

Then he, she or it comes across a source of stimulus: let us make it a pleasant one. It may be food, it may be sex, it may be anything which gives a 'buzz'. This event makes life worth living. It makes everything more pleasant. It is the equivalent of finding a treasure. The fruit just found tastes more delicious, just as the million dollars stands for something which can procure numerous pleasurable stimuli. Knowledge, study, anthropology do not give anything like that.

Beyond the immediate pleasure-seeking comes the phase when reason comes into it, or knowledge. Reason says that one needs a shelter. It is not exciting to build a shelter, not, certainly, as exciting as a pleasurable input like finding a delicious taste, smell or sight. There is a hierarchy of importance here.

More Anthropology

If you treat people in Europe and North America as if they were unsophisticated 'natives' they will react appropriately.

For instance, you can engage them in conversation on abstruse matters, or on things which are their supposedly important concerns, and they will respond accordingly.

But . . . you may get the most sophisticated intellectual and tell him that you are about to write his name in Arabic letters, and you will have him entrapped in an instant as surely as if he was an African or Asian having his first sight of a Polaroid camera's product.

I have reduced many a professor, engineer, scientist or business man to silence and pliant eagerness – by saying, as a demonstration of this, that I could read his or her character from the palm of a hand.

There are lots of other indications, too, which show that people will react according to how you treat them.

How The World Works

Since I have been emphasising the need for people to discern their own emotional ebb and flow, and to come to an understanding of it, so that they operate it, and not it them, there has been a great deal of comment. People say, of course, that because emotion moves them this is the only way in which it can work. Those who idolise it even imagine that it would be 'spoilt' if it did not come upon them unawares. This, of course, does not stop them using emotion if they can . . .

But there is a very ancient allegory connected with this belief that things are set in a certain way in the world and that nobody can change them. It is the

TALE OF THE WEEPING PUPPY

There was once a man who wanted to deceive a woman into believing that a certain dog was her former husband rein-carnated, so that he could sell it to her and make a large profit from what was a worthless mongrel.

So, every day for some weeks, he fed the puppy with bread covered in mustard whenever it was hungry. Naturally, this brought tears to its eyes.

Then he went to see the woman, and said that he simply had to sell her the animal, since he had had a vision that it was her dead husband in another guise.

When she looked doubtful, he said:

'Let us put it to the test, for you need not believe me without seeing something with your own eyes. You remember that you used to feed your dear husband, and that he liked your food? Let us remind him. Bring out a piece of bread, offer it to the dog, and if he shows unusual interest, you will know that what I say is true.'

The woman produced a scrap of bread and offered it to the puppy who, instead of gobbling it up, looked at her with reproachful eyes, which filled with tears.

So she bought the dog and cherished it, and nothing would ever convince her that it was not her husband: had she not had proof?

Chewing

Q: *I do not get any satisfaction from my life as a whole, but I do enjoy many things which I do, which makes my life worth living. Can there be anything wrong with that, so long as I do not harm anyone else?*

A: It does depend upon what the consequences of what you are doing ultimately are. If you know this, you are already wise, and would, I fancy, not be asking the question.

So I cannot comment, except to remind you of the mouse which was asked why it was chewing the insulation off a high-voltage electric cable. It said: 'I enjoy doing this, and besides, I am doing nobody any harm, am I?'

The Fisherman's Neighbour

There was once a poor fisherman, who just managed to keep body and soul together, through his work.

One day he cast his net and brought up a fish with a golden ring in it. He took this ring to the King, as that was all he could think of doing with it.

The King, who was delighted, gave him much more than the ring was worth, but in the form of bags of small change, which were more useful to a fisherman, and, moreover, something which he could understand better.

When he got home, the fisherman asked his small son to go to the neighbours to borrow his weights and scales, to weigh the money.

The neighbour, thinking himself very clever, and having decided to find out whatever he could about the fisherman, smeared some fat on the pan of the scales. 'Whatever he has, some of it will stick to the fat and I'll know what he has in the house,' he thought.

Sure enough, when the scales were returned, there was a silver coin sticking to the fat.

Now the neighbour decided that he must discover how the fisherman had got hold of money: so much money, indeed, that he had to weigh it. He and his wife took it in turns to lurk outside the fisherman's window, so that they could hear what they could hear.

Now they were both a bit deaf, but would not admit it.

While he was listening, the neighbour heard the fisherman discussing with his wife what he had done. He understood everything except that instead of 'a gold ring taken to the King', he thought the fisherman had said: 'a whole load of cats' – because, in their language, the two phrases sounded very similar.

He went home at once, and spent several days rounding up as many cats as he could. Then he took them to the King. When they were released in the throne-room, they went wild, bit people and scratched the valuable draperies. The fisherman's neighbour was, of course, flung into a dungeon.

Entering into an enterprise without the requisite basis will, more often than not, turn out something like this.

People do not understand this because they attribute other causes to what is always, in fact, their own lack of correct preparation. In the case of the fisherman's neighbour, of course, he did not learn a lesson from his greed and deafness, since he was able to blame the fisherman for 'knowing that he was there and deliberately deceiving him'.

But *we* are not like that, are we?

Denunciation

There was once a Dervish who had a small house in a town where people used to visit him from time to time, to benefit from his teaching.

One day he was sitting there when someone arrived from a distant country and asked whether he could sit at his feet.

'Enter, and welcome,' said the Dervish.

Now the visitor had heard for years of the wisdom and sanctity of that Dervish, and had saved for many months to accumulate enough money to make the journey to see him.

Now he was beginning to fear that he had been wrong in thinking highly of the man.

Every time he went to see the Dervish, the holy man merely sat there, giving out no wisdom and ignoring the guest. Even more perplexing, the Dervish did nothing about the constant shouting and banging which came from the house next door. It was caused by a drunkard who never seemed to be sober.

Finally the visitor plucked up enough courage to say to the Dervish: 'Pray, Sir, why do you not denounce the alcoholic in the next house, for he interrupts your repose; and moreover it is against the law here to drink and it is therefore a social as well as a personal duty to inform the police.'

The Dervish heaved a great sigh and answered: 'It is hard to do your social duty at the expense of your selfishness. The man next door is addicted to drink. I, in turn, am addicted to denouncing people. If I denounce him, I shall be feeding and making worse my own addiction. Let those whose social duty is fulfilled or unnecessary denounce others.'

'But should he continue to suffer, when he could be cured?' asked the guest.

'When my addiction becomes less I shall worry about that of others,' said the Dervish.

And that is why the traveller became convinced that the Dervish was selfish and therefore unworthy.

Trifles

A Sufi and his disciple were resting on a high rock one day when they saw two men being attacked by robbers.

They were too far away to intervene, and the thieves made off at once.

The Sufi and his companion made their way down to where

the two merchants had been, to find them limping back onto the road. They bound up their wounds and offered them some of their own scant refreshment, and then the disciple was amazed to see the Sufi kiss the hands of both of them.

'Baba, why do you kiss this man's hand?' he asked him.

'Because he, like a real man, struggled with the robbers, in spite of age, before they put him to flight.'

'But, in that case,' said the disciple, 'I cannot see why you kissed the hand of this other man. After all, he ran off and left the elder one to fight alone.'

'The younger man,' said the Sufi, 'did not need valour, for he had perception. He knew two things that nobody else present perceived. First, that if all four had fought, three people's eyes would have been put out: for the fight would have taken a different form. Second, that his own bravery would have produced such admiration in all the others that they would never have liberated themselves from dependence upon emotion, and would seek it thenceforward everywhere, in love and war, in commerce and crime, in games and trifles. They would all have ceased the work of the spirit.'

Humility

A certain missionary, obsessed by humility, went to a contemporary Dervish, and the following dialogue ensued:

'Is there anything worse than lack of humility?'

'Yes, drawing attention to lack of humility in others is worse.'

'And what is better than modesty?'

'Asserting yourself when self-assertion is necessary.'

'And when is it necessary?'

'When jealous people want you to be "humble" so that they can silence you.'

307

Advisable

Now and again sanity breaks through, even under the most hidebound and bureaucratic circumstances. This may be one reason why humour is so important. Tyrants, oppressing others and themselves oppressed by ideas and training, hardly ever have any humour. So seek to find and to encourage humour.

I once arrived at the immigration control desk of a certain country, to find a grim-faced official who read an interminable list of questions out to me.

He had just finished asking about the name of my father's grandmother when he burst out laughing.

I waited politely. When he had composed himself somewhat, he said:

'Once, when I asked someone the next question, "Have you been certified insane?" he said, very dolefully, "No, but I'll be ready for it after this!"'

Analogy

Q: *Can you give me an analogy of our situation in the sense of the existence of another dimension which we cannot really grasp?*

A: Analogy is really almost useless by itself; that is to say, until the individual can correctly grasp the analogy. To you I can only indicate the possibility in terms of a familiar experience, but this is no real analogy. Here it is however:

You are sitting in an aircraft, eating a sandwich. The aircraft, you and the sandwich are hurtling through the air at several hundred miles an hour. You are completely unaware of this unless you look out of the window and see a fixed point below.

For practical purposes you discount the hurtling, because it does not seem to affect you.

The speed is there, unperceived.

Nice

A wise man once said to me:

A certain scholar, suffused with jealousy and insecurity, once ascended a pulpit and attacked me.

Afterwards, at a dinner, my host asked me why the scholar had been so bitter – what had I done to annoy him so much.

Before I could reply, another guest, a real sage, interrupted:

'Master,' he said to our host, 'if you knew the scholar as well as I do, you would not have put the question in that way!'

'Indeed?' said our host; 'and what is it that you know about the scholar that would so change the question?'

'If you knew him as I do,' continued the sage, 'you would realise that the scholar was actually trying to be NICE!'

Consciousness of Good

Q: *You told a story about telling a man off on the telephone. It was funny. The man who told the girl off did not seem to gain much. Neither did the girl, because she was not herself responsible for the situation. What good did it do?*

A: What, indeed? An apple fell off a tree. What good did it do?

309

A man picked it up and ate it. What good did it do? The seeds germinated when the core rotted, and a tree grew. What good did it do? More apples fell, were eaten, provided seeds which grew, and so on. What good is anything doing? Do you think that a thing like this can be worked out like that?

Remember, 'Two wrongs don't make a right'. Well, what do two wrongs make? What does a right make? And two 'rights'? What exactly are you talking about? You are actually *talking* about something which can only be *perceived*. As long as you go on picking up snippets of things and trying to relate them to a sort of individual 'good' you will be unable to know what good and bad are. 'How lucky? I have won a fortune.' 'What a pity! I have now drunk myself to death with the money!' 'What a pity! Someone has robbed him of the lot.' 'Every cloud has a silver lining.' 'It's an ill wind that blows nobody any good.'

Q: *Yes, but I KNOW that there is, somewhere inside of me, a feeling for good and a rejection of evil.*

A: If you know that, stop trying to equate it with superficially assessed, fragmented and artificially 'frozen in motion' 'good'. Follow the 'good' which is inside and use it. How can you do both? If you are afraid that the inner sense of good is not really there, of course, you will merely comfort yourself that it 'could be used if I wanted to use it' – and carry on assessing things in the old and absurd way.

Q: *But does this not give a personal license for doing anything, saying that there is some good in it; or that at least there is no 'evil' which is really evil?*
A: Not if you have a cognition of the pattern, a REAL consciousness of *good*, which is a palpable experience within you. With this developed, you will follow the 'independent' (objective) good and not the imaginary one. If you have not an experience of this kind, follow the 'assessed good'. But don't try to work it out, because you can't. You are using a rule of thumb: recognise that and you will at least have attained something. You may or may not be able to progress from there. The hardest

310

thing for man is to know where the starting-point is. He tries to start far beyond where he is ready to start.

How Many Miles . . . ?

Q: *You often complain about unauthorised or unenlightened people dealing in Sufic materials. Surely there can be nothing wrong in this? Surely any information is better than none? Surely the accumulation of facts and arguments must be useful?*

A: Hold on a moment, you are asking question after question, and what you say begins to sound like rhetoric.

Sufic knowledge is not accumulation of facts or arguments: it is experience.

More and more information about the Sufis or Sufic experience is quite unnecessary. The more you have, the cruder the result, and the Sufic content disappears.

Do you know how thick a sheet of paper becomes if it starts at a thousandth of an inch thick and is then doubled over fifty times?

Q: *An inch?*

A: No. Try again.

Q: *Twenty inches?*

A: No.

Q: *I give up.*

A: You see – you can't even imagine anything like the correct answer to something which is strictly material, let alone something more subtle. The answer is that if you double a sheet a thousandth of an inch thick, upon itself fifty times – supposing that this were possible – you would end up with a pile of paper more than 17,000,000, yes, seventeen million miles thick.

'Doubling' inert facts only increases the dead weight of them.

Patience, Faith and Honour

In the East, as in many countries of the West, there is no rule of primogeniture. This means that the sons of kings and other nobles do not automatically inherit their rank, but must earn it. The father decides as to which of the candidates is the most worthy.

There was once a king who had three sons. When he felt that it was time to nominate his successor, he told his three sons to go into the world on a quest.

'Each one of you,' he said, 'must find a wife; for it is necessary that the heir to the Throne should have a consort. Whoever brings back the most valuable gift with his bride shall be my successor.'

The three young men went forth, each with his own ideas. The first Prince returned within a few days with a Princess from a neighbouring country, bearing an immense treasure: three thousand camel-loads of silver, gold and precious stones. 'These are for the strengthening of the Kingdom,' he told his father. 'I doubt whether the others can produce anything so splendid.'

The second son was still searching for a fabulously rich bride when word reached him of the success of the first young man. He realised that he would not be able to compete on those terms, and set himself to think. Eventually he chose a brilliant woman as his bride. She was a poetess, a philosopher and skilled in every kind of science.

'This lady,' he informed his father, 'will be more precious than treasure to our country and its people.'

312

The third son, who had never set much store by wealth or intellect, simply followed his camel's nose, penetrating deeper and deeper into the jungle, awaiting what his fate might bring him, and how he would deal with it.

After many days, the Prince found himself in a country full of fine buildings and abundant crops. Before he could discover anything more about the place, he was captured by a band of monkeys, and taken to the palace, where he was locked into a deep dungeon.

Little by little, as food was brought to him and he was taken out for exercise, he realised that this kingdom was populated, and ruled, entirely by monkeys such as the ones who had seized him.

The monkeys, unlike any of whom he had ever heard, behaved largely like human beings. They tilled the soil, carried out debates, passed laws and even read books. They did all this in their own way, however, and many of their habits appalled him. Further, he was unable to understand more than a few words of their language, which was based on grunts, laughter and groans.

There were, as he discovered, other human beings among the monkeys, all of them captives like himself. He was not allowed to speak to these unfortunate people, and he found it impossible to escape.

One night, lying in his cell, he heard a voice, the voice of a woman, saying, 'Prince, will you marry me?'

At first he thought that it was a delusion, but, when the voice repeated its question night after night, he came to believe that it must be real. The voice had a strange and compelling beauty, and, without having seen its owner, the Prince fell in love. Finally he answered, 'Yes, of course I will marry you.'

The following morning the monkeys took the Prince from his prison, fed and washed him, and took him to the Palace. There he saw a heavily-veiled form sitting on deep cushions, surrounded by all the requirements of a wedding. The human captives assembled included a Mulla and witnesses, while human servants brought rose-water and delicious fruits for all.

At the appropriate point in the ceremony, the bride's veil was removed so that the Prince could see her for the first time. He looked at the owner of the melodious voice and saw – a monkey!

Forgetting her voice, the Prince at first sprang back, appalled. Then he thought, 'I have given my word, and as a Prince, I must stand by it. Patience will rescue me, if there is any value in patience. At all events, my honour demands that I fulfil my undertaking.'

So saying, he put his name to the marriage contract.

The moment he had signed, he saw that the lady monkey had been transformed into a human princess of ravishing beauty. The large monkey on the throne, her father, was seen to have become a human king, who said: 'Know, O Prince, that we are really human beings. We were turned into monkeys by a magician as a punishment for faithlessness. We had to wait until a human being with patience, honour and faith might appear. That is why we have been capturing as many humans as we could, looking for such a man.' And he embraced his new son-in-law with delight and gratitude.

Now the young Prince with his bride and escorted by a huge band of monkey attendants – for most of the people had not resumed their natural shape – returned to the Prince's homeland.

When they stood at the foot of the Throne and related their adventures to the King, he plunged the head of reflection into the pocket of wisdom. Then he said:

'The best of all the three gifts which my sons have brought is yours, my son and successor! For this gift – patience, faith and honour – is to be valued far above materiality or intellect.'

At these words, all the monkeys who were the Prince's escort were miraculously transformed into human beings again. Their leader addressed the King saying:

'O Fountain of wisdom! Know that while many of our fellow-citizens were freed of their enchantment by your noble son's thoughts and actions, some of us were not. We had to await the occasion of someone actually valuing certain thoughts and deeds over wealth or cunning; someone who, like you,

would prove that he valued these things in a practical way.'
Then he kissed the hand of the King's son in homage.

And, strange to tell, after that all the people in the country
who were worshippers of pedantry or empty thought, of money
or goods, found that they had been turned into monkeys
themselves.

When the good King died, the Prince and his bride ruled over
their land for many years in happiness and justice. And the
release of the remaining malefactors of word or deed who had
become monkeys had to wait until the appearance of another
saviour, after they had had enough time to ponder their
evildoing.

The Valiant Trader-Knight

There was once a rich man whose experience of life was limited
to buying what pleased him, to profiting from the effect which
his possessions had upon others, and to inventing work for
himself.

One day his wife, seeing that he lacked some of the experiences of life such as other people have, suggested that he might
try his luck at trade.

'By all means,' he said, 'if you arrange for me to be fitted up
with transport and merchandise, I would be glad to try my luck
at trade. After all, my luck and prudence have brought me to
where I am – why should they not carry me even further?'

She arranged for him to buy some sacks of grain, dressed him
in a merchant's guise, and sent him off to try his luck, mounted
on a fine horse with bags of grain for trade slung on either side of
a mule.

When he had been travelling for some time, night began to
fall, and the new merchant tethered his animals and lay down to
sleep behind an outcrop of rocks beside the road.

Just near his chosen sleeping-place was the entrance to a cave, where a party of merchants, burdened with many valuable treasures, planned to spend the night. When they arrived, they placed a trumpet near the entrance so that whoever heard any suspicious sound during the night might lose no time in sounding it, so that they could wake and defend themselves and their merchandise against robbers.

But, of course, the traders had not seen the sleeping new merchant, and he had not woken at their approach. He rolled about in his sleep, and the trumpet rolled on the uneven ground until, wonder of wonders, its mouthpiece met his mouth as he puffed his way through a deep dream. Presently the breath sounded the alarm and the traders woke up in great fear, while he still remained asleep.

Inside the cave, the merchants saw that none of them was missing: so who had sounded the alarm? They concluded that they must be surrounded by an audacious and powerful band of thieves, who were challenging them and might at any moment burst in and massacre everyone. Crazed with panic, the merchants broke from the cave and ran away in all directions, leaving their goods behind.

One of the traders, seeing the horse of the would-be merchant, leapt upon it and fled from the imaginary robbers. This noise woke the new merchant up. When it was light, he found his horse gone, and a great quantity of merchandise left behind.

'They were in rather a hurry to trade with me, but I reckon that this is a fair exchange,' he said to himself. He took all the goods left behind and went back to his home town, to the applause of the multitude, who cried: 'Surely he was born under a lucky star! But he must also be a master merchant, to turn one horse into a king's ransom!'

Our new trader was accordingly convinced that he was a master merchant. Only his wife, who knew him well, realised that there must be something in the story which her husband had not noticed.

But people only look at the obvious explanation, and the rich man accepted his own imaginings about the cause-and-effect of his experiences. Now he said to his wife:

'You were right about my having to extend my experiences. Now that I have shown that I can be a merchant, I think that I shall become a hunter.'

His wife agreed. But she wanted to find out the reality which she was sure lay behind appearances. After equipping him with the necessary arms and horse, she bade him farewell, only warning him:

'One may go hunting, but there are perils on the road. An armed man can fall foul of mighty warriors. They patrol the roads, anxious to prove their supremacy and challenge all comers!'

But the rich man who had become a merchant and who was now a hunter also saw himself as a warrior. He said:

'Touched though I am by your concern for me, yet I do not need either warnings or support: let any champion approach – I shall know how to put him to flight!'

The newly-created hunter set off.

No sooner was he out of sight than his wife disguised herself as a warrior and bound the lower part of her face with a turban-end to conceal her features. She leapt upon a fast horse and made her way to a spot where she knew her husband would have to pass.

As she came up to him she waved a sword and cried, in a deep voice:

'Stand and fight, if you call yourself a man!'

The husband was terrified. Throwing himself upon the ground, he stripped off his armour and offered it, with his arms and his horse, to the challenger. The disguised wife collected the loot and rode away, hiding the items carefully before her husband arrived home, many hours later, covered in dust.

'And what has happened to you?' asked his wife, 'you look as if you have had a terrible time, my poor husband . . .'

'Not at all, woman!' thundered the hero. 'I met the most fierce and dangerous knight in all the world, with his face covered: and I vanquished him with the greatest of ease, putting him to flight!'

317

'But what happened to your horse, your arms?' she asked.

'Do you not remember, woman, that when I made a fortune at trading I abandoned it and turned to the profession of arms? This time, having vanquished the greatest knight of the road, I had no need for the equipment, and I threw it to him as compensation for his disgrace!'

'And now?' his wife asked.

'Now, I am ready for fresh adventures!'

Hoard

There was once a much-revered Dervish, who lived in a small cell on a caravan route, occupied with religious exercises.

One day a number of merchants brought a large quantity of gold and left it at his door. In the morning it was gone, but the travellers had told the people of the neighbouring town of their offering, and people wondered whether the Dervish had appropriated the gold for himself.

Many years later the Dervish died; and people started to build a tomb (*maqbara*) incorporating his cell. As they were working on it, a wall crumbled and the hoard of gold fell out.

With it, written on a board, was this message:

'This has been hoarded to prevent temptation. Take care that you, too, are not tempted.'

This tale is told by dervishes to show how their fellows are often misunderstood, and how hard they work on overcoming temptation and also on preventing others from being tempted.

But the tale is also told by Sufis and others to illustrate the difference between the Sufi and the Dervish. The Dervish is the man of rules, who has to stick to beliefs and practices because he does not actually know anything. The Sufi is the one who knows how, for example, to detach from temptation and also how to use gold if it is offered to him.

Let it not be thought that, in this respect, the Sufis and Dervishes are opposed. The dervish represents the highest moral exemplar of the ordinary man, and the Sufi the highest exemplar of the conscious man.

Music and Goodness

Q: *It is now widely realised that the Sufis insist that music has to be performed and heard very selectively if it is not to have undesirable effects, and that random audiences hearing it are unwittingly influenced in an undesirable way. Is there any evidence to this effect that can persuade ordinary people of its truth? After all, apart from Sufi circles, music is generally considered to be connected with goodness and higher things . . .*

A: The Sufis do not make a big issue of this, because when something is stated so authoritatively, it does not have to be 'proved'. Further, nobody is trying to 'persuade' anyone of its truth.

This said, however, it is certainly a fact now known to those who have researched it, even on a lower level. If you were listening to the BBC between 7 and 8 a.m., on 24 December 1981, during the annual constant repetition of Christmas carols, you would have heard about it.

The broadcast quoted a Canadian researcher as reporting an experiment with Christmas carols which he carried out in 1981.

He took two groups of people. One heard carols, the others were left in silence. Then he described to the members of each group a 'crime', and asked what sentence they would pass on the offender.

Those who had *not* listened to the music said 'five years' imprisonment'. The people who *had* been exposed to the carols preferred to give a sentence of eleven years.

Peace and goodwill are not caused by singing about them: indeed, in this instance we may be seeing the 'law of reverse effect' in operation.

What is happening, from the Sufi point of view, is that the emotional, not the spiritual, pitch is being raised, and the result, acting on the unregenerate self, brings out the characteristics which are present in the mind, and which have been both left untouched by earlier training and also unimproved (perhaps exacerbated) by the music and song allegedly related to goodness.

Inner Value of Music

Q: *I am very fond of music. I feel that the great composers and orchestras give us an additional dimension in life, something which is very precious to me. Can you tell me something about the place of music in teachings designed to awaken higher consciousness?*

A: Always remember two things. First, that people get out of something the nutrition which they are equipped and prepared to receive from it. Second, that music which is a product of a certain kind of mind, or a mind in a certain condition, will reflect that mind. I find that contemporary musicians and lovers of music take virtually no interest in these factors, if indeed they have ever heard of them. I will amplify.

Music can be used, and has been so used, to increase the milk-yield of cows. This is a factor which operates in the case of cows. In other instances, where human beings are concerned, there is merely the sensation that the music 'gives' something. In some of these cases, what the music is 'giving' is a vehicle or instrument whereby emotional tension can be released. In order for music to exercise a function in the formative or development area, it must be composed and performed, and experienced, on the basis of knowledge of its value for such a process. This brings us to the question of the understanding of music as a very much more important phenomenon than most people realise. Music can be used, and is in fact sometimes used, merely as a training or 'conditioning' element, linked with certain emotions. The individual writing, playing or hearing this music may conclude, largely through social habit, that he is deriving something from the music which may, in fact, be far removed from what he is actually deriving, or could derive.

Music can only be understood and participated in, by higher perception, by a mind which is capable of getting out of the music what it really contains. This can only happen if the person:

> Knows about this fact;
> Knows how to listen and understand;
> Listens at times and under conditions suitable for the desirable development.

Behind the Image

Q: *We all know that people judge others by appearances and the developing of a good or effective 'image' is thought more important than the person behind the image. What is, however, wrong with 'image'?*

A: There is nothing wrong with an image in this sense, but if there is nothing but 'image' there, it can be lack of courage, and succeed only too well, as in the case of the philosopher and the street of ill-fame.

THE PHILOSOPHER AND THE STREET OF ILL-FAME

There was once a philosopher who believed that appearances reflected reality to the extent that if people *did* things which *seemed* good, they would be *good*. He also believed that one should avoid looking bad, in case people believed that one was, in fact, bad.

A Sufi once said to him:

'But if good appearances can be taken as goodness, what name do we give to real goodness? If, on the other hand, people think that something is bad just because it looks bad, what term do we use for something which is good but looks bad or is bad but looks good?'

The philosopher, however, said:

'This is a matter of verbal contortions. I believe that doing good is *good*.'

It so happened that the philosopher was very short-sighted, and he seldom ventured out of his house alone for that reason. One day he decided to walk through the city in which he lived, in spite of his disability.

Thus it was that he strayed down a lane which led only to a house of ill-fame: and was seen doing so by many respectable people of the town.

Within an amazingly short space of time, everyone had heard that the philosopher had been seen where he should not be.

His disciples crowded around him and clamoured for an explanation.

The philosopher said:

'My dear friends, I can only say that I have made a mistake due to my weak eyesight. I recommend that you listen to the words of the Sufi on this matter and this kind of suspicion and judgement.'

But the disciples cried:

'Let us abandon this despicable man without delay! Not only has he done something which brings dishonour on us all; he supports that notorious Sufi, who, as we all know, claims that appearances do not matter!'

The philosopher, of course, lost his reputation in the town. He also lost all his pupils – because he had taught them too well, to look only at appearances. Because they had listened to him, they could not in the end understand him.

Path of Blame

Q: *You have spoken of the Path of Blame. Can you say more about this?*

A: The Path of Blame is known in Persian as the *Rahimalamat*. Although called a 'Path' it is in fact a phase of activity, and has many applications. Most of these applications are unsuspected in the West. Some of the uses of the Malamati (blameworthy) system are known only to its adherents or those carrying on a course of Malamatism.

The Malamati method is used in many Mulla Nasrudin stories. It is also said to have close affinities with Masonic ideas. Masons coming into contact with Malamati people in Turkey have said that they have ritualistic affinities with them.

The teacher incurs 'blame'. He may, for instance, attribute a bad action to himself, in order to teach a disciple the way to behave without directly criticising him. Direct criticism of a bad characteristic cannot always be used to overcome that obstacle. This is where the Malamati expertise comes in.

If you say 'I have such a bad habit of doing or thinking such and such' you remove the personal aspect and prevent the remark from being fought off or absorbed by the learner's self-esteem.

Many people follow Malamati (blameworthy) behaviour, even making themselves out to be wrongdoers, in order to highlight these characteristics in others. The reason for this is that when a person sees someone saying or doing something, he will tend to judge him by himself. This is what Rumi and others call 'Holding up a mirror to oneself and calling the image the other person.'

The temptation to apply the technique in a mass form is one which characterises *Gumrahi* (strayed) or small-potential instructors. Malamati behaviour can only be used with great care.

The first person to make public this system was Dhun-Nun

Misri, the 'Lord of the Fish', who is associated with the interpretation of Egyptian teachings from ancient times.

Perspective

Q: *You say that you do not like the use of books to find omens and answers to questions. But I have found that whenever I am anxious about something it makes me feel much better if I open a certain divining-book at random and read the message in it. And I generally find that there is good advice there, too.*

A: About omens and so on: you should be aware that when people born, say, 'under Gemini', are shown the 'reading' for people 'born under Aries' or Taurus or anything else – they overwhelmingly affirm that it describes them. Providing, that is, that they have been told that it is their own sign involved, and not told that it is someone else's. So we are dealing here with the power of suggestion.

As for the value of something, however fanciful, making one feel better, you do not take into account whether something which makes you feel better is not also contributing to making you not *feel*, but *be* worse.

There is a short tale about this, which is intended to indicate a perspective which people in your position lack:

There was once an old lady who took a hen to market, determined to get rid of it as it had stopped laying. Nobody wanted it. Finally she had an idea. She went to a dentist and said: 'Would you draw one of my teeth in exchange for this hen? After all, it will not cost you anything to exercise your skill, and you will get a hen.'

The dentist agreed. But when he had pulled the tooth, he said:

'Why did you make me draw this tooth – there is nothing wrong with it!'

'Well,' said the woman, 'I had to get rid of the hen, didn't I?'

You may have 'got rid of the hen', but at what price?

Spirituality and Materialism

Q: *Is spirituality preferable to materialism, since this Work is performed in the world, and is associated with material things?*

A: I shall deal with this question as well as several similar ones which have recently been asked.

First of all you must realise that what the ordinary man calls 'spirituality' is usually a vague aspiration towards something 'higher', or perhaps an indulgence in certain forms of emotion, hallowed only by custom, because of their historical or associative connection with what have been assumed or claimed for a long time to be spiritual things. We are not working with this false element at all.

'Materialism', again, is regarded as attachment to the acquisition of material things, or the use of them in a certain manner. Nobody asks whether this is the only way in which to approach or perceive that which is commonly assumed to be 'material'.

The actual fact is that such crude attitudes are not a basis of any real kind for the approach to our problem.

Within the confused mass generally called spirituality there are elements which are of developmental value. This is the portion of spirituality with which we are dealing. Within the dynamic of material there are elements with which we work. The question, as put, can be likened to that of a savage who might ask whether he should sniff the fuel in a cigarette lighter, or admire the sheen on its metallic surface. When someone tells him that the purpose or use of the lighter is something total and different from his assumptions about it, he may be confused, hostile, amazed or uninterested. His experiences so far have been in terms of smelling and looking – petrol and reflected light. These have served him well in the past. Why should he take a step further and seek a fresh range of experience?

Possession and Possessing

Q: *Are possessions and possessing things mixed up in peoples' minds with 'relationships'? And is this connected with self-will?*

A: Yes, they are mixed up. Just think of the various uses of the possessive form of 'my', linked as it is with what we think to be ourselves. At random: my father, my son. You are in a different relationship to each, but you use the same word for these two. Then there is my money, something over which you are supposed to have control – and my cup, something out of which you happen to be drinking, and which, for that period, is considered to be yours.

From our point of view, we can see here a tremendous inefficiency of the mental working which, because of the associations of the word 'my', will carry over one kind of 'my' from one situation to another, thus confusing itself. Again, there are qualified and absolute – apparently – 'mys'. A person gets caught on them, too. 'My duty' for instance, is not absolute unless it is a kind of duty with which few people are really familiar. But since the word 'duty' has been taken to mean something continuous, the mental mechanism is confused and not always able to know when a duty has really been discharged. So people go on trying to carry out duties which are duties no longer (if 'duty' means something continuous to them); or sometimes look at a long-term duty as a short-term one.

This is not playing with words. It is pointing out that playing with words vitiates the thinking capacity of the human mind. There is no established accurate method of cerebration in wide use. The mind which deals in such inefficient materials cannot grasp more refined, that is, more accurate or really objective ones.

Problems of The World

Q: *Our society is in a ferment, and people say quite openly that this is a sick civilisation. I am aware of the injustices which surround us, and also of the material threats which could at any moment destroy us. There are whole communities at each others' throats and evils which we thought we had put down are rising in stronger forms. While I am prepared to do my bit, and while I do support good causes and as far as possible, the weak against the strong if the weak are right, I want to know how we are going to be able to survive at all, if indeed we are going to survive. One of the things which worries me most is that fair-minded people make such blunders when they try to act for the best, or from objective moral principles.*

A: If there is no knowledge, only information, people will act in accordance with that range of information available to them – at the best. At the worst, and more frequently, they will act in accordance with impulse or emotion linked with intellect and set off by what you call objective moral principles. Objective moral principle, of course, is a phrase which seems to mean something but in fact does not mean more than chosen assumptions.

If you look at the people deeply concerned about right and the right thing to do, you will note that their dominating characteristics are that they are worriers. They worry about nuclear bombs, about injustices, and so on. They make decisions as a result of worrying. Naturally you get a lop-sided result.

They have no real feel of what is to happen as a result of certain actions, so they act on the spur of the moment. Naturally the consequences of their actions produce further worry-causing developments. They do not stop to think that recognition of an evil is one thing; worrying oneself to a point of action about it is another. People worry about poverty. They banish poverty, and the crime rate climbs. So they worry about the crime rate again, worry because they were wrong.

They do not say 'There may be something wrong with the very way in which we look at things, which causes us continually to make these terrible mistakes'. Such people are those who learn nothing and forget nothing. Until they seek in the right way for the right understanding of their situation they will continue along the same inevitable path.

Exchange

Q: *Why do people work for Sufis, doing things which seem to have no connection with their studies? For example, I have seen disciples waiting hand and foot on a Sufi and his guests, or looking after his house, and so on ...*

A: Because the Sufi is doing, in exchange, what he can do for them. You would not think it odd if a plumber mended your water-supply and you did something for him in return, would you? Would it seem to merit comment if a baker gave a loaf of bread to a butcher who gave him meat in exchange? Would you say 'Why does the baker give the bread, why does the butcher accept it?'

The reason why you ask this question at all is because you doubt whether the disciples are getting anything in exchange for their services. You doubt this only because they are not receiving something which you can measure in return. This, therefore, is your problem, not theirs or anyone else's. Your problem is to get to the stage when you can perceive the less crude return which is given by the teacher. If, for instance, you were deaf but not blind, and you saw something being given but could not hear the *quid pro quo*, which might be something only heard and not seen (like information) you might make a similar remark. And, in such a case, the only answer to you, which you might feel to be impolite but which would nevertheless be the truth, would be: 'Since you are deaf, you will not know unless you can hear.'

The Diamond

As many people know, it is customary to take a present when visiting a spiritual figure. This is usually both an indication of respect, a proof of personal sacrifice and an object which can be used by the recipient in charitable or other work.

It is widely believed – and I have often seen it happen – that presents, in kind or money, given to a Sufi will enter the realm of truly important operations and human service: releasing, in turn, something for the giver.

But that this 'alchemy' only happens with real Sufis may be borne out by several incidents, of which I can mention a typical example.

A man once found a large diamond, which he had cut and polished, and presented to a dervish, not to a Sufi. A dervish may be taken as roughly equivalent to what is called, in the West, a friar. In the East, such people are only thought of as aspirants to high knowledge by most people. Others, like the man who found the diamond, imagine them to be people of sanctity.

This dervish was no thief, though he was, for all his

imaginings, no spiritual individual either. He gave the diamond to a woman who had recently been widowed, and who had several children to bring up. Because, it is related, the vehicle, the dervish, could not so place the diamond as to ensure its working in the 'truly important realm', she failed to recognise that it was real. She handed it to one of the children. This little girl used it in her games until she was grown up. The family had hard times, and the diamond lay in a sewing-box.

Over twenty years later the man who had found it happened to notice it among a bundle of trifles in a market stall, and bought it for the price of a loaf of bread. He took it to a Sufi, who said, 'What did you pay for this?' The other man said, 'The equivalent of a loaf of bread.' 'Good,' said the Sufi, 'because things of this world are not worth more. However, with it we can avert a war.' How that came to pass is another story: but it really did happen.

Irritated

Q: *Which are the most irritating letters you get?*

A: The most irritating of all are from people who want to know why I am not irritated by something which irritates them, ranging from politics to criticisms of me. A close second are those who are irritated because I don't answer their letters or, more likely, because I don't give them the answers they wanted. As they get more irritated they write more and more letters, thus supplying so many letters that I would be able to do nothing else if I were to answer them, which of course ensures that they get no answer and are able to become even more irritated.

How To Get A Job

Q: *You continually say that people do not really know what they are doing, and that many actions are subconsciously intended to have an effect which the individual does not himself understand. There are many examples of people behaving like this in Sufi literature. But are there no occasions when people really are aware of the deceit in their characters, and make deliberate use of it?*

A: Yes, indeed. Sometimes, as in the case of the Kaftan-seller whom I quoted in *Learning How to Learn*, they allow it to operate, while being aware of it. Other cases are like that of the professor who asked me to employ him as a personal assistant. I told him that I would not do so. So he said:
   'Well, give me a letter offering me the job, in any case!'
   I said:
   'What earthly use could such a letter be to you?'
   'Well,' he answered, 'if I show it to such-and-such a person, who is an admirer of yours, he will give me a job at once, because he will think himself lucky to have beaten you to it!'
   This kind of deliberate deceit, which ordinarily happens on the non-conscious level, is generally only found otherwise in jokes and in stories attributed to 'clever idiots'. But it is my experience that it is known at all because people have observed this behaviour and have passed its knowledge on as 'jokes', both for illustrative and for informational purposes.

The Demon and The Happy Couple

There was once a happily married couple, whom a demon decided to separate. He went first to the wife, in the guise of an

331

old woman, and muttered that her spouse was behaving in a distraught fashion because he was in love with another woman. Then he went to the husband, in the form of a palmist, and told him that his wife was secretly involved with another man.

When the husband went home from his work that evening, it was quite natural that he should be uncomfortable with his wife, and she with him. Because of this tension, however, each concluded that there must be some truth in what he or she had been told.

Of course they were not certain about their suspicions; and the demon knew this and developed another phase of his attack. He told the woman that he had a spell which would reclaim her husband's fidelity. 'This,' he said, 'can be accomplished by cutting three hairs from his beard. Here is a razor with which to do it.'

Now he told the husband, who was starting to question the truth of the soothsayer's readings, that his wife would attempt to kill him that very night.

When the man got home, his wife asked him to lie down and rest and he did so, pretending to go to sleep. As soon as she thought it was safe, she took out the razor and advanced upon him with it – and the husband opened his eyes to see this 'proof' of her murderous intentions.

The husband, so continues the story, killed his wife, and the neighbours, alarmed and infuriated and panicking, killed him. Finally, everyone in their town took sides and there was a clash in which almost everyone there was also killed.